Sentencing Referen
2009

Sentencing

Referencer

2009

by **David Thomas**
Q.C., LL.D

SWEET & MAXWELL  **THOMSON REUTERS**

Published in 2009 by
Thomson Reuters (Legal) Limited
(Registered in England & Wales, Company No 1679046.
Registered Office and address for service:
100 Avenue Road, London, NW3 3PF)
trading as Sweet & Maxwell
For further information on our products and services, visit
www.sweetandmaxwell.co.uk
Typeset by LBJ Typesetting Ltd
of Kingsclere
Printed and bound in Great Britain by Athenaeum Press, Gateshead

No natural forests were destroyed to make this product; only farmed timber was used and replanted.

A CIP catalogue record of this book is available from the British Library.

ISBN 9781847037909

Preface

2008 was an eventful year for sentencing legislation. The year began quietly, with the Criminal Justice and Immigration Bill making its way slowly through the parliamentary process. By early January the Bill had completed its Committee Stage in the House of Commons when suddenly the government introduced a long list of amendments to be considered at short notice on Report Stage and Third Reading. By far the most important of these was a series of amendments to the disastrous dangerous offender provisions of the Criminal Justice Act 2003. The new legislation marked a welcome about turn in the Government's ill-considered policy of mandatory sentences. The mandatory element in the original version of the dangerous offender provisions was effectively removed, but unfortunately the pendulum swung too far in the opposite direction with the creation of new restrictive qualifying conditions for "dangerous offender" sentences which may prevent courts using the powers in cases for which they would be appropriate.

One aspect of the new dangerous offender provisions which deserves mention is the extreme difficulty in sorting out the text of the amended legislation. This requires an exercise in editorial reconstruction by reference to the Criminal Justice Act 2003 itself, the Criminal Justice Act 2003 (Commencement No.8 and Transitional and Saving Provisions) Order 2005, the Criminal Justice Act 2003 (Sentencing) (Transitory Modifications) Order 2005, the Criminal Justice and Immigration Act 2008, the Criminal Justice and Immigration Act 2008 (Commencement No.2 and Transitional and Saving Provisions) Order 2008, and the Criminal Justice and Immigration Act 2008 (Transitory Provisions) Order 2008. It is absurd that establishing the operating text of a relatively recent piece of legislation requires reference to two statutes and four statutory instruments. The need for transitory modifications of the legislation results from the fact that the government is still unable to make up its mind whether to implement s.61 of the Criminal Justice and Court Services Act 2000, which would abolish the sentence of detention in a young offender institution and lower the minimum age of imprisonment from 21 to 18. Although this amendment was a matter of urgent government policy when the Act was passed, eight years later it has not yet been brought into force, but virtually all sentencing legislation since that date has been written on the assumption that either it has been or will be brought into force, with the result that the new legislation must be modified to suit the current temporary position.

A second important change made by the Criminal Justice and Immigration Act 2008 was intended to assimilate the position of long-term prisoners serving sentences for offences committed before April 4, 2005, to that of those serving similar sentences for offences committed after that date. Under the position as it was following the commencement of the early release provisions of the 2003 Act, offenders serving sentences of four years or more for offences committed before April 4, 2005 (whenever the sentence was imposed) remain subject to the early release provisions of the Criminal Justice Act 1991, and become eligible for release on licence (but not entitled) after serving half of the sentence; they become entitled to release only after serving two-thirds of the sentence. Whenever released, they remain on licence until three-quarters of the sentence has elapsed. Those sentenced for offences committed on or after April 4, 2005, are entitled to be released after serving half of the sentence, but remain on licence for the whole term of the sentence pronounced in court. The 2008 Act amended the early release provisions of the 1991 Act by providing that when a long-term prisoner had served half of the sentence he would be entitled to be released, but would remain on licence until the end of the nominal term of the sentence. What had been given was immediately taken away for the vast majority of offenders serving long-term sentences, as the amendment of the 1991 Act was qualified so as to exclude those serving sentences for the 153 offences which are "specified offences" within Sch.15 of the Criminal Justice Act 2003. As the overwhelming majority of offenders serving sentences of four years or more have been convicted of "specified offences", the number of offenders benefiting from the change is a relatively small proportion of the population of prisoners serving long-term sentences under the 1991 Act. The principal beneficiaries of the change will be drug dealers and large-scale fraudsters, some of whom will find the custodial element in their sentences very substantially reduced. A man serving a sentence of 24 years for importing vast quantities of drugs in the year 2000 might well have expected to spend 16 years in custody, with little chance of discretionary early release under the early release provisions of the 1991 Act; now he can look forward confidently to release after serving 12 years under the amended provisions, at the cost of a longer period on licence.

The principal effect of this amendment seems to be to increase the complications in working out the effective length of the period to be served in custody under sentences of four years or more imposed for offences committed before April 4, 2005, as some will and some will not attract the amended early release provision. Those offenders who benefit from the early release provision will benefit a second time by the fact that the power to order their return to custody under the Powers of Criminal Courts (Sentencing) Act s.116, in the event of the commission of a further offence following release during the whole term of the sentence, ceases to apply to them.

One of the innovations made by the 2008 Act is the provision for offenders to be given credit against a custodial sentence in respect of time spent on remand on bail subject to a "qualifying curfew condition". A qualifying curfew condition is in essence a requirement to remain in a particular place for period of at least nine hours on any one day, subject to electronic monitoring. Reduced to its essentials, the new scheme requires the sentencing court to calculate a "credit period" which is in effect half of the number of days which the offender has spent on bail subject to a qualifying curfew condition, and then direct that the credit period should be treated as having been served as part of the sentence, unless it would be just not to give such a direction. Unlike the corresponding provision of s.240 of the Criminal Justice Act 2003, which applies only to sentences imposed for offences committed on or after April 4, 2005, the new scheme applies to sentences for offences committed before that date, although instead of "directing" that the time will count, the court in the case of a pre-April 2005 offence must simply "specify" the credit period which will then be deducted automatically from the sentence imposed. Again, the statutory text is not easy to find. The provisions relating to sentences for offences committed on or after April 4, 2005 are inserted into the Criminal Justice Act 2003, as new s.240A, but the provisions relating to offences committed before the date are concealed in Sch.6 of the Criminal Justice and Immigration Act 2008.

The new scheme is complicated enough at face value, but its operation is likely to be confused by what appears to be a drafting error in The Remand on Bail (Disapplication of Credit Period) Rules 2008. These rules specify various periods which cannot be treated as having been served. Rule 2 deals with the case of an offender who is ordered to serve more than one sentence following a period of remand on bail. The intended effect of the provision seems to be that where a defendant has been on bail in respect of a number of offences, and has qualified for a credit period, the credit period should be counted against only one of the resulting sentences, and that the defendant should not get the credit twice over. Unfortunately in r.(2)(1)(b), reference is made to a term of imprisonment which is "ordered to be served consecutively on, or wholly or partly concurrently with, another term of imprisonment". If the credit period has been counted against one sentence, it cannot be counted against the other. This makes perfect sense where the sentences are consecutive. If the defendant's credit period has been counted against sentence A, it obviously should not be counted a second time against consecutive sentence B. However the reference to concurrent sentences seems to defeat the purpose of the legislation. If a defendant has acquired a credit period and receives concurrent sentences, he will be allowed to count the credit period against one sentence, but not the other; the time which he gains against one of the sentences will be lost against the other, and he will have to serve it. Sentencers who find this all confusing may reflect on the fact that a qualifying curfew must be for at least nine hours on any day. A curfew period of eight hours does not count. A curfew period of eight hours, from perhaps 8pm until 4am the next day, may be just as effective in preventing further crime as a curfew period of 11 hours, from 8pm until 7am. Few offenders will bother to go out looking for trouble at 4am, when everyone else has gone home. An eight-hour curfew period avoids the complications of the statutory scheme, and the sentencing court can give some credit by reducing the length of the sentence.

One positive change which deserves mention is the amendment of the definition of "mental disorder" in the Mental Health Act 1983, made by the Mental Health Act 2007. The most important practical effect of this change is to make available to courts the power to make a "hospital and limitation" direction in conjunction with a sentence of imprisonment. This power, introduced by the Crime (Sentences) Act 1997, has remained virtually unused for a decade, as it was limited to offenders suffering from psychopathic disorder whose condition could be alleviated by treatment. The power is now available for offenders suffering from any form of mental disorder, and may provide a useful solution in cases where the choice between a hospital order and a sentence of imprisonment is difficult.

There remains a large body of legislation enacted but not yet in force. The "custody plus" provisions of the 2003 Act seem to be receding into history and there is happily as yet no positive sign that the complicated provisions of Sch.3 of the 2003 Act, governing mode of trial and committal for sentence, will be brought into force. The future of community orders for young offenders is no clearer than it was. Although the 2003 Act provisions for community orders will be extended to those between 16 and 18 on April 4, 2009, by virtue of the Criminal Justice Act 2003 (Commencement No.8 and Transitional and Saving Provisions) (Amendment) Order 2007, the 2008 Act creates a new sentence, a youth rehabilitation order, which will replace these forms of sentence if and when it comes into force.

At the time of writing, details of the proposed Law Reform, Victims and Witnesses Bill are awaited. The Bill promises "a structured, coherent and transparent sentencing framework that will allow the drivers of demand on prison and probation resources to be addressed and managed in a more consistent and predictable manner". The precise details of how this is to be achieved have not been disclosed.

As with previous editions, this edition is intended to help users find a path through the maze of legislation. It does not purport to deal with every problem that can arise, or to resolve problems of statutory interpretation. References are provided, wherever possible, to Current Sentencing Practice and to Archbold (2009 edition). This edition attempts to state the law as at December 1, 2008, but some provisions which were not in force on that date, but which may come into force within the life of the edition, are included.

D A Thomas
November 2008

Contents

Part 1—Sentencing Topics

Part 2—Maximum Sentences (Indictable Offences)

Part 3—Charts and Tables

Part 1:

Sentencing topics

Action Plan Order

P.C.C.(S.)A., ss.69, 70

References: Current Sentencing Practice E12–1; Archbold 5–175

An action plan order may be made only if the court has been notified that arrangements for implementing the order are in force.

An action plan order may be made in respect of an offender under 18 convicted of an offence for which the sentence is not fixed by law.

The court must be satisfied that it is desirable to make an action plan order in the interests of *securing his rehabilitation or preventing the commission of further offences*.

The court must observe the general requirements for making a youth community order. (See **Community Orders—Criminal Justice Act 2003—General Criteria.**)

An action plan order requires the offender be under supervision for three months and to comply with any of the following requirements:

(a) to participate in specified activities;

(b) to present himself to a specified person or persons at a specified place or places and at a specified time;

(c) to attend at an attendance centre for a specified number of hours;

(d) to stay away from a specified place or places;

(e) to comply with any specified arrangements for his education;

(f) to make specified reparation to a person or persons or to the community at large; and

(g) to attend any hearing fixed by the court.

Drug treatment and testing requirements may be included if they are recommended, suitable arrangements are available, and the offender consents. The power to include a drug treatment and testing requirement is available to certain courts only and applies only to offences committed on or after December 1, 2004.

An offender may be required to attend at an attendance centre only if the offence is punishable with imprisonment, and reparation requirements may be made in respect of a specified individual only if that individual has been identified as the victim of the offence and consents to the reparation requirement being made.

An action plan order may not be made if an action plan order is already in force, or if the court proposes to pass a custodial sentence, or make a community order or a referral order.

Before making an action plan order, the court must obtain and consider a written report. (The court must obtain and consider a presentence report unless it considers it unnecessary to do so on the ground that the court has considered an earlier report). The consent of the offender is not necessary.

The court may direct a further hearing not more than 21 days after the making of the order to receive a report from the supervising officer.

Adjournment

MAGISTRATES' COURTS ACT 1980, s.10

References: Current Sentencing Practice L7–1; Archbold 5–15

A **magistrates' court** may adjourn after conviction to enable enquiries to be made or to determine the most suitable method of dealing with the case. The adjournment must not be for more than four weeks at a time, or three weeks if the offender is in custody.

The **Crown Court** may adjourn after conviction for similar purposes; there is no statutory limitation. The Crown Court may adjourn part of the sentence only.

(Where the court postpones hearings in connection with confiscation orders, the total period of postponement must not exceed six months or two years from the date of conviction, according to which statutory scheme applies, unless there are exceptional circumstances: see **Confiscation Orders—Postponement of Proceedings.**)

The Bail Act 1976, s.4 applies if the court adjourns for inquiries.

On adjourning, the court should avoid giving the offender any reason to expect that he will be dealt with by means of a sentence not involving custody. If the offender is given the impression that the court will deal with him without sending him to custody, it may not be open to the court which adjourns, or any other court dealing with the offender subsequently, to impose a custodial sentence.

A magistrates' court which adjourns after convicting a defendant of an either way offence should avoid giving the defendant any reason to expect that he will not be committed to the Crown Court for sentence.

Advance Indication of Sentence

R. v Goodyear [2006] 1 Cr.App.R(S.) 6 (p.23)

Current Sentencing Practice L1–1; Archbold 5–79b

A judge may give an advance indication of the maximum sentence which would be imposed **if a plea of guilty were tendered at the stage the indication is sought**.

The judge should not give an advance indication unless one is sought by the defendant. The judge retains an unfettered discretion to refuse to give an advance indication. The judge may reserve his position until he feels able to give an advance indication of sentence, for instance where reports on the defendant are expected.

Once an advance indication of sentence is given, it is binding on the judge and any other judge who becomes responsible for the case. If the defendant does not plead guilty within a reasonable time after the advance indication has been given, the indication will cease to have effect.

The process of seeking an advance indication should be initiated by the defence; the defence advocate should have written instructions from the defendant. An indication should not be sought while there is any uncertainty about an acceptable plea or the factual basis of sentencing.

The judge should not become involved in discussions which link the acceptable plea to the sentence which is likely to be imposed. Advance indications should not be given on alternative bases.

Particular care should be taken in cases where the defendant is charged with one or more specified offences. Counsel should inform the judge that one or more of the offences is a specified offence. The judge may decline to give any indication; it he does give an indication, it may in qualified terms, depending on the outcome of the assessment of the defendant's dangerousness.

The right of the Attorney General to refer a sentence to the Court of Appeal on the ground that it is unduly lenient is not affected by the giving of an advance indication of sentence.

Hearings relating to advance indications of sentence should normally take place in open court.

Age of Offender

P.C.C.(S.)A. 2000, s.164(1)

References: Current Sentencing Practice E2–2AA

For the purposes of liability to custodial sentences and community orders, community rehabilitation orders, community punishment orders, community punishment and rehabilitation orders, curfew orders, drug abstinence orders, drug treatment and testing orders, exclusion orders, supervision orders and attendance centre orders **the age of the offender is his age on the day of conviction**, except in the exceptional cases listed below.

For the purposes of sentences of imprisonment, detention in a young offender institution, detention under the P.C.C.(S.)A. 2000, s.91 or detention and training orders, **the age of an offender is deemed to be what it appears to the court to be**, after the court has considered any available evidence, but where it is apparent that the age of the offender is in doubt or dispute, the court should adjourn and obtain proper evidence of age before sentencing.

Exceptional cases

An offender committed to the Crown Court for sentence under the P.C.C.(S.)A. 2000, ss.3, 4 or 6, must be sentenced on the basis of his age on the day he appears before the Crown Court. *This does not apply to an offender committed for sentence under the P.C.C.(S.)A. 2000, s.3C (dangerous young offenders).*

An offender subject to a community rehabilitation order, community punishment order, community punishment and rehabilitation order, curfew order, drug abstinence order, drug treatment and testing order, or exclusion order, who is convicted by the Crown Court, or who appears before the Crown Court for sentence, while the community order is in force, must be sentenced on the basis of his age when he appears before the Crown Court if the Crown Court revokes the community order and passes a further sentence for the offence.

An offender who is found to be in breach of a community rehabilitation order, community punishment order, community punishment and rehabilitation order, curfew order, drug abstinence order, drug treatment and testing order, or exclusion order and in whose case the order is revoked must be sentenced on the basis of his age when he appears before the court which revokes the order.

An offender who is subject to a community order made under the Criminal Justice Act 2003 in whose case the community order is revoked following a breach or subsequent conviction must be sentenced on the basis of his age when the original order was made.

Where an offender who has been the subject of a conditional discharge is convicted of a further offence and the conditional discharge is revoked and a sentence imposed for the original offence, he must be sentenced on the basis of his age when he is sentenced.

An offender convicted at any age of a murder committed when he was under 18 must be sentenced to be detained during Her Majesty's Pleasure.

The power to make a disqualification order depends on the offender's age when he committed the offence.

The obligation to impose a required minimum sentence under the Firearms Act 1968, s.51A depends on the offender's age when the offence was committed.

Aggravated Drug Trafficking

MISUSE OF DRUGS ACT 1971, s.4A

References: Current Sentencing Practice A19–1A; Archbold 27–28a

If an offender over 18 is convicted of an offence of supplying or offering to supply a controlled drug, and either the offence was committed in the vicinity of a school at any time when the premises were in use, or one hour before or after such time, or the offender used a courier who was under the age of 18, the court must treat that fact as an aggravating factor and must state in open court that the offence was so aggravated.

This provision applies to offences committed on or after January 1, 2006.

Alteration of Sentence

P.C.C.(S.)A. 2000, s.155; MAGISTRATES' COURTS ACT 1980, s.142

References: Current Sentencing Practice L10–1; Archbold 5–940

The Crown Court may vary or rescind a sentence which it has imposed or an order which it has made, **within specified time limits**. *The Crown Court must be constituted as it was when the original sentence was imposed or order was made*, except that if the court included one or more justices of the peace, one or all of them may be omitted.

A magistrates' court may vary or rescind a sentence or order at any time after the sentence has been passed or the order made, unless the Crown Court or the High Court has determined an appeal against the sentence or the conviction on which it is based. *There is no time limit for magistrates' courts.*

The time limit for the Crown Court is **56 days beginning with the day on which the sentence was imposed or the order was made**. Where orders have been made on different dates in respect of the same conviction the period of 56 days begins to run on the day on which the particular order which it is proposed to vary was made.

The relevant time limit must be strictly observed, but where a sentence has been passed or order made which is defective in form, it may be permissible to correct the error after the expiration of the relevant time limit, so long as the correction can be treated as a matter of form rather than substance.

If the Crown Court rescinds a sentence within the permitted period for variation or rescission, without imposing a further sentence, it may adjourn sentence for such period as may be appropriate, without regard to the time limit.

There is no restriction on the nature of the variation in sentence which may be made. In appropriate circumstances the court may substitute a sentence or order which is more severe than the sentence originally passed. The power is not limited to the correction of slips of the tongue or minor errors made when sentence was originally passed.

It is permissible to correct a sentence which is unlawful in the form in which it has been passed.

Where the court has been persuaded to pass a particular form of sentence, or a sentence of a particular length, on the basis of the existence of specific mitigating factors, the court may review the sentence and substitute a more severe sentence if it subsequently appears that the court has been misled and that the mitigating factors did not exist. Such a decision should not be made without proper inquiry and giving the offender an opportunity to dispute the allegation that he has deceived the court.

It is wrong for a sentencer to increase a sentence simply because on reflection he considers that the sentence he has passed was too lenient. There is no objection to reducing a sentence because on second thoughts it appears to have been too severe.

It is wrong to vary a sentence which has been passed on the ground that the offender has reacted to the sentence by misbehaving in the dock and addressing abusive comments to the judge or other persons present.

It is not clear whether a sentence which has been varied once can be varied a second time.

As a general rule, the power to vary a sentence should be exercised only in open court and in the presence of the offender after hearing his counsel, who should be advised of the nature of the alteration which the court proposes to make.

Where the Crown Court passes part of a sentence and expressly postpones passing some other part of the sentence, the time limits do not apply.

Antecedents Statements

See Consolidated Criminal Practice Direction, para.III.27.

Anti-Social Behaviour Order on Conviction

CRIME AND DISORDER ACT 1998, s.1C

References: Current Sentencing Practice H10–1A; Archbold 5–881

A court dealing with an offender for any offence committed on or after December 2, 2002, may make an order if it considers that the offender has acted, at any time since April 1, 1999, in a manner that *caused or was likely to cause harassment, alarm or distress to one or more persons not of the same household as himself and that an order is necessary to protect persons in any place in England and Wales from further anti-social acts by him.*

The order may prohibit the offender from doing anything described in the order.

The test for making an order under s.1C is one **of necessity to protect the public from further anti-social acts by the offender**.

The terms of the order must be precise and capable of being understood by the offender.

The findings of fact giving rise to the making of the order must be recorded.

The order must be explained to the offender.

The exact terms of the order must be pronounced in open court and the written order must accurately reflect the order as pronounced.

The order may be for a specified period (not less than two years) or indefinite.

The court may make an order if the prosecutor asks it to do so, or if the court thinks it is appropriate to do so.

For the purpose of deciding whether to make an order under this section the court may consider evidence led by the prosecution and the defence, whether or not the evidence would have been admissible in the proceedings in which the offender was convicted.

An order should not be made simply for the purpose of subjecting the offender to an increased maximum sentence for conduct which would otherwise be a summary offence.

An order may be made only in addition to a sentence imposed for the offence, or a conditional discharge.

An order may be suspended during any period when the offender is detained in legal custody.

An offender subject to an order, the DPP or the relevant authority, may apply to the court which made the order for it to be varied or discharged. An order may not be varied or discharged within two years on the application of the offender unless the DPP consents. An order may not be varied or discharged within two years on the application of the DPP or the relevant authority unless the offender consents.

If an offender is convicted of a breach of an antisocial behaviour order as a result of conduct which would amount to the commission of a distinct criminal offence, the sentence for the breach of the order is not limited to the maximum sentence which would be available for the criminal offence.

Assistance to Prosecutor

<small>SERIOUS ORGANISED CRIME AND POLICE ACT 2005, S.73</small>

References: Current Sentencing Practice A20–1; Archbold 5–94a

If a defendant who has **pleaded guilty** in proceedings in the Crown Court, or who has been committed to the Crown Court for sentence following a plea of guilty, has entered a **written agreement** with a specified prosecutor, to assist or offer to assist the investigator or prosecutor in relation to the offence to which he has pleaded guilty *or any other offence*, the court may take into account the extent and nature of the assistance given or offered in determining what sentence to pass.

The extent to which the assistance given or offered may affect the sentence is a matter within the discretion of the sentencing court.

If the court passes a sentence which is less than it would otherwise have passed, the court must **state in open court that it has passed a lesser sentence than it would otherwise have passed, and what the greater sentence would have been**. *This obligation does not apply if the court thinks that it would not be in the public interest to disclose that the sentence has been discounted.* Where no statement is made in open court, the court must give written notice of the fact that it has passed a lesser sentence, and what the greater sentence would have been, to the prosecutor and to the defendant.

Nothing in any enactment which requires that a "minimum sentence" is passed in respect of any offence or an offence of any description or by reference to the circumstances of any offender affects the power of a court to take into account the extent and nature of this assistance given or offered.

In a case of **murder**, nothing in any enactment which requires the court to take into account "certain matters" for the purposes of making an order which determines or has the effect of determining the minimum period of imprisonment which the offender must serve affects the power of the court to take into account the extent and nature of the assistance given or offered.

Where the defendant has been sentenced in the Crown Court, and has received a discounted sentence as a consequence of having made a written agreement to give assistance to the prosecutor or investigator of an offence, but has *knowingly failed "to any extent" to give assistance in accordance with the agreement*, a specified prosecutor may refer the case back to the court if the person concerned is still serving his sentence, and the prosecutor thinks that it is in the interest of justice to do so. The case so referred must if possible be heard by the judge who passed the original sentence. If the court is "satisfied" that a person whose sentence has been discounted has "knowingly failed to give the assistance", it may substitute for the sentence which has been referred "such greater sentence" as it thinks appropriate, provided that the new sentence does not exceed the sentence which it would have passed if the agreement had not been made.

Where the defendant has received a discounted sentence in consequence of having entered a written agreement to give assistance, and having given the assistance in accordance with the original agreement makes a further written agreement to give further assistance, the defendant's sentence may be referred to the Crown Court.

Where the defendant has received a sentence which is not discounted, but in pursuance of a written agreement made subsequently to the imposition of sentence, gives or offers to give assistance to the prosecutor or investigator, the defendant's sentence may be referred to the Crown Court, whether or not he pleaded guilty to the offence (except where he was convicted of murder following a trial).

On such a reference, the court may take into account the extent and nature of the assistance given or offered, and substitute for the original sentence "such lesser sentence as it thinks appropriate".

Where an offender who has pleaded guilty to murder offers or gives assistance after sentence, his case may be referred if the prosecutor chooses to do so.

On the hearing of a reference, or any other proceedings arising in consequence of a reference, the court may exclude from the proceedings anyone other than an officer of the court, a party to the proceedings or legal representatives of the parties, and may give such directions as it thinks appropriate prohibiting the publication of any matter relating to the proceedings, including the fact that the reference has been made. Such an order may be made only to the extent that it is necessary to do so to protect the safety of any person, and is in the interests of justice.

The statutory provisions do not replace the conventional practice by which a defendant who is unable or unwilling to enter onto a written agreement may ask the prosecuting or investigating body to produce a "text" setting out the details of the assistance or information provided by the defendant.

Attendance Centre Order

P.C.C.(S.)A., s.60

References: Current Sentencing Practice E7–1A; Archbold 5–162

An attendance centre order may be made in respect of an offender **under 16** who is convicted of an offence which is punishable with imprisonment whenever the offence was committed.

An attendance centre order may be made in respect of an offender **between the ages of 16 and 18** who is convicted of an offence which is punishable with imprisonment committed before **April 4, 2009.**

An attendance centre order may be made in respect of an offender **under the age of 21** who is convicted of an offence which is punishable with imprisonment committed before **April 4, 2005.**

Before making an attendance centre order, the court must comply with the general statutory provisions relating to community orders. (See **Community Orders—Criminal Justice Act 2003—General Criteria.**)

The court must obtain and consider a pre-sentence report unless it considers it unnecessary to do so on the ground that the court has considered an earlier report.

An attendance centre order is normally for 12 hours. The court may specify less than 12 hours if the offender is under the age of 14 and the court considers that 12 hours would be excessive, having regard to his age and any other circumstances.

The court may specify more than 12 hours if the court considers that 12 hours would be inadequate. If the offender is under 16 the maximum number of hours is 24. If the offender is over 16 the maximum number of hours is 36.

The court must not make an attendance centre order unless it is satisfied that the attendance centre to be specified is reasonably accessible to the person concerned, having regard to his age, the means of access available to him, and any other circumstances.

The times at which the offender is required to attend shall be such as to avoid interference so far as is practicable, with the offender's school hours or working hours.

The offender must not be required to attend at an attendance centre on more than one occasion on any one day, or for more than three hours on any occasion.

An attendance centre order may be made even though the offender is still subject to an existing attendance centre order.

Breach of the requirements of an attendance centre order may lead to revocation of the order. Commission of an offence while subject to an attendance centre order does not give rise to any power in respect of the attendance centre order.

Automatic Life Sentence

P.C.C.(S.)A., s.109

References: Current Sentencing Practice A14–1; Archbold 5–251i

Note: the P.C.C.(S.)A. 2000, s.109, is repealed by the Criminal Justice Act 2003, s.303, but saved in respect of offences committed not later than April 3, 2005.

The court must pass an automatic life sentence on an offender convicted of a "serious offence" if:

(a) the offender was 18 years or older when he committed the offence;

(b) the offence was committed on or after October 1, 1997 and not later than April 3, 2005; and

(c) the offender has been convicted on a previous occasion of a serious offence.

The following offences are "serious offences":

(i) attempted murder, conspiracy to murder, incitement to murder, soliciting murder;

(ii) manslaughter;

(iii) any offence under Offences against the Person Act 1861, s.18;

(iv) rape or attempted rape, unlawful sexual intercourse with a girl under 13;

(v) an offence under ss.1 or 2 of the Sexual Offences Act 2003 (rape, assault by penetration);

(vi) an offence under s.4 of the Sexual Offences Act 2003 (causing a person to engage in sexual activity without consent), where the activity caused involved penetration within subs.(4)(a) to (d) of that section;

(vii) an offence under ss.5 or 6 of the Sexual Offences Act 2003 (rape of a child under 13, assault of a child under 13 by penetration);

(viii) an offence under s.8 of the Sexual Offences Act 2003 (causing or inciting a child under 13 to engage in sexual activity), where an activity involving penetration within subs.(3)(a) to (d) of that section was caused;

(ix) an offence under s.30 of the Sexual Offences Act 2003 (sexual activity with a person with a mental disorder impeding choice), where the touching involved penetration within subs.(3)(a) to (d) of that section;

(x) an offence under s.31 of the Sexual Offences Act 2003 (causing or inciting a person, with a mental disorder impeding choice, to engage in sexual activity), where an activity involving penetration within subs.(3)(a) to (d) of that section was caused;

(xi) an attempt to commit any of the offences against the Sexual Offences Act 2003 mentioned above;

(xii) offences under ss.16, 17 and 18 of the Firearms Act 1968;

(xiii) robbery, where the offender had in his possession at some time during the commission of the offence a firearm or imitation firearm.

Attempts to commit these offences (other than those specifically mentioned) are not "serious offences".

Corresponding offences committed in Scotland (of which the offender has been convicted before the High Court) and Northern Ireland, and corresponding offences under service law, are "serious offences".

An offence committed outside the United Kingdom of which the offender was convicted by court martial is not a "serious offence."

It is not necessary for the serious offences to be the same.

The offender must have been convicted of the first serious offence before he committed the second.

A conviction which has been followed by a conditional or absolute discharge does not count for these purposes. A conviction which has been followed by a probation order made before October 1, 1992 does not count. A finding of guilt by a youth court or juvenile court does count.

An offender convicted on the same occasion of a number of serious offences committed over a period of time does not qualify for an automatic life sentence.

The court need not pass an automatic life sentence if it is of the opinion that there are "exceptional circumstances" relating to either of the offences or the offender which justify the court in not imposing a life sentence. *The fact that the sentence is "unjust" is not an exceptional circumstance.* The fact that the offender is mentally ill and eligible for a hospital order is not an exceptional circumstance. If the court refrains from imposing a life sentence, it must state what the exceptional circumstances are.

If the offender does not represent an unacceptable risk to the community, there may be "exceptional circumstances".

If the court passes an automatic life sentence, it must fix a period to be served in accordance with P.C.C.(S.)A. 2000, s.82A. (See **Minimum Term.**)

Banning Orders

FOOTBALL SPECTATORS ACT 1989, s.14

References: Current Sentencing Practice H6–1; Archbold 5–822

If an offender is convicted of a **relevant offence** and the court is satisfied that there are *reasonable grounds to believe that a banning order would help to prevent violence or disorder at or in connection with any regulated football matches*, it **must** make a banning order. If the court is not so satisfied, it **must** state that fact in open court and give its reasons.

A banning order prohibits the offender from attending a regulated football match in England and Wales, and requires him to report when required to a police station when football matches are being played outside England and Wales. A banning order may include other requirements. The order must require the offender to surrender his passport in connection with matches played outside England and Wales.

If the offender is sentenced to custody, the banning order must be for at least 6 years and not more than 10 years.

If the offender is not sentenced to custody, the banning order must be for at least three years and not more than five years.

A banning order may be made only in addition to any other form of sentence or in addition to a discharge.

The following offences are relevant offences:

(a) any offence under the Football Spectators Act 1989, ss.14J(1) or 21C(2);

(b) any offence under ss.2 or 2A of the Sporting Events (Control of Alcohol, etc.) Act 1985 (alcohol, containers and fireworks) committed by the accused at any regulated football match or while entering or trying to enter the ground;

(c) any offence under **s.4A** or s.5 of the Public Order Act 1986 (harassment, alarm or distress) or any provision of Pt III of that Act (racial hatred) committed during a period relevant to a regulated football match at any premises while the accused was at, or was entering or leaving or trying to enter or leave, the premises;

(d) **any offence involving the use or threat of violence by the accused towards another person committed during a period**

relevant to a regulated football match at any premises while the accused was at, or was entering or leaving or trying to enter or leave, the premises;

(e) **any offence involving the use or threat of violence towards property committed during a period relevant to a regulated football match at any premises while the accused was at, or was entering or leaving or trying to enter or leave, the premises;**

(f) any offence involving *the use, carrying or possession of an offensive weapon or a firearm* committed during a period relevant to a regulated football match at any premises while the accused was at, or was entering or leaving or trying to enter or leave, the premises;

(g) any offence under s.12 of the Licensing Act 1872 (persons found drunk in public places, etc.) of being found drunk in a highway or other public place committed while the accused was on a journey to or from a regulated football match applies in respect of which the court makes a declaration of relevance;

(h) any offence under s.91(1) of the Criminal Justice Act 1967 (disorderly behaviour while drunk in a public place) committed in a highway or other public place while the accused was on a journey to or from a regulated football match in respect of which the court makes a declaration of relevance;

(i) any offence under s.1 of the Sporting Events (Control of Alcohol, etc.) Act 1985 (alcohol on coaches or trains to or from sporting events) committed while the accused was on a journey to or from a regulated football match in respect of which the court makes a declaration of relevance;

(j) any offence under **s.4A or s.5 of the Public Order Act 1986** (harassment, alarm or distress) or any provision of Pt III of that Act (racial hatred) committed while the accused was on a journey to or from a regulated football match in respect of which the court makes a declaration of relevance;

(k) any offence under ss.4 or 5 of the Road Traffic Act 1988 (driving, etc. when under the influence of drink or drugs or with an alcohol concentration above the prescribed limit) committed while the accused was on a journey to or from a regulated football match in respects of which the court makes a declaration of relevance;

(l) **any offence involving the use or threat of violence by the accused towards another person committed while one or each of them was on a journey to or from a regulated football match in respect of which the court makes a declaration of relevance;**

(m) **any offence involving the use or threat of violence towards property committed while the accused was on a journey to or** from a regulated football match in respect of which the court makes a declaration of relevance;

(n) **any offence involving the use, carrying or possession of an offensive weapon or a firearm committed while the accused was on a journey to or from a regulated football match in respect of which the court makes a declaration of relevance;**

(o) any offence under the Football (Offences) Act 1991;

(p) any other offence under **s.4A or s.5 of the Public Order Act 1986** (harassment, alarm or distress) or any provision of Pt III of that Act (racial hatred) which was committed during a period relevant to a regulated football match in respect of which the court makes a declaration that the offence related to that match or to that match and any other football match which took place during that period;

(q) **any other offence involving the use or threat of violence by the accused towards another person which was committed during a period relevant to a regulated football match in respect of which the court makes a declaration that the offence related to that match or to that match and any other football match which took place during that period;**

(r) any other offence involving the use or threat of violence towards property which was committed during a period relevant to a regulated football match in respect of which the court makes a declaration that the offence related to that match or to that match and any other football match which took place during that period;

(s) any other offence involving the use, carrying or possession of an offensive weapon which was committed during a period relevant to a regulated football match in respect of which the court makes a declaration that the offence related to that match or to that match and any other football match which took place during that period;

(t) any offence under s.166 of the Criminal Justice and Public Order Act 1994 (sale of tickets by unauthorised persons) which relates to tickets for a football match.

The **period relevant** to a football match is the period beginning 24 hours before the start of the match, or the advertised start, and ending 24 hours after the end of the match. If the match does not take place, the period is the period beginning 24 hours before the time at which it was advertised to start, and ending 24 hours after that time.

*The court may not make a **declaration of relevance** unless the prosecutor gave notice to the defendant five days before the first day of the trial that it was proposed to show that the offence related to football matches, unless the offender consents to waive* *the requirement or the court is satisfied that the interests of justice do not require more notice to be given.*

A regulated football match is an association football match in which one or both of the participating teams represents a club which is for the time being a member (whether a full or associate member) of the Football League, the Football Association Premier League or the Football Conference, or represents a club from outside England and Wales, or represents a country or territory; and which is either played at a sports ground which is designated by order under s.1(1) of the Safety of Sports Grounds Act 1975, or registered with the Football League or the Football Association Premier League as the home ground of a club which is a member of the Football League or the Football Association Premier League at the time the match is played; or is played in the Football Association Cup (other than in a preliminary or qualifying round).

The prosecution may appeal against the failure of a court to make a banning order.

Binding Over

JUSTICES OF THE PEACE ACT 1968, s.1(7)

References: Current Sentencing Practice D10–1; Archbold 5–119

A person who has been convicted of an offence may be bound over to come up for judgment when called, on such conditions as the court may specify.

A person "who or whose case" is before the Crown Court or a magistrates' court may be bound over to keep the peace and to be of good behaviour, whether or not he has been charged with or convicted of an offence.

A witness who has not given evidence is not liable to be bound over.

A person who has not been charged with an offence should not be bound over without being given the opportunity to make representations before being bound over.

A person who refuses to be bound over may be committed to prison. A person under 18 may consent to be bound over, but may not be committed to custody if he refuses to be bound over.

Where a court proposes to bind over a person in a substantial amount, it should allow him to address the court on the amount.

Where a person is bound over to keep the peace and be of good behaviour, there is no power to insert additional specific conditions.

Where a person who has been bound over to keep the peace and be of good behaviour fails to comply with the terms of the binding over, he is liable to be ordered to pay the amount in which he has been bound over, but cannot be sentenced to custody.

Breach of Community Orders

P.C.C.(S.)A., Sch.3

References: Current Sentencing Practice D6–1

Note: this section summarises the law relating to breaches of community orders made under the P.C.C.(S.)A. 2000. For breaches of orders made under the Criminal Justice Act 2003, see **Community Orders—Criminal Justice Act 2003—Breaches of Orders and Re-offending**.

These provisions apply to community rehabilitation orders, community punishment orders, community punishment and rehabilitation orders, drug treatment and testing orders, and drug abstinence orders. *They do not apply to supervision orders and attendance centre orders*.

Where it is proved that an offender subject to a community order made by a magistrates' court has failed without reasonable excuse to comply with any of the requirements of the relevant order, the court may either:

(a) impose a fine not exceeding £1,000;

(b) make a community punishment order for not more than 60 hours;

(c) if the order is a community rehabilitation order or a community punishment and rehabilitation order and the offender is under 21, make an attendance centre order;

(d) if the order is a curfew order and the offender is under 16, make an attendance centre order;

(e) revoke the order and deal with him, for the offence in respect of which the order was made, in any manner in which it could deal with him if he had just been convicted by the court of the offence.

If the court makes a community punishment order in respect of an offender who is already subject to a community punishment order, the aggregate of the hours must not exceed 240.

If the court revokes the order and passes a different sentence, the court must *take into account the extent to which the offender has complied with the requirements of the relevant order*. If the offender has wilfully and persistently failed to comply with the order, the court may pass a custodial sentence, whether or not the other criteria for a custodial sentence are satisfied.

If a custodial sentence is passed, the court should allow for any time spent in custody on remand before a community rehabilitation order or community punishment order was made, which will not count as part of the sentence.

Where a community order made by a magistrates' court is revoked, the magistrates' court which revokes the order may not commit the offender to the Crown Court to be sentenced for the original offence.

If the community order was made by the Crown Court, the magistrates' court may make any of the orders above but may not revoke the order. The court may commit the offender to the Crown Court. If the Crown Court which made the community order, directed that any breach should be dealt with by the Crown Court, the offender must be brought before the Crown Court.

When the offender appears before the Crown Court, the breach of the order must be proved to the satisfaction of the Crown Court. If the breach is proved, the Crown Court may:

(a) impose a fine not exceeding £1,000;

(b) make a community service order for not more than 60 hours;

(c) if the order is a community rehabilitation order or a community punishment and rehabilitation order and the offender is under 21, make an attendance centre order;

(d) if the order is a curfew order and the offender is under 16, make an attendance centre order;

(e) revoke the order and deal with him, for the offence in respect of which the order was made, in any manner in which it could deal with him if he had just been convicted by the court of the offence.

If the court makes a community punishment order in respect of an offender who is already subject to a community service order, the aggregate of the hours must not exceed 240.

If the court revokes the order and passes a different sentence, the court *must take into account the extent to which the offender has complied with the requirements of the relevant order.* If the offender has wilfully and persistently failed to comply with the order, the court may pass a custodial sentence, whether or not the other criteria for a custodial sentence are satisfied.

If a custodial sentence is passed, the court should allow for any time spent in custody on remand before a community rehabilitation order or community punishment order was made, which does not count as part of the sentence.

An offender who is convicted of a further offence while a community order is in force is not for that reason liable to be dealt with for a failure to comply with any requirement of the order.

Breach of Supervision Order

P.C.C.(S.)A., SCH.7

References: Current Sentencing Practice E6–1F; Archbold 5–217

If an offender who is subject to a supervision order made by a youth court or magistrates' court is found by a youth court or magistrates' court to be in breach of the order, the court may impose a fine not exceeding £1,000, make an attendance centre order or make a curfew order. Alternatively the court may revoke the supervision order and deal with the offender for the offence in any manner in which he could have been dealt with by the court which made the order if the order had not been made.

If an offender who is subject to a supervision order made by the Crown Court is found by a youth court or magistrates' court to be in breach of the order, the court may impose a fine not exceeding £1,000, make an attendance centre order or make a curfew order. Alternatively the youth court or magistrates' court may commit the offender to the Crown Court. *If it is proved to the satisfaction of the Crown Court that the offender has not complied with the requirements of the order, the Crown Court may deal with the offender in any way in which it could have dealt with him if it had not made the supervision order.*

Commission of a further offence during the supervision order is not a breach of the order.

Committal for Sentence

P.C.C.(S.)A. 2000, ss.3–7

References: Current Sentencing Practice L12–1; Archbold 5–24

Note: the Criminal Justice Act 2003, Sch.3, enacts new versions of the P.C.C.(S.)A. 2000, s.3, and adds new ss.3A, 3B and 3C. Of these sections, only s.3C was in force on December 1, 2008. The effect of s.3C is summarised below. Otherwise this section summarises the effect of the Powers of Criminal Courts (Sentencing) Act 2000, ss.3 to 7 as originally enacted.

Either way offences (P.C.C.(S.)A. 2000, s.3)

An offender **aged 18 or more** who has been convicted by a magistrates' court of an either way offence may be committed to the Crown Court for sentence if either the magistrates' court considers that the offence or the combination of the offence and one or more offences associated with it is so serious that greater punishment should be inflicted for the offence than the court has power to impose, or the offender has been convicted of a **violent or sexual** offence and the court is of opinion that a custodial sentence for a term longer than the court has power to impose is necessary to protect the public from serious harm from him.

It is not necessary for the magistrates' court to have information before it which was not available to the court when the court decided to proceed with a summary trial.

The magistrates' court may commit for sentence if it is of the opinion that the Crown Court should be able to pass a sentence not involving custody which is beyond the powers of the magistrates' court, such as a compensation order for an amount greater than the magistrates' court can order, or a confiscation order.

When the offender appears before the Crown Court, the conviction in the magistrates' court and the committal should be formally proved and the defendant identified. The defendant should be asked whether he intends to appeal against the conviction; if he does so, he should not be sentenced on the committal until the appeal has been determined.

The Crown Court may deal with the offender in any manner in which it could deal with him if he had just been convicted of the offence on indictment before the court. The Crown Court is not bound to pass a sentence which would have been beyond the powers of the magistrates' court.

If the offender intends to ask the Crown Court to take into consideration offences other than those of which he has been convicted, the normal procedure for taking offences into consideration must be followed in the Crown Court.

Where the case has been adjourned in the magistrates' court in such a way as to give rise to a reasonable expectation by the offender that he will not be sentenced to custody, a custodial sentence should not be passed in the Crown Court.

Where the case has been adjourned in the magistrates' court in such a way as to give rise to a reasonable expectation by the offender that he will not be committed to the Crown Court for sentence, he should not normally be committed for sentence.

A magistrates' court may not commit an offender for sentence under s.3 if it is dealing with him for a breach of a community order which it has made on an earlier occasion following a summary conviction for an either way offence.

Indicated plea (P.C.C.(S.)A. 2000, s.4)

If a magistrates' court has committed an offender for trial for some offences, but has to deal with the offender for other either way offences **in relation to which he has indicated an intention to plead guilty**, the magistrates' court may commit the defendant to the Crown Court for sentence for those offences, provided that they are offences which could be included in the same indictment as the first offences.

The offender may be committed for sentence even though the court is not satisfied that greater punishment should be inflicted than the magistrates' court has power to inflict, or that the offence is a violent or sexual offence and a sentence longer than the court has power to impose is necessary to protect the public from serious harm.

If the magistrates' court commits an offender under this provision, it should state whether it has power also to commit the offender under P.C.C.(S.)A. 2000, s.3.

If the offender is convicted of the offences for which he has been committed for trial, or if the magistrates' court on committing him for sentence has stated that it has power to commit him for sentence for the other offences under P.C.C.(S.)A. 2000, s.3 the Crown Court may impose any sentence for the offences for which he has been committed for sentence which it would have power to impose if the offender had just been convicted on indictment.

If the defendant is not convicted of those offences for which he has been committed for trial, and the magistrates' court has not stated

that it had power to commit him under P.C.C.(S.)A. 2000, s.3, the Crown Court must deal with the offender for the offences for which he has been committed for sentence in a manner in which the magistrates' court could deal with him if it had just convicted him.

This procedure should not be used unless the defendant has been committed for trial for related offences. A defendant who has been convicted by a magistrates' court after indicating an intention to plead guilty in other circumstances should be committed under s.3.

Subsidiary offences (P.C.C.(S.)A. 2000, s.6)

Where an offender is committed for sentence under either of these provisions, or various other provisions relating to existing sentences, the magistrates' court may commit the offender for other offences for which he could not be committed under the principal provision. If the offence is a summary offence, it must be punishable with imprisonment or with disqualification from driving under ss.34, 35 or 36 of the Road Traffic Offenders Act 1988. The power may be exercised in conjunction with other powers of committal. The section does not apply in the case of an offender subject to a community order made under the Criminal Justice Act 2003 who is committed to the Crown Court under the Criminal Justice Act 2003, Sch.8, para.22, following his conviction by a magistrates' court of an offence while a community order made by the Crown Court is in force.

Where an offender is committed under s.6, **the Crown Court must observe all limits which would apply to a magistrates' court passing sentence for those offences, both in relation to the maximum term of imprisonment which the magistrates' court may pass for the individual offences, and** *the limitations on the aggregate maximum term* **of imprisonment which the magistrates' court may impose for all the offences. See Magistrates' Courts Powers—custodial sentences.**

Committal of dangerous young defendant (P.C.C.(S.)A. 2000, s.3C)

A defendant under 18 who has been convicted by a magistrates' court of a **specified offence committed on or after April 4, 2005,** must be committed to the Crown Court if the court considers that there is a significant risk of serious harm to the public caused by further specified offences committed by him, and that the criteria for the imposition of a sentence of detention for life, detention for public protection, or an extended sentence of detention would be met.

Where a young defendant is committed for sentence the Crown Court shall "inquire into the circumstances of the case and may deal with the offender in any way in which it could deal with him if he had just been convicted of the offence on indictment before the court". The Crown Court is not bound to deal with the defendant under the Criminal Justice Act 2003, ss.226 or 228, unless it considers that there is a significant risk of serious harm to the public caused by further specified offences committed by him. If it does not so consider, the Crown Court may impose any other sentence which is open to the court for an offender of the defendant's age.

The age of the defendant for the purpose of determining the sentencing powers of the Crown Court is his age on the date on which he was convicted. If a defendant is convicted by a magistrates' court at the age of 17 and is committed for sentence, but attains the age of 18 before he appears before the Crown Court, the Crown Court must deal with him as a 17–year-old.

Defective committals

Where an offender is committed to the Crown Court for sentence, and it is alleged that the committal is unlawful for want of jurisdiction or otherwise, the normal remedy is by way of judicial review. The Crown Court may decline to pass sentence only if the committal is obviously bad on its face.

The Crown Court has no power to remit the case to the magistrates' court where it appears that the defendant is not guilty of the offence for which he had been committed, but it may allow him to withdraw or change his plea and then remit the case to the magistrates' court.

Community Orders—Criminal Justice Act 2003—
Breaches of Orders and Re-offending

CRIMINAL JUSTICE ACT 2003, SCH.8

References: Current Sentencing Practice D14–1; Archbold 5–180

Note: these provisions apply only to community orders made under the Criminal Justice Act 2003. They do not apply to youth community orders.

Breach of requirement of order

Where it is proved to a magistrates' court that an offender subject to a community order has failed without reasonable excuse to comply with any of the requirements of the relevant order, the court may either:

(a) impose more onerous requirements than the original order; or

(b) if the order was made by a magistrates' court, deal with him, for the offence in respect of which the order was made, *in any manner in which it could deal with him if he had just been convicted by the court of the offence.*

In dealing with the offender, the court must take into account the extent to which the offender has complied with the requirements of the relevant order. If the offender has wilfully and persistently failed to comply with the order, the court may pass a custodial sentence, *whether or not the offence is punishable with imprisonment and the other criteria for a custodial sentence are satisfied.*

If the magistrates' court deals with the offender in any other manner than by imposing more onerous requirements, it must revoke the order. (*There is no power to impose a fine for the breach and allow the order to continue*).

If the community order was made by the Crown Court, the magistrates' court may commit the offender to the Crown Court, as an alternative to imposing more onerous requirements.

When the offender appears before the Crown Court, the breach of the order must be proved to the satisfaction of the Crown Court. If the breach is proved, the Crown Court may:

(a) impose more onerous requirements than the original order contained; or

(b) deal with him, for the offence in respect of which the order was made, *in any manner in which he could have been dealt with by the court which made the original order if the order had not been made.*

In dealing with the offender, the court must take into account the extent to which the offender has complied with the requirements of the relevant order.

If the offender is 18 or over and has wilfully and persistently failed to comply with the order, the court may pass a custodial sentence, whether or not the offence is punishable with imprisonment and the other criteria for a custodial sentence are satisfied.

If the court deals with the offender in any other manner than by imposing more onerous requirements, it must revoke the order. (*There is no power to impose a fine for the breach and allow the order to continue.*)

Commission of further offence

If an offender in respect of whom a community order made by a magistrates' court is in force is convicted by magistrates' court, and the magistrates' court considers it in the interests of justice to do so, the magistrates' court may either simply revoke the community order, or revoke the order and deal with the offender in any way in which he could have been dealt with by the court which made the order.

If an offender in respect of whom a community order made by the Crown Court is in force is convicted by magistrates' court, the magistrates' court may commit the offender to the Crown Court.

If an offender appears before the Crown Court having been committed by the magistrates' court following a conviction by the magistrates' court, or if the offender is convicted of an offence before the Crown Court while he is subject to a community order, whether the order was made by the magistrates' court or by the Crown Court, the Crown Court may either revoke the order, or revoke the order and deal with the order in any way in which he could have been dealt with by the court which made the order.

The power to deal with the offender depends on his being convicted while the order is still in force; it does not arise where he is convicted after the order has expired of an offence committed while the order was current.

The offender must be sentenced on the basis of his age when the original order was made, not on his age at the date of sentence. If the offender is convicted before the Crown Court while he is subject to a community order made by a magistrates' court, the Crown Court may impose only a sentence which would have been open to the magistrates' court which convicted him.

In sentencing the offender, the Crown Court must take account of the extent to which he has complied with the requirements of the order.

Community Orders—Criminal Justice Act 2003—General Criteria

CRIMINAL JUSTICE ACT 2003, s.148

References: Current Sentencing Practice D 13–1; Archbold 5–125

Note: these provisions apply only to community orders made under the Criminal Justice Act 2003, including youth community orders.

A court may not impose a community sentence unless it is of the opinion that:

(a) the offence or the combination of the offence and one or more offences associated with the offence are "**serious enough to warrant such a sentence**";

(b) the particular requirements or combination of requirements are "**the most suitable for the offender**"; and

(c) the restrictions on liberty imposed by the order are "**commensurate with the seriousness of the offence**" or the combination of offences for which the sentence is imposed.

In considering the seriousness of an offence or combination of offences, the court must have regard to the offender's previous convictions and offending while on bail, a guilty plea, and any racial or religious aggravation or aggravation based on the victim's sexual orientation or disability, among other things.

The fact that the offence is serious enough to warrant a community order or the proposed requirements are commensurate with the seriousness of the offence or the combination of offences for which the order would be imposed, does not mean that the court is required to make a community order or to impose those restrictions.

A community sentence may not be passed where the sentence is fixed by law, or a custodial sentence is required by the Firearms Act 1968, s.51A, the P.C.C.(S.)A. 2000, ss.110 or 111, or the Criminal Justice Act 2003, ss.225 to 228.

A community order may not be made in respect of an offence which is not punishable with imprisonment by the court which makes the order.

A community order must specify the petty sessions area in which the offender resides or will reside. Copies of the order must be given to the offender, and to an officer of a local probation board or (in the case of an offender under 18) either an officer of a local probation board or a member of a youth offending team, and to others concerned with the operation of the order. The offender must keep in touch with the responsible officer and notify him of any change of address.

The Crown Court may include in the order a direction that any breach of the order is to be dealt with by a magistrates' court. If no such direction is made, any breach will be dealt with by the Crown Court.

Loss of benefit: a court which makes a community order must explain to the offender that if he is found to be in breach of the order, he may be liable to the stoppage or reduction of any social security benefits to which he is entitled. This warning must be given whether or not the offender is in receipt of benefit at the time when the order is made. *Note: this provision applies only to offenders likely to be supervised in specified areas.*

Community Orders—Criminal Justice Act 2003— Offenders Previously Remanded in Custody

CRIMINAL JUSTICE ACT 2003, s.149

References: Current Sentencing Practice D13–1; Archbold 5–127

Note: these provisions apply only to community orders made under the Criminal Justice Act 2003.

Where a court makes a community order in respect of an offender who has previously been remanded in custody, it may have regard to any period during which the offender has been remanded in custody in connection with the offence for which the order is made, or any offence founded on the same facts or evidence, in determining the restrictions on liberty to be imposed on the offender.

The court has a discretion; there is no obligation to make any allowance in the terms of the order for time spent in custody on remand. *A court which takes account of remand time in determining the terms of a community order should say that it has done so, and to what extent, for the information of any court which may have to deal with the offender at a later stage if the order is revoked.*

Community Orders—Criminal Justice Act 2003—
Requirements

CRIMINAL JUSTICE ACT 2003, ss.199–214

References: Current Sentencing Practice D13–1; Archbold 5–135

**Note: these provisions apply only to community orders made under the
Criminal Justice Act 2003.**

There is no restriction on the requirements which may be combined in
the same community order, but the court must consider whether the
requirements are compatible with each other.

The requirements of a community order shall, as far as is practicable,
avoid any conflict with the offender's religious beliefs or the requirements
of any other community order to which he may be subject, and any
interference with the times at which he normally works, or attends school
or an educational establishment.

Unpaid work requirements

An unpaid work requirement requires the offender to perform unpaid
work for a number of hours, not less than 40 and not more than 300,
specified in the order. An unpaid work requirement may not be made
unless the court is satisfied that the offender is a suitable person to
perform work under such a requirement.

Where an offender is convicted of more than one offence, an unpaid
work requirement may be made in respect of each offence, and may direct
that the hours of work specified in any of the requirements should be
concurrent with or in addition to the hours of work required by the other
requirement, but the total number of hours which are not concurrent must
not exceed the permissible maximum of 300.

The work must normally be completed within 12 months, but the
requirement remains in force until all the hours of work have been
completed.

It is not necessary for the offender to consent to the making of an unpaid
work requirement. (This requirement is subject to availability: see s.218.)

Activity requirements

An activity requirement requires the offender either to present himself
to a person or persons specified in the order at a place or places specified

on such number of days as may be specified, or to participate in activities specified in the order on the number of days specified. An activity requirement may not be included in an order unless the court has consulted an officer of a local probation board and is satisfied that it is "feasible to secure compliance with the requirement".

The aggregate of the number of days on which the offender may be required to present himself to a person or participate in activities must not exceed 60. (This requirement is subject to availability: see s.218.)

Programme requirements

A programme requirement requires the offender to participate in an "accredited programme" at a place or places specified on such number of days as may be specified, or to participate in activities specified in the order on the number of days specified. A programme requirement may not be included in an order unless the programme has been recommended as being suitable for the offender by an officer of a local probation board and the court is satisfied that the programme is available.

There is no restriction on the number of days on which the offender may be required to participate in a programme requirement.

Prohibited activity requirements

A prohibited activity requirement requires the offender to refrain from participating in activities specified in the requirement on a day or days specified in the order or during a period specified in the requirement. A prohibited activity requirement may not be included in an order unless the court has consulted an officer of a local probation board.

The prohibited activity requirements may include requirements relating to possessing, carrying or using firearms.

Curfew requirements

A curfew requirement requires the offender to remain, for periods specified in the requirement, at a place specified in the order The periods specified must be not less than 2 hours and not more than 12 hours, in any day. The requirement may specify different places or different periods for different days.

All the specified periods must fall within the period of six months beginning with the day on which the order is made.

Before making a curfew requirement, the court must obtain and consider information about the place to be specified in the order and the attitude of persons likely to be affected by the enforced presence there of the offender.

The court must impose an electronic monitoring requirement in accordance with the general provision for electronic monitoring in s.215.

Exclusion requirements

An exclusion requirement prohibits the offender from entering any place specified in the order for a period not exceeding two years (whatever the length of the community order). The prohibition may operate continuously or only during specified periods and different places may be specified in the order for different periods or days.

The court must impose an electronic monitoring requirement in accordance with the general provision for electronic monitoring in s.215. *As an alternative to an exclusion requirement, courts will in many cases be able to achieve the same effect with an order under the Crime and Disorder Act 1998, s.1C, which does not require electronic monitoring.*

Residence requirements

Before making an order containing a residence requirement, the court must consider the home surroundings of the offender. The requirement may provide for the offender to reside at a place other than the place specified. A hostel or other institution may not be specified as the place of residence except on the recommendation of an officer of a local probation board.

Mental health treatment requirements

A court may not include a mental health treatment requirement in an order unless it is satisfied, on the evidence of an approved medical practitioner, that the mental condition of the offender is such as requires and is susceptible to treatment, but does not warrant his detention under a hospital order.

The court may not include such a requirement in the order unless the offender expresses his willingness to comply with it.

The requirement relating to treatment may be for the whole period of the order, or for any part of the period of the order.

The treatment required by the order may be either treatment as a resident patient in an independent hospital or care home, or a hospital under the Mental Health Act 1983, other than a hospital where high security services are provided, or treatment as a non-resident patient at such institution or place as may be specified in the order, or treatment by or under the direction of a medical practitioner or chartered psychologist specified in the order.

The court must be satisfied that arrangements have been or can be made for the proposed treatment, including arrangements for the offender's reception as a resident patient, where treatment as a resident is proposed.

The medical nature of the treatment is not specified in the order.

Drug rehabilitation requirements

A drug rehabilitation requirement may be made only if the court is satisfied that the offender is dependent on or has a propensity to misuse drugs; and that his dependency or propensity is such as requires and may be susceptible to treatment. The treatment and testing period must be at least six months.

A drug rehabilitation requirement requires the offender to submit, during the treatment and testing period, to treatment by a specified person with a view to the reduction or elimination of the offender's dependency on or propensity to misuse drugs. The treatment may be treatment as a resident in a specified institution or place, or treatment as a non-resident in a specified institution or place. The nature of the treatment is not specified in the order.

The requirement must also require the offender to provide samples during the treatment and testing period at times and in circumstances determined by a responsible officer or person providing treatment, for the purpose of ascertaining whether he has any drug in his body during the treatment and testing period.

A court must not make a drug rehabilitation requirement unless it is satisfied that arrangements have been or can be made for the treatment intended to be specified in the order, and the requirement has been recommended by an officer of a local probation board.

A requirement may not be included in an order unless the offender expresses his willingness to comply with the requirement.

A drug rehabilitation requirement may (and must if the treatment and testing period is more than 12 months) provide for the order to be reviewed periodically at intervals of not less than one month at a hearing held for the purpose by the court responsible for the order. The offender may be required to attend each review hearing (and must if the period is more than 12 months).

At a review hearing the court, after considering the responsible officer's report, may amend any requirement or provision of the order. The court may not amend the treatment or testing requirement unless the offender expresses his willingness to comply with the amended requirement, and must not reduce the treatment and testing period below the minimum of six months. If the offender fails to express his willingness to comply with the amended order, the court may revoke the order, and deal with him, for the offence in respect of which the order was made, in any manner in which it could deal with him if he had just been convicted by the court of the offence.

If at a review hearing the court is of the opinion that the offender's progress under the order is satisfactory, the court may so amend the order as to provide for each subsequent review to be made by the court without a hearing, but this may be reversed.

Alcohol treatment requirements

An alcohol treatment requirement may be made if the court is satisfied that the offender is dependent on alcohol, and that his dependency is such as requires and may be susceptible to treatment. The requirement may specify that the offender shall submit during the specified period to treatment by or under the direction of a person having the necessary qualifications with a view to the reduction or elimination of the offender's dependency on alcohol. The period of treatment must be not less than six months.

The court may not include or make an alcohol treatment requirement unless the offender expresses his willingness to comply with the requirement.

The treatment required by the alcohol treatment requirement may be either treatment as a resident in such institution or place as may be specified in the order, treatment as a non-resident in such institution or place as may be specified in the order, or treatment by or under the direction of a qualified person specified in the order.

The court may not make an alcohol treatment requirement unless it is satisfied that arrangements have been made for the proposed treatment, including arrangements for the offender's reception where he is required to submit to treatment as a resident.

Supervision requirements

A supervision requirement may be made for the purpose of promoting the offender's rehabilitation. A supervision requirement requires the offender to attend appointments with the responsible officer.

Attendance centre requirements

An attendance centre requirement may be made in respect of an offender under 25. It requires the offender to attend an attendance centre order for a total of not less than 12 hours and not more than 36 hours. The court must not make an attendance centre requirement unless it is satisfied that the attendance centre to be specified is reasonably accessible to the person concerned, having regard to the means of access available to him, and any other circumstances.

The times at which the offender is required to attend shall be such as to avoid interference so far as is practicable, with the offender's school hours or working hours.

The offender must not be required to attend at an attendance centre on more than one occasion on any one day, or for more than three hours on any occasion.

(This requirement is subject to availability: see s.218.)

Electronic monitoring requirements

A court which makes a community order may include in the order a requirement for securing the electronic monitoring of the offender's compliance with any other requirements of the order. An electronic monitoring requirement may not be included without the consent of any person without whose co-operation monitoring cannot be secured. An electronic monitoring requirement must include provision for making a person of a specified description responsible for the monitoring.

An electronic monitoring requirement must be included in any community order which includes a curfew requirement or an exclusion requirement. (This requirement is subject to availability: see s.218.)

Community Orders—Powers of Criminal Courts (Sentencing) Act 2000—General Requirements

P.C.C.(S.)A., ss.33–36

References: Current Sentencing Practice D1–1

Note: the requirements set out below apply to community orders made under the P.C.C.(S.)A. 2000.

The following requirements apply when a court makes any of the following orders: a community rehabilitation order, a community punishment order, a community punishment and rehabilitation order, a drug treatment and testing order, a supervision order, a curfew order, an attendance centre order, a drug abstinence order, an exclusion order.

The court may not make any of the following community orders *without obtaining and considering a pre-sentence report*, unless it considers a pre-sentence report unnecessary:

(a) a community rehabilitation order which includes additional requirements, authorised by P.C.C.(S.)A. 2000, Sch.2;

(b) a community punishment order;

(c) a community punishment and rehabilitation order;

(d) a supervision order which includes requirements;

(e) a drug treatment and testing order.

In the case of an offender under the age of 18 years, the court must not make any of these community orders without considering a pre-sentence report.

The court may not make a community order unless each of three statutory criteria is satisfied.

The first is that the offence or the combination of the offence and other offences associated with it was *serious enough to warrant a community order*. In assessing the seriousness of an offence or offences, the court must take account of information about the circumstances of the offence, including aggravating or mitigating circumstances of the offence. The court must not take account of information about the offender. The court may take into account any previous convictions of the offender and his response to previous sentences.

The second requirement is that the community order chosen is in the opinion of the court the *most suitable for the offender*, taken together with any other form of order which the court intends to make in respect of the offender. In forming this opinion the court must take into account information about the circumstances of the offence, including aggravating or mitigating circumstances of the offence and any information which is available about the offender.

The third requirement is that *the restrictions on liberty imposed by the community order and any other orders which the court makes against the offender, must be commensurate with the seriousness of the offence* or the combination of the offence and other offences associated with it. In assessing the seriousness of an offence or combination of offences the court must take account of information about the circumstances of the offence, including aggravating or mitigating circumstances of the offence. The court may not take into account information about the offender, but may take into account any previous convictions of the offender, or any failure to respond to previous sentences.

The court may mitigate the sentence by taking into account any such matters as in the opinion of the court are relevant in mitigation of sentence.

A court which imposes a suspended sentence may not make a community order against the same offender for a different offence.

Electronic monitoring: a court which makes a community order may include in the order requirements for securing the electronic monitoring of the offender's compliance with any other requirements of the order. Such a requirement may not be included in any community order unless the court has been notified that suitable arrangements are available in the relevant area and that the necessary provision can be made.

An electronic monitoring requirement may not be included without the consent of any person without whose co-operation monitoring cannot be secured.

Where an electronic monitoring requirement is included in an order, the requirement must include provision for making a person of a specified description responsible for the monitoring.

Where the *Crown Court makes a community order*, the Crown Court may direct that any breach of the order shall be dealt with by the Crown Court.

Loss of benefit: a court which makes a community order must explain to the offender that if he is found to be in breach of the order, he may be liable to the stoppage or reduction of any social security benefits to which he is entitled. This warning must be given whether or not the offender is in receipt of benefit at the time when the order is made. *Note: this provision applies only to offenders likely to be supervised in specified areas.*

Community Orders—Powers of Criminal Courts (Sentencing) Act 2000—Subsequent Offence

P.C.C.(S.)A. 2000, Sch.3, para.11

References: Current Sentencing Practice D7–1

Note: these provisions apply to offences during orders made under the Powers of Criminal Courts (Sentencing) Act 2000.

These provisions apply to persons subject to the following orders: community rehabilitation orders, community punishment orders, community punishment and rehabilitation orders, curfew orders, drug treatment and testing orders, drug abstinence orders and exclusion orders. They do not apply to supervision orders or attendance centre orders.

The power to revoke the community order may be exercised by the Crown Court only if one of the following conditions is satisfied:

(a) the offender is convicted before the Crown Court while the community order is still in force;

(b) the offender appears before the Crown Court for sentence following a committal for sentence while the order is still in force;

(c) the offender is committed following an application to vary the order.

It does not matter when the offence was committed.

The court may revoke the order without imposing any further sentence for the original offence or revoke the order and impose any sentence which it could impose if the offender had just been convicted.

If the court passes a further sentence for the offence in respect of which the community order was made, it should take into account the extent to which the offender has complied with the requirements of the order. All statutory restrictions on the imposition of a custodial sentence must be observed. (See **Custodial Sentences—P.C.C.(S.)A. 2000—Statutory Criteria.**)

If the court revokes a community rehabilitation order or a community punishment order and imposes a custodial sentence for the original offence, the offender should be given credit for any time spent in custody on remand before the order was made, which will not count as part of the sentence. (See **Time on Remand.**)

If the community order was made by a magistrates' court, the sentence which the court passes should be one which would have been within the powers of the magistrates' court. (See **Magistrates' Courts Powers— Custodial Sentences.**)

A community order made by a magistrates' court may be revoked by a magistrates' court which has convicted the offender of an offence if the magistrates' court is not the court which is responsible for the order, the magistrates' court imposes a custodial sentence on the offender, the offender or the responsible officer applies to the magistrates' court for the revocation of the order, and the magistrates' court decides that it is in the interests of justice to revoke the order. *The court may not impose any sentence for the offence in respect of which the order was made.* If the order was made by the Crown Court, the magistrates' court may commit the offender to the Crown Court; the Crown Court may revoke the order but *may not impose any sentence for the offence in respect of which the order was made.*

Community Punishment Order

P.C.C.(S.)A. 2000, s.46

References: Current Sentencing Practice D3–1

Note: a community punishment order may be made in the case of a person aged 18 or over convicted of an offence committed before April 4, 2005, or a person under the age of 18 convicted of an offence committed before April 4, 2009.

A community punishment order is a community order and may not be made unless the general requirements for a community order are satisfied; see **Community Orders—P.C.C.(S.)A. 2000—General Requirements)**.

The minimum age for a community punishment order is 16 years. A community punishment order may be made only if the offence concerned is punishable with imprisonment.

A community punishment order must specify the number of hours of unpaid work which the offender must perform. The minimum number of hours of work is 40; the maximum number of hours of work is 240. The court does not specify the nature of the work which is to be performed.

A community punishment order may be passed as the only sentence for the offence, or combined with any other form of sentence except an immediate custodial sentence, an activated suspended sentence, a suspended sentence, or a community rehabilitation order.

Before making the order, the court must explain to the offender the purpose and effect of the order, the consequences which may follow if he fails to comply with the order, and the power of the court to review the order on the application of the offender or a probation officer.

It is not necessary for the offender to consent if the order is made for an offence committed on or after October 1, 1997.

A court which imposes a suspended sentence may not make a community punishment order against the same offender for a different offence.

Drug abstinence requirement: the order may include a drug abstinence requirement, if the offender was 18 or over on the day of conviction, and the court is of the opinion that the offender is dependent on or has a propensity to misuse specified Class A drugs and that the misuse of those drugs by the offender contributed to the offence.

If these conditions are satisfied and the offence is a "trigger offence" any community punishment order must include a drug abstinence requirement, whether or not the use of drugs contributed to the offence.

The following offences are "trigger offences": theft, robbery, burglary, aggravated burglary, taking a vehicle without consent, aggravated vehicle taking, obtaining property by deception, or going equipped for theft, fraud, possession of articles for use in frauds, making or supplying articles for use in frauds, and producing or supplying a controlled drug, possession of a controlled drug with intent to supply, or possession of a controlled drug committed in relation to specified Class A drugs.

An offender subject to a drug abstinence requirement must abstain from misusing Class A drugs of the kind specified, and must provide when instructed to do so an appropriate sample for the purpose of ascertaining whether he has any specified Class A drug in his body.

A drug abstinence requirement may not be included in a community punishment order if the offender is sentenced at the same time to a drug treatment and testing order or a drug abstinence order.

A drug abstinence requirement may be included in an order only if the sentencing court has been notified that arrangements for implementing such requirements are available.

Community Punishment and Rehabilitation Orders

P.C.C.(S.)A. 2000, s.51

References: Current Sentencing Practice D4–1

Note: a community punishment order and rehabilitation order may be made in the case of a person aged 18 or over convicted of an offence committed before April 4, 2005, or a person under the age of 18 convicted of an offence committed before April 4, 2009.

A community punishment and rehabilitation order may be made in respect of a person of or over the age of 16 convicted of an offence punishable with imprisonment.

The order may involve a requirement that the offender be under supervision for a period not less than 12 months nor more than three years; and to perform unpaid work for a period not less than 40 nor more than 100 hours.

The court must be of the opinion that a community punishment and rehabilitation order is desirable in the interests of securing the rehabilitation of the offender or protecting the public from harm from him or preventing the commission by him of further offences.

Provisions relating to community rehabilitation orders apply to the rehabilitation element of the order; provisions relating to community punishment orders apply to the punishment element of the order.

A community punishment and rehabilitation order is a community order and the general requirements relating to community orders must be satisfied. (See **Community Orders—P.C.C.(S.)A. 2000—General Requirements.**)

Before making a community punishment and rehabilitation order, the court must give the explanations required for community rehabilitation orders and community punishment orders.

There is no requirement for consent if the offence was committed on or after October 1, 1997.

A court which imposes a suspended sentence may not make a community punishment and rehabilitation order against the same offender for a different offence.

Community Rehabilitation Order

P.C.C.(S.)A. 2000, s.41

References: Current Sentencing Practice D2–1

Note: a community rehabilitation order may be made in the case of a person aged 18 or over convicted of an offence committed before April 4, 2005, or a person under the age of 18 convicted of an offence committed before April 4, 2009.

A community rehabilitation order is a community order. A court may not make a community rehabilitation order unless the general requirements for a community order are satisfied. (See **Community Order— P.C.C.(S.)A. 2000—General Requirements.**)

The minimum age for a community rehabilitation order is 16 years.

A community rehabilitation order may be made only if the court is of the opinion that *supervision of the offender is desirable in the interests of securing the rehabilitation of the offender; or of protecting the public from harm from him; or of preventing the commission by him of further offences.*

Before making a community rehabilitation order, the court must explain to the offender the purpose and effect of the order, the consequences which may follow if he fails to comply with the order, and the power of the court to review the order on the application of the offender or a probation officer.

A community rehabilitation order may be for any period not less than six months and not more than three years. The order may include such additional requirements as the court considers desirable in the interests of securing the rehabilitation of the offender; or of protecting the public from harm from him; or of preventing the commission by him of further offences. The offender may be required to comply with such requirements during the whole or any part of the order period.

Special statutory rules apply to requirements relating to the following matters:

(a) residence;

(b) participation in specified activities;

(c) refraining from participation in specified activities;

(d) attending at a probation centre;

(e) submitting to treatment for a mental condition;

(f) submitting to treatment for drug or alcohol dependency;

(g) drug abstinence;

(h) curfew;

(i) exclusion.

The court may not make a community rehabilitation order including a requirement of this kind without obtaining and considering a pre-sentence report, unless it considers the pre-sentence report unnecessary. In the case of an offender under the age of 18 years, the court must not make such an order without considering a pre-sentence report, unless one of the offences is triable only on indictment, or there is a previous pre-sentence report in respect of the offender and the court has had regard to the information contained in that report.

Residence: before making an order containing a residence requirement, the court must consider the home surroundings of the offender. If the offender is to be required to reside in an approved hostel or other institution, the period for which he is to reside in the hostel or institution must be specified in the order.

Specified activities: the order may require the offender to present himself to a person specified in the order at a place specified in the order and to participate in activities specified in the order on a day or days specified in the order or during the period of the order, or such portion of it as may be specified. Such a requirement may not be included in an order unless the court has consulted an officer and is satisfied that it is feasible to secure compliance with the requirement and any person whose co-operation is involved in the requirement has consented. The offender may be required to attend on not more than 60 days in all. If the offender has been convicted of a sexual offence, the court may direct that he may be required to attend on a greater number of days; the greater number of days must be specified in the order. The place specified in the order must be approved as providing facilities suitable for persons subject to community rehabilitation orders.

Negative requirements: the order may require the offender to refrain from participating in activities specified in the order on a day or days specified in the order or during the period of the order, or such portion of it as may be specified. Such a requirement may not be included in an order unless the court has consulted an officer and is satisfied that it is feasible to secure compliance with the requirement.

Community rehabilitation centre: the order may require the offender to attend a community rehabilitation centre during a period specified in the order, provided that the court has consulted an officer and the court is satisfied that arrangements can be made for the offender's attendance at the centre and that the person in charge of the centre consents to the inclusion of the requirement. The offender may not be required to attend on more than 60 days in all. If the offender has been convicted of a sexual offence the court may direct that he may be required to attend on a greater number of days; the greater number of days must be specified in the order.

Psychiatric treatment: the order may include a requirement that the offender submit to treatment under the direction of a qualified medical practitioner with a view to the improvement of his mental condition.

Before including such a requirement, the court must be satisfied, on the evidence of an approved medical practitioner, that the mental condition of the offender is such as requires and is susceptible to treatment, but does not warrant his detention under a hospital order.

The court may not include such a requirement in the order unless the offender expresses his willingness to comply with it.

The requirement relating to treatment may be for the whole period of the order, or for any part of the period of the order. A community rehabilitation order may be for any period not less than six months and not more than three years.

The treatment required by the order may be either treatment as a resident patient in a mental hospital or mental nursing home, other than a special hospital, or treatment as a non-resident patient at such institution or place as may be specified in the order, or treatment by or under the direction of a practitioner specified in the order.

The court may not make a community rehabilitation order including a requirement for psychiatric treatment unless it is satisfied that arrangements have been made for the proposed treatment, including arrangements for the offender's reception as a resident patient, where such treatment is proposed.

The medical nature of the treatment is not specified in the order.

Drug or alcohol dependency: if the offender is dependent on drugs or alcohol, and the court is of the opinion that his dependency caused or contributed to the offence in respect of which the order is to be made, and that his dependency is such as requires and may be susceptible to treatment, the order may include a requirement that the offender shall submit during the whole of the period of the order or such part of it as is specified in the order to treatment by or under the direction of a person having the necessary qualifications with a view to the reduction or elimination of the offender's dependency on drugs or alcohol.

The court may not include such a requirement in the order unless the offender expresses his willingness to comply with the requirement.

The treatment required by the order may be either treatment as a resident in such institution or place as may be specified in the order, treatment as a non-resident in such institution or place as may be specified in the order, or treatment by or under the direction of a qualified person specified in the order.

The court may not make a community rehabilitation order including a requirement for treatment for drug or alcohol dependency unless it is satisfied that arrangements have been made for the proposed treatment, including arrangements for the offender's reception where he is required to submit to treatment as a resident.

A court may not make a community rehabilitation order including a requirement for treatment for drug dependency if it has been notified that arrangements for drug treatment and testing orders are available.

Drug abstinence requirement: the order may include a drug abstinence requirement, if the offender was 18 or over on the day of conviction, and the court is of the opinion that the offender is dependent on or has a propensity to misuse specified Class A drugs and that the misuse of those drugs by the offender contributed to the offence.

If these conditions are satisfied and the offence is a "trigger offence" any community rehabilitation order must include a drug abstinence requirement, whether or not the use of drugs contributed to the offence.

The following offences are "trigger offences": theft, robbery, burglary, aggravated burglary, taking a vehicle without consent, aggravated vehicle taking, obtaining property by deception, or going equipped for theft, and producing or supplying a controlled drug, possession of a controlled drug with intent to supply, or possession of a controlled drug committed in relation to specified Class A drugs.

An offender subject to a drug abstinence requirement must abstain from misusing Class A drugs of the kind specified, and must provide when instructed to do so an appropriate sample for the purpose of ascertaining whether he has any specified Class A drug in his body.

A drug abstinence requirement may not be included in a community rehabilitation order if the order contains a requirement relating to treatment for drug abuse, or if the offender is sentenced at the same time to a drug treatment and testing or a drug abstinence order.

A drug abstinence requirement may be included in an order only if the sentencing court has been notified that arrangements for implementing such requirements are available.

Curfew requirements: a community rehabilitation order may include a curfew requirement. The curfew requirement must not extend beyond the period of six months beginning with the day on which the order is made.

The period of curfew on each day must be at least two hours and not more than 12 hours. Curfew periods must as far as practical avoid conflict with the offender's religious beliefs or the requirements of any other community order to which he is subject, and any interference with his attendance at school or any an educational establishment.

A curfew requirement must include provision for monitoring the offender's whereabouts during the curfew period. Curfew requirements may not be included in a community rehabilitation order unless the court has been notified that arrangements for monitoring the order are available in the place to be specified in the requirement.

A curfew requirement may not be included in a community rehabilitation order if the offender is sentenced on the same occasion to a curfew order.

Exclusion requirements: a community rehabilitation order may include an "exclusion requirement."

The maximum period of the exclusion requirement is two years (the maximum duration of a community rehabilitation order is three years). The requirement may operate only during periods specified in the order and the requirement may specify different places or different periods or days. The requirement must so far as practical avoid conflict with the offender's religious beliefs or the requirements of any other community orders to which he may be subject and avoid interference with his attendance at school or any other educational establishment.

An exclusion requirement must include provision for monitoring the offender's whereabouts during the period when the prohibition applies. An exclusion requirement may not be included in a community rehabilitation order unless the court has been notified that arrangements for monitoring the offender's whereabouts are available in the relevant area.

An exclusion requirement may not be included in a community rehabilitation order if the offender is sentenced on the same occasion to an exclusion order.

Note: it is not necessary for the offender to express his willingness to comply with a community rehabilitation order if it is made in respect of an offence committed on or after October 1, 1997, except where the order contains requirements relating to psychiatric treatment or treatment for drug or alcohol dependency.

A court which imposes a suspended sentence may not make a community order against the same offender for a different offence.

Compensation Order

P.C.C.(S.)A. 2000, s.130

References: Current Sentencing Practice J2–1; Archbold 5–411

A compensation order may be made in respect of any *personal injury, loss or damage* which results from an offence of which the offender is convicted or from any offence which is taken into consideration.

A compensation order may be made as the only sentence for an offence, or in addition to most other forms of sentence.

If the court has power to make a compensation order, but does not exercise the power, it must state its reasons for not doing so.

Magistrates' courts

A magistrates' court may order a maximum of £5,000 in respect of any one offence. If compensation is ordered to be paid in respect of offences taken into consideration, the total amount of the compensation must not exceed the total amount which the court could order in respect of all the offences of which the offender has been convicted (that is, £5,000 multiplied by the number of offences of which he has been convicted).

Death

Where a person has died as a result of an offence, a compensation order may be made for funeral expenses or bereavement in respect of death, except in the case of a death due to an accident arising out of the presence of a motor vehicle on a road. A compensation order in respect of funeral expenses may be made for the benefit of anyone who incurred the expenses. A compensation order in respect of bereavement may be made only for the benefit of a person for whose benefit a claim for damages for bereavement could be made under the Fatal Accidents Act 1976, s.1A. The amount of compensation in respect of bereavement must not exceed £11,800 (or £10,000 if the death occurred before January 1, 2008).

Road accidents

If personal injury, loss or damage arises out of an accident caused by the presence of a motor vehicle on a road, a compensation order may be made only if either *the damage can be treated as damage arising out of an offence under the Theft Act 1968* (this would include any damage to a vehicle which has been stolen or taken without consent, whoever has actually caused the damage, so long as the damage occurred while the vehicle was out of the owner's possession) or the offender is *uninsured in respect of the personal injury, loss or damage concerned and compensation is not payable under the Motor Insurer's Bureau Agreement*.

In practice the effect of this is that a compensation order may be made in respect of damage to property up to a maximum of £300, unless the claimant was driving a vehicle which was itself not insured for the purposes of the Road Traffic Acts, or the claimant was a person who at the relevant time knew or ought to have known that the vehicle in which he was travelling had been stolen or unlawfully taken, or was not covered by insurance. In these cases the claimant is not covered by the MIB Agreement and the court may make a compensation order for the full amount of the loss, damage or personal injury. The court may also make a compensation order in favour of a claimant claiming by virtue of a right of subrogation.

General

The court must be satisfied that the injury, loss or damage which has occurred, is attributable to the offence in respect of which the compensation order is made.

The court must determine the amount of compensation which it considers appropriate, having regard to any evidence and to any representations that are made by or on behalf of the prosecutor.

If the value of the personal injury, loss or damage is not agreed by the defendant it must be established by evidence.

If the amount of the compensation due to the defendant cannot be established without complicated enquiries, it may be appropriate for the court to decline to make a compensation order and leave the victim to civil remedies.

A compensation order may be made in respect of a loss which is not itself actionable and may if appropriate contain an element of interest.

If the victim of an assault has provoked the assault by his own violent behaviour towards the offender, the amount of the compensation order may be reduced.

In determining whether to make a compensation order, or the amount of such an order, the **court must have regard to the means of the**

offender so far as they appear or are known to the court. *It is wrong in principle to impose a compensation order when there is no realistic possibility that the compensation will be paid within a reasonable time.*

If the compensation cannot be paid out of resources immediately available to the offender the court should determine the amount that he can reasonably pay out of income and order payment by instalments. The period of payment by instalments may extend to two years, or three years in exceptional circumstances.

The fact that the offender has been sentenced to custody does not necessarily mean that a compensation order is inappropriate, but a compensation order should not be made on the basis that the compensation will be paid out of future income unless the offender has clear prospects of employment on release from custody and the obligation to pay compensation will not be an encouragement to commit further offences.

If it is proposed to raise the necessary funds by selling assets, the court should satisfy itself that the assets do exist and should ensure that the assets have been valued by a competent person, before acting on the valuation. It is rarely appropriate to make a compensation order on the assumption that the necessary funds will be raised by the sale of the offender's matrimonial home.

The offender may be ordered to pay compensation even though he has not profited from the offence and his available assets are not themselves the proceeds of crime.

If the offender has been convicted of more than one offence, a separate order should be made in respect of each offence. If more than one offender has been convicted, a separate order should be made against each offender. If more than one offender has been convicted, but not all of them have the means to pay compensation, it is permissible to make an order against one offender for the whole amount of the loss, damage or injury.

The court does not fix any term of imprisonment in default, but may allow time for payment or fix payment by instalments.

If the amount of the compensation order exceeds £20,000, the Crown Court has power to enlarge the powers of the magistrates' court responsible for enforcing the order if it considers that the maximum default term of 12 months is inadequate. The court should make an order that the maximum term of imprisonment in default should be a figure taken from the table below:

Amount not exceeding:	Maximum term:
£50,000	18 months
£100,000	24 months
£250,000	36 months
£1 million	60 months
Over £1 million	120 months

If the court has made a confiscation order under Criminal Justice Act 1988 or the Proceeds of Crime Act 2002, the court should consider whether to make an order under Criminal Justice Act 1988, s.72(7) or the Proceeds of Crime Act 2002, s.13(6), which allows the court to direct that if the offender is unable to satisfy the compensation order because his means are inadequate, the deficiency shall be made good from the proceeds of the confiscation order.

Conditional Discharge

P.C.C.(S.)A. 2000, s.12

References: Current Sentencing Practice D11–1; Archbold 5–113

The court may grant a discharge for any offence other than murder or an offence in respect of which the court is obliged to pass a mandatory custodial sentence under the P.C.C.(S.)A. 2000, ss.109, 110 or 111, the Firearms Act 1968, s.51A, or the Criminal Justice Act 2003, ss.225, 226, 227 or 228.

The court must be of the opinion, having regard to the circumstances including the nature of the offence and the character of the offender, that it is *inexpedient to inflict punishment*.

The discharge may be absolute or conditional. A conditional discharge may be for any period not exceeding three years. There is no minimum period.

It is not necessary for the offender to consent.

The following orders may be made in conjunction with a discharge: a compensation order, a disqualification from driving, an order to pay prosecution costs, a recommendation for deportation, a banning order or an order under the Crime and Disorder Act 1998, s.1C (anti-social behaviour).

An offender who has been warned under the Crime and Disorder Act 1998, s.65 may not be conditionally discharged for an offence committed within two years of the warning, unless there are exceptional circumstances.

Conditional Discharge—Subsequent Conviction

P.C.C.(S.)A. 2000, s.13

References: Current Sentencing Practice D11–1; Archbold 5–114

The power to deal with an offender subject to a conditional discharge arises when he is convicted of an offence *committed during the period of the discharge,* whether or not the discharge is still effective when he appears before the court.

If the conditional discharge was granted by the Crown Court, the offender may be dealt with only by the Crown Court. A magistrates' court may commit the offender to the Crown Court to be dealt with in respect of the conditional discharge, and to be sentenced for the latest offence. (See **Committal for Sentence.**)

If the conditional discharge was granted by a magistrates' court, the offender may be dealt with either by the Crown Court or by a magistrates' court.

The court may deal with the offender as if he had just been convicted of the offence.

The offender should be sentenced on the basis of his current age, not his age on the date of conviction.

If the conditional discharge was granted by a magistrates' court, the court may deal with the offender for the offence in respect of which the conditional discharge was granted **in any way in which a magistrates' court could deal with him** for the offences concerned if it had just convicted him of that offence. *The Crown Court must observe the relevant limitations on the powers of the magistrates' court, in relation to maximum terms of imprisonment, aggregate terms of imprisonment, and financial penalties.*

If the offender is subject to two conditional discharges, the court may impose separate sentences for each of the offences in respect of which the orders were made.

If the court imposes a custodial sentence for the latest offence it will normally be appropriate for the court to impose a sentence for the original offence, which will terminate the conditional discharge, but there may be exceptional cases where it will be appropriate to leave the conditional discharge in effect.

Confiscation Order—Criminal Justice Act 1988
(Offences Committed before November 1, 1995)

CRIMINAL JUSTICE ACT 1988, s.71

References: Current Sentencing Practice J5–1001

The Criminal Justice Act 1988, as amended by the Criminal Justice Act 1993, but not as amended by the Proceeds of Crime Act 1995 applies to proceedings instituted on or after February 3, 1995 in which the offender has been convicted of at least one offence committed before November 1, 1995.

The Crown Court may proceed with a view to making a confiscation order if the defendant has been convicted of an offence triable on indictment other than a drug trafficking offence and the prosecutor has given **written notice that if the court considered that it ought to make such an order, it would be able to make an order requiring the offender to pay at least the minimum amount**.

A magistrates' court may proceed with a view to making a confiscation order if the defendant has been convicted of an offence listed in Criminal Justice Act 1988, Sch.4 (as amended) and the prosecutor has given written notice.

If the prosecutor gives notice, the court is not obliged to proceed with a view to making a confiscation order, but may decide to do so at its discretion.

If the court decides to proceed to make a confiscation order, the court must determine the amount of the defendant's benefit from the offences of which he has been convicted and any offences taken into consideration. The burden of proof is on the prosecution to the civil standard.

The court may postpone all questions relating to confiscation, or may determine that the offender has benefited from any relevant criminal conduct, and postpone the determination of the amount to be recovered in his case. The court may grant repeated postponements, but may not postpone the determinations for a total period of more than six months from the date of conviction unless there are exceptional circumstances. A postponement may be made on the application of either party, or by the court on its own motion. (See **Confiscation Order—Postponement of Proceedings**.)

If the court does postpone the inquiry, the court may proceed to sentence, but must not impose a fine or other financial order, or forfeiture order, but may make a compensation order.

If the defendant has been served with a statement tendered by the prosecutor, the court may ask the defendant to admit or challenge the allegations in the statement. Assumptions may not be made.

If the court has determined the value of the defendant's benefit and the defendant alleges that the amount that might be realised is less than the value of his benefit, the court must determine the amount that might be realised.

If the defendant establishes on the balance of probabilities that the amount that might be realised is less than the value of his benefit, the court may make a confiscation order for an amount not less than £10,000 and not more than the amount that might be realised.

If the defendant does not establish that the amount that might be realised is less than the value of his benefit, the court may make a confiscation order for an amount which is not less than £10,000 and not more than the amount which has been assessed as the value of the defendant's benefit from the offences of which he has been convicted or has asked to be taken into consideration.

The court has a discretion to determine the amount of the confiscation order, between the minimum amount, and either the value of the defendant's benefit or the amount which might be realised, whichever is the less.

The court must fix a term of imprisonment in default, whether or not property to value of the confiscation order has been seized. The term must be served consecutively to any custodial sentence imposed for the offences in respect of which the confiscation order is made. For default terms, see **Default Terms—Crown Court**.

The confiscation order must be left out of account in sentencing the offender except in considering a fine or order involving payment of costs or forfeiture of property. **A compensation order may be made**.

If the offender has already been sentenced, the court may make an order under P.C.C.(S.)A. 2000, s.143 or impose a fine within the normal time limit for varying a sentence, beginning on the day the confiscation order was made.

If the court makes a confiscation order and a compensation order, the court may order the sums recovered under the confiscation order to be applied to satisfy the compensation order.

The order or sentence may be varied by the Crown Court within the time limits allowed by P.C.C.(S.)A. 2000, s.155. (See **Alteration of Sentence.**)

Confiscation Order—Drug Trafficking Act 1994

DRUG TRAFFICKING ACT 1994

References: Current Sentencing Practice J7–1

The Drug Trafficking Act 1994 applies in the case of a defendant convicted of a drug trafficking offence in circumstances in which the Proceeds of Crime Act 2002 does not apply. (See Confiscation Order— Proceeds of Crime Act 2002.)

If the defendant has been convicted on indictment of a drug trafficking offence, or committed for sentence under P.C.C.(S.)A. 2000, s.3, the Crown Court must proceed with a view to a confiscation order if either the prosecutor asks the court to do so or the court decides that it is appropriate to do so.

If the prosecution ask the court to proceed with a view to a confiscation order, the prosecutor must provide a prosecutor's statement to the court; if the court decides to proceed, the court may require the prosecutor to provide a prosecutor's statement. If the defendant has been served with the prosecutor's statement, the court may ask the defendant to admit or challenge the allegations in the statement.

The court may direct the defendant to give such information as may be specified by the court.

The court may postpone all questions relating to confiscation, or may determine that the offender has benefited from drug trafficking, but postpone the determination of the value of his proceeds of drug trafficking and the amount that might be realised. The court may grant repeated postponements, but may not postpone the determinations for a total period of more than six months from the date of conviction, unless there are exceptional circumstances. A postponement may be made on the application of either party, or by the court on its own motion. If the court does postpone the inquiry, it may proceed to sentence, but must not impose a fine or other financial order, or forfeiture order. (See **Confiscation Order— Postponement of Proceedings.**)

If the prosecution establish on the balance of probabilities that the defendant has held property since his conviction, or that property has been transferred to him within the relevant six-year period, or that the defendant has made expenditures in the relevant six-year period, the court must **make the required assumptions**, unless the assumption is *shown to be incorrect or there would be a serious risk of injustice.*

If the court determines that the defendant has benefited from drug trafficking at any time, the court must assess the value of the defendant's proceeds of drug trafficking (*the gross value of all payments or rewards received by the defendant in connection with drug trafficking, adjusted for any change in value*); the defendant may not deduct or set off expenses. If drugs have been found in the possession of the defendant, the value of the drugs is not counted in determining the value of his proceeds of drug trafficking, but the court may assume that the drugs were bought with the proceeds of earlier drug trafficking.

If the defendant alleges that the amount that might be realised (the value of his assets and gifts caught by the Act) is less than the value of his proceeds of drug trafficking, the court must determine whether that amount is less than the value of his proceeds. The burden of proof that the amount that might be realised is less than the value of his proceeds is on the defendant.

If the defendant fails to establish that the amount that might be realised is less than the value of his proceeds, the court must make a confiscation order for the amount which it has assessed as the value of his proceeds.

If the defendant satisfies the court that the amount that might be realised is less than the value of his proceeds, the court must make a confiscation order for the amount that might be realised. If the amount is nil, an order for a nominal amount must be made.

The court may issue a certificate in relation to its determinations, and must so do if it makes an order for less than the value of the defendant's proceeds.

The court must fix a term of imprisonment in default, whether or not property of the value of the confiscation order has been seized. (See **Default Terms—Crown Court.**)

The default term must be served consecutively to any custodial sentence imposed for the offences in respect of which the confiscation order is made. *Service of the default term does not cancel the confiscation order.*

If the court has not already sentenced the offender, the court proceeds to sentence for the offence. The confiscation order must be left out of account except in considering a fine or order involving payment or forfeiture of property.

If the offender has already been sentenced, the court may impose a fine or financial order, or make an order under Misuse of Drugs Act 1971, s.27 or P.C.C.(S.)A. 2000, s.143 within the normal time limit for varying a sentence, beginning on the day the confiscation order was made.

The order or sentence may be varied by the Crown Court within the normal time limits. (See **Alteration of Sentence.**) Alternative procedures allow the confiscation order to be reopened after it has been made.

Confiscation Order—Postponement of Proceedings

CRIMINAL JUSTICE ACT 1988, s.72A; DRUG TRAFFICKING ACT 1994, s.3, PRO-
CEEDS OF CRIME ACT 2002, s.11

References: Current Sentencing Practice J10; Archbold 5–541

**Note: this section sets out a summary of decisions on postpone-
ment of confiscation proceedings under the Criminal Justice Act 1988
and the Drug Trafficking Act 1994. The statutory provisions governing postponement under the Proceeds of Crime Act 2002 are different from those under the two earlier Acts, but some of these
decisions may apply to that Act.**

***All decisions on the postponement of confiscation orders must be consid-
ered in the light of the decision of the House of Lords in Soneji and Bullen
[2006] 1 Cr.App.R.(S.) 79 (p.430).***

The Crown Court must make the decision to proceed with a view to
confiscation and to postpone the determination of the relevant matters,
before sentencing the defendant.

A postponement of the determinations need not be for a specific period.

The decision to postpone is a judicial act, which must be performed in
open court in the presence of both parties.

The decision to postpone requires the exercise of judicial discretion,
which must be shown to be exercised.

If a court proposes to postpone inquiries for a period exceeding six
months (two years where the Proceeds of Crime Act 2002 applies) from the
date of conviction, it must identify "exceptional circumstances" for doing
so and order the postponement before the end of the six-month period.

If the court properly postpones the determinations for a period which
exceeds six months from the date of conviction on the grounds that there
are "exceptional circumstances", it is not necessary for the court to find
further exceptional circumstances for subsequent postponements.

The determination whether the circumstances which are relied on to
justify a postponement beyond the period of six months from the date of
conviction is a matter within the discretion of the sentencing judge, and
the Court of Appeal, Criminal Division will not readily interfere with the
judge's exercise of the discretion.

The period of six months beginning with the date of conviction includes the day on which the defendant is convicted itself.

A court which postpones the relevant determinations and proceeds to sentence the defendant before making a confiscation order should not make an order for the payment of prosecution costs before making the confiscation order, but it may make a compensation order.

Confiscation Order—Proceeds of Crime Act 1995
(Offences Committed on or after November 1, 1995)

CRIMINAL JUSTICE ACT 1988, SS.71–83, AS AMENDED BY CRIMINAL JUSTICE ACT 1993 AND PROCEEDS OF CRIME ACT 1995

References: Current Sentencing Practice J9–1

The Criminal Justice Act 1988, as amended by the Proceeds of Crime Act 1995, applies only if every offence of which the offender has been convicted was committed on or after November 1, 1995. *If any of the offences of which the offender has been convicted in the same proceedings was committed before November 1, 1995, the amended version of the Criminal Justice Act 1988 does not apply.*

The Criminal Justice Act 1988 as amended by the Proceeds of Crime Act 1995 does not apply where the Proceeds of Crime Act 2002 applies (see *Confiscation Order—Proceeds of Crime Act 2002*).

The Crown Court may proceed with a view to a confiscation order if the offender has been convicted of an offence triable on indictment, other than a drug trafficking offence or an offence under the Prevention of Terrorism (Temporary Provisions) Act 1989 or the Terrorism Act 2000, and either the prosecutor has given written notice that it would be appropriate to initiate confiscation proceedings or the court considers that it is appropriate to do so. **The court may initiate confiscation proceedings even though the prosecution has not given written notice.** *If the prosecution has given written notice, the court must proceed with a view to a confiscation order.*

The powers may be exercised if the offender has been committed for sentence under the P.C.C.(S.)A. 2000, ss.3, 4 or 6.

A magistrates' court may proceed with a view to a confiscation order if the offender has been convicted of an offence listed in Sch.4 to the Act.

If the prosecutor serves notice, the prosecutor must tender a statement to the court setting out matters relevant to determining whether the offender has benefited, and the value of his benefit; if the court decides to initiate confiscation proceedings, the court may require the prosecutor to provide such a statement.

If the offender has been served with a statement tendered by the prosecutor, the court may ask the offender to admit or challenge the allegations in the statement. *The court may direct the offender to give such information as may be specified.*

The court may postpone all questions relating to confiscation, or may determine that the offender has benefited from any relevant criminal conduct, and postpone the determination of the amount to be recovered in his case. The court may grant repeated postponements, but may not postpone the determinations for a total period of more than six months from the date of conviction unless there are exceptional circumstances. A postponement may be made on the application of either party, or by the court on its own motion. (See **Confiscation Order—Postponement of Proceedings**).

If the court postpones the confiscation proceedings, the court may proceed to sentence, but must not impose a fine or other financial order, or forfeiture order. The court may make a compensation order.

The court must determine whether the offender has benefited from any relevant criminal conduct (the offences of which the offender has been convicted and any offences taken into consideration) and assess the value of the offender's benefit. The burden of proof is on the prosecution to the civil standard.

If the offender alleges that the amount that might be realised is less than the value of his benefit from relevant criminal conduct, the court must determine the amount that might be realised. If the offender establishes on the balance of probabilities that the amount that might be realised is less than the value of his benefit from relevant criminal conduct, the court must make a confiscation order for the amount that might be realised, unless the victim is taking or has taken civil proceedings against the offender, in which case the order may be for a lesser amount.

If the offender does not establish that the amount that might be realised is less than the value of his benefit, the court must make a confiscation order for the amount which it has assessed as the value of the offender's benefit from relevant criminal conduct, unless the victim is taking or has taken civil proceedings against the offender, in which case the order may be for a lesser amount.

There is no minimum amount. The court may issue a certificate in relation to its determinations.

The court must fix a term of imprisonment in default, whether or not property to the value of the confiscation order has been seized. (See **Default Terms—Crown Court.**) The term must be served consecutively to any custodial sentence imposed for the offences in respect of which the confiscation order is made. *Service of the default term does not cancel the confiscation order*.

If the court has not already sentenced the offender, the court proceeds to sentence for the offence. The confiscation order must be left out of account except in considering a fine or order for payment of costs or forfeiture of property.

The confiscation order must be left out of account in considering whether to make a compensation order. If the court makes a confiscation order and a compensation order, the court may order the sums recovered under the confiscation order to be applied to satisfy the compensation order.

If the offender has already been sentenced, the court may make an order under the P.C.C.(S.)A., s.143, or impose a fine within the normal time limit for varying a sentence, beginning on the day the confiscation order was made.

If the prosecutor has given a written notice which contains a declaration that the case is one in which s.72AA should be applied, and either the offender has been convicted in the present proceedings of at least two offences from which he has benefited, committed on or after November 1, 1995, (other than a drug trafficking offence or a Prevention of Terrorism (Temporary Provision) Act 1989 or Terrorism Act 2000 offence), or the offender has been convicted in the present proceedings of at least one offence (other than a drug trafficking offence or a terrorism offence) from which he has benefited, and has been convicted on a previous occasion during the six years immediately before the institution of the present proceedings of at least one such offence, the court may make if it thinks fit the permitted assumptions in determining the value of the offender's benefit from relevant criminal conduct. *The court has a discretion whether or not to make the permitted assumptions.*

The Court must not make any of the permitted assumptions if it is *shown to be incorrect*, or to relate to property which has been the subject of a previous confiscation order, or would involve the *risk of serious injustice*.

Where the court makes any such assumption, the offences in relation to which the assumption is made are treated as part of the relevant criminal conduct. The court determines the amount of the offender's benefit on the basis that all the property or expenditure in respect of which assumptions have been made is derived from offences of which he has been convicted in the present proceedings.

Sentencing Referencer

Confiscation Order—Proceeds of Crime Act 2002

PROCEEDS OF CRIME ACT 2002

References: Current Sentencing Practice J11–1; Archbold 5–527

The confiscation order provisions of the Proceeds of Crime Act 2002 apply only where all of the offences of which the offender has been convicted (but not those which he asks the court to take into consideration) were committed on or after March 24, 2003. *Where an offence has been committed over a period of two or more days, or at some time during a period of two or more days, it is taken to have been committed on the earliest of those days.*

To qualify for a confiscation order, the defendant must either have been:

> convicted of an offence or offences in proceedings before the Crown Court;

> committed to the Crown Court for sentence in respect of an offence or offences under the Powers of Criminal Courts (Sentencing) Act 2000, ss.3, 4 or 6;

> or committed to the Crown Court under the Proceeds of Crime Act 2002, s.70.

If the defendant absconds after conviction, the Court may proceed under Proceeds of Crime Act 2002, s.27.

The court must proceed with a view to a confiscation order if it is asked to do so by the prosecutor, or if the court believes "it is appropriate for it to do so".

If the court believes that any victim of the offence has initiated, or intends to initiate, civil proceedings against the defendant, it is not bound to institute confiscation proceedings, but may do so in its discretion.

If the Crown Court embarks on confiscation proceedings, it must first decide whether the defendant has a "**criminal lifestyle**".

A person has a "criminal lifestyle" if either:

> he is convicted of one of the offences specified in Sch.2 of the Act; or

> the offence constitutes "conduct forming part of a course of criminal activity"; or

if the offence was committed over a period of at least six months and the defendant has benefited from the conduct.

An offence constitutes part of a course of criminal conduct if either:

the defendant has been convicted in the same proceedings of at least four offences, he has benefited from at least four offences, and his "relevant benefit" is at least £5,000; or

the defendant has been convicted on at least two separate occasions during the period of six years ending with a day when the proceedings for the present offence were started and has benefited from the offences in respect of which he was convicted on both of those occasions, and the "relevant benefit" amounts to at least £5,000. The latest offence must have been committed on or after March 24, 2003, but it is not necessary that the two earlier offences should have been.

If the Court decides that the defendant has a **"criminal lifestyle"** it must decide whether he has benefited from his **"general criminal conduct"**. "General criminal conduct" is "all his criminal conduct", and it is immaterial whether the conduct occurred before or after the passing of this Act or whether property constituting a benefit from conduct was obtained before or after the passing of the Act.

In making this decision, the Court **must** make any of the **assumptions** required by s.10 which apply, *unless the assumption is "shown to be incorrect" or there would be a "serious risk of injustice" if the assumption were made.*

The first assumption is that any property transferred to the defendant within the period of six years ending on the day on which proceedings were started against the defendant was obtained by him as a result of his general criminal conduct.

The second assumption is that any property held by the defendant at any time after the date of conviction was obtained by him as a result of his general criminal conduct.

The third assumption is that any expenditure incurred by the defendant within a period of six years ending with the date on which the proceedings were started against him was met from property obtained by him as a result of his general criminal conduct.

The fourth assumption is that any property obtained or assumed to have been obtained by the defendant was free of any other interest in the property.

If the court decides that the defendant **does not have a "criminal lifestyle"**, the court must then decide whether the defendant has benefited from his "**particular criminal conduct**". "Particular criminal conduct" is "all his criminal conduct" which "constitutes the offence or offences concerned", or "constitutes the offences of which he was convicted in the same proceedings as those in which he was convicted of the offence or offences concerned", or "constitutes offences which the court will be taking into consideration in deciding his sentence for the offence or offences concerned". **Benefit arising from offences committed before March 24, 2003, and which are taken into consideration, must be disregarded**.

Any question arising in connection with whether the defendant has a criminal life style or whether he has benefited from his general or particular criminal conduct must be decided on a "balance of probabilities".

The court must make an order for the amount which it has assessed to be the defendant's benefit, unless either:

> it believes that a victim of the offence has started or intends to start civil proceedings against the defendant (in which case the amount of the order is such amount "as the court believes is just", but the amount must not exceed the amount of the defendant's benefit;

> or the defendant shows that the "available amount" is less than the benefit (in which case the amount of the confiscation order is either the "available amount" itself, or a nominal amount).

The "**available amount**" includes the total of the values of all "free property" held by the defendant at the time the confiscation order is made, and the total value of all "**tainted gifts**".

If the Crown Court is proceeding with a view to a confiscation order on the application of the prosecutor, the prosecutor must give the Crown Court a statement of information. If the Crown Court is proceeding with a view to confiscation on its own initiative, it may order the prosecutor to give such a statement.

Where a statement of information has been given to the Court and a copy served on the defendant, the Crown Court may order the defendant to indicate to what extent he accepts the allegations made in the statement, and in so far as he does not accept an allegation, "to give particulars of any matters he proposes to rely on". If the defendant accepts any allegation, the Crown Court may treat that acceptance as conclusive. If the defendant fails to comply with an order, he may be treated as accepting every allegation in the statement of information other than an allegation in respect of which he has complied with the requirement, or an allegation that he has benefited from his general or particular criminal conduct.

No acceptance of an allegation by the defendant is admissible in evidence in proceedings for an offence.

The Crown Court may order the defendant to give it the "information specified in the order". There is no restriction on the kind of information which may be specified. If the defendant fails "without reasonable excuse" to comply with an order, the court "may draw such inference as it believes is appropriate" from the failure.

When the Crown Court makes a confiscation order it must make the following orders:

Appoint receiver (ss.50–55)

The Court may appoint an "enforcement receiver" on the application of the prosecutor.

Empower the receiver

The Court must confer on the enforcement receiver whichever of the powers under ss.51 or 53 is relevant.

Transfer from management receiver to enforcement receiver (s.64)

Where a receiver has been appointed in connection with a restraint order, and the Crown Court makes a confiscation order and a receiver is appointed under s.50, the Crown Court must order the "management receiver" appointed in connection with the restraint order to transfer to the "enforcement receiver" appointed in connection with the confiscation order all property held by the first receiver by virtue of the exercise of his powers.

Allow time for payment (s.11)

If the defendant shows that he needs time to pay the order, **the court may make an order allowing payment to be made within a specified period *which must not exceed six months* from the day on which the confiscation order is made**.

If the defendant makes a further application to the Crown Court within the specified period and Court believes that there are "exceptional circumstances" it may make an order extending the period. *The extended period must not extend beyond 12 months from the day on which the confiscation order was made.*

Although the second application must be made within the original six-month specified period, the order extending the period may be made after the end of that period, but not after the end of the period of 12 months starting with the day on which the confiscation order was made.

It is not open to the Crown Court to make an order allowing 12 months for payment on the defendant's initial application, even though the defendant shows that there are exceptional circumstances in which this would be appropriate. The defendant must make a further application within the six-month period.

Fix term of imprisonment in default (ss.35, 36)

The Crown Court must fix a term of imprisonment to be served in default of the order, taking the terms from the table set out in the P.C.C.(S.)A. 2000, s.139(4); (See **Default Terms—Crown Court.**)

Sentencing the defendant for the offence (ss.13, 15, 71)

If the court postpones the confiscation proceedings under s.14, it may sentence the defendant in the normal way but must not make any of the orders specified in subs.(2). (These orders include a compensation order).

Where the defendant has been sentenced and subsequently a confiscation order is made following a postponement, the sentence originally passed may be varied by the addition of one of the orders mentioned in subs.(3) within 28 days starting with the last day of the period of postponement. This does not necessarily mean the day on which the confiscation order is actually made.

If the Crown Court makes a confiscation order before sentencing the defendant, the Crown Court when sentencing the defendant must take account of the confiscation order before imposing a fine, making any order involving payment by the defendant other than a compensation order, or making the other orders of forfeiture or deprivation specified in the section. *A court which has made a confiscation order may leave the confiscation order out of account in deciding whether to make a compensation order in favour of the victim of the offence and in deciding the amount of the order. It is open to the Crown Court to make a confiscation order and a compensation order in respect of the same offence, even though this means that the defendant will be required to pay twice the amount involved in the offence.*

In deciding the appropriate sentence for the offence, where it is not a financial penalty, the confiscation order must be left out of account. *The defendant cannot claim that his sentence should be mitigated because a confiscation order has been made.*

If the defendant has been committed for sentence under s.70 for an either way offence, the powers of the Crown Court to deal with the offender for the offence depend on whether the magistrates' court at the time of committal stated in accordance with s.70(5) that it would have committed the defendant for sentence under the P.C.C.(S.)A. 2000, s.3. If it did, the Crown Court must inquire into the circumstances of the case and may deal with the defendant in any way in which it could deal with him if he had just been convicted of the offence on indictment. If the magistrates' court did not make a statement under s.70(5) in respect of an either way offence, or the offence is not an either way offence, the Crown Court, having inquired into the circumstances of the case, may deal with the defendant in any way in which the magistrates' court could deal with him if it had just convicted him of the offence.

Enforcing the default term (ss.35–39)

All questions relating to serving the default term will be dealt with in the magistrates' court, in the same way as a fine, subject to the amendments made by s.35(3) to the normal procedure.

Consecutive Sentences

CRIMINAL JUSTICE ACT 2003, s.265

References: Current Sentencing Practice A5–1; Archbold 5–388

Consecutive sentences of imprisonment should not normally be passed in respect of offences which arise out of the same transaction or incident, but may be passed in exceptional circumstances in such cases.

Consecutive sentences should normally be passed in the following cases:

- (a) where a burglar uses violence towards an occupant of premises who interrupts him;

- (b) where violence is used to resist arrest for the primary offence;

- (c) where an offender is convicted of an offence under the Firearms Act 1968 committed by having a firearm with him at the time of another offence;

- (d) where one offence is committed while the offender is on bail in connection with the other offence;

- (e) where a community order is revoked following the offender's conviction of a further offence;

- (f) where a suspended sentence is activated following the offender's conviction of a further offence;

- (g) where an offender is convicted of doing an act tending to pervert the course of justice in relation to the other offence.

In all cases, whether or not the sentences are passed on the same occasion or by the same sentencer, the court should have regard to the principle of totality and review the aggregate sentence to ensure that it is just and appropriate for the offender's behaviour, taken as a whole.

A sentence of life imprisonment or imprisonment for public protection should not be imposed to run consecutively to any other sentence, and no sentence may be ordered to run consecutively to a sentence of life imprisonment or imprisonment for public protection. If a court imposes such a sentence in circumstances in which the sentence would normally be consecutive to another sentence, it should make an appropriate adjustment to the minimum term. (See **Minimum Term.**) If an offender who is serving the minimum term of an indeterminate sentence falls to be sentenced for another offence, the court may impose a determinate sentence to begin at the expiry of the minimum term of the indeterminate sentence.

If a court makes an order under the P.C.C.(S.)A. 2000, s.116 ordering an offender to return to custody to serve the balance of a sentence from which he has been released, the court must order him to serve the s.116 period before (or concurrently with) any new sentence for the later offence.

A court must not order a term of imprisonment to commence on the expiration of any other sentence of imprisonment from which the offender has already been released and in respect of which his licence has been revoked. This does not prevent the court from ordering a sentence of imprisonment to run consecutively to an order under P.C.C.(S.)A. 2000, s.116, where that section applies (see Return to Custody).

Curfew Order

P.C.C.(S.)A. 2000, s.37

References: Current Sentencing Practice D5–1

Note: a curfew order may be made in respect of a person aged 18 or over only if the offence was committed before April 4, 2005. A curfew order may be made in respect of a person between the ages of 16 and 18 only if the offence was committed before April 4, 2009. A curfew order may be made in respect of a person under 16 irrespective of the date of the offence.

A curfew order may not be made unless the general requirements for a community order are satisfied. (See **Community Orders—Criminal Justice Act 2003—General Criteria.**)

A curfew order may be made only by a court which has been notified that appropriate arrangements have been made.

The court must obtain and consider a presentence report unless it considers it unnecessary to do so on the ground that the court has considered an earlier report.

A curfew order is an order requiring the offender to remain, for periods specified in the order, at a place specified in the order. A curfew order may specify different places or different periods for different days.

All the specified periods must fall within the period of six months beginning with the day on which the order is made. If the offender is under 16, the period is three months. The periods specified must be not less than 2 hours, and not more than 12 hours.

The requirements of the order shall, as far as is practicable, avoid any conflict with the offender's religious beliefs or the requirements of any other community order to which he may be subject and any interference with the times at which he normally works, or attends school or an educational establishment.

A curfew order must include provision for making a person of an authorised description responsible for monitoring the offender's whereabouts during the periods specified in the order.

Before making the order, the court must explain to the offender the effect of the order, the consequences which may follow if he fails to comply with the order, and the power of the court to review the order on the application of the offender or a probation officer.

The consent of the offender is not necessary if the offence was committed on or after October 1, 1997.

Before making a curfew order the court must obtain and consider information about the place to be specified in the order and the attitude of persons likely to be affected by the enforced presence there of the offender.

Custodial Sentences—Criminal Justice Act 2003— General Criteria

CRIMINAL JUSTICE ACT 2003, ss.152, 153, 156

References: Current Sentencing Practice A2A; Archbold 5–262

Note: these provisions apply only to sentences imposed for offences committed on or after April 4, 2005.

A court must not pass a custodial sentence unless it is of the opinion that the offence or the combination of the offence and one or more offences associated with it **was so serious that neither a fine alone nor a community sentence can be justified for the offence**.

This requirement does not apply to sentences fixed by law, mandatory or required minimum sentences under the P.C.C.(S.)A. 2000, ss.110 and 111, and the Firearms Act 1968, s.51A, or sentences of life imprisonment, imprisonment (or detention) for public protection, or extended sentences of imprisonment or detention.

It is not a justification for a discretionary custodial sentence that the offence is a sexual or violent offence and only a custodial sentence would be adequate to protect the public from serious harm from the offender. An offender to whom this would apply will normally qualify for one of the sentences provided for dangerous offenders convicted of specified offences. (See **Specified Offences—Adult Offenders.**)

A custodial sentence may be passed for an offence which is not "so serious that neither a fine alone nor a community sentence can be justified" if the offender refuses to express his willingness to comply with a proposed requirement of a community order which requires him to express his willingness to comply. *The relevant requirements are a mental health treatment requirement, a drug rehabilitation requirement, and an alcohol treatment requirement.* It is not necessary for the offender to express his willingness to comply with an unpaid work requirement.

A custodial sentence may also be passed for an offence which is not "so serious that neither a fine alone nor a community sentence can be justified" if the offender fails to comply with an order to take a pre-sentence drug test.

Length of discretionary custodial sentences

A custodial sentence must be for the **shortest term (not exceeding the permitted maximum) that in the opinion of the court is commensu-**

rate with the seriousness of the offence, or the combination of the offence and one or more offences associated with it.

The restriction does not apply to a sentence fixed by law, a required minimum sentence under the P.C.C.(S.)A. 2000, ss.110 or 111, or the Firearms Act 1968, s.51A, or a sentence of imprisonment (or custody or detention) for life, or imprisonment (or detention) for public protection. The restriction applies to the custodial term of an extended sentence of imprisonment or detention in a young offender institution, but may not apply to the custodial term of an extended sentence of detention.

No provision is made for a "longer than commensurate" sentence to be passed where such a sentence is considered necessary for the protection of the public from serious harm from the offender. In such cases, the court should pass either a sentence of imprisonment (or detention) for public protection, or an extended sentence. (See **Specified Offences—Adult Offenders.**)

Information

The court must take account of all available information about the circumstances of the offence when forming an opinion about the seriousness of the offence, for the purpose of deciding whether the offence is so serious that a custodial sentence is necessary and what is the shortest term which is commensurate with the seriousness of the offence.

Reports

If a court proposes to impose a custodial sentence on an offender over the age of 18 on any ground other than the failure of an offender to express his willingness to comply with one of the orders mentioned in s.152(3) it must "obtain and consider" a pre-sentence report unless it is of the opinion "that it is unnecessary" to do so.

In the case of an offender under the age of 18, a pre-sentence report is mandatory before the court imposes a custodial sentence (other than on the basis of a failure to express willingness under s.152 (3). (*The exception in the P.C.C.(S.)A. 2000, s.81 for cases where one of the offences for which the offender is to be sentenced is triable only on indictment is not repeated in this provision*).

If the sentencing court does not obtain a pre-sentence report, where such a report is required, the failure does not affect the validity of the sentence or order of the court, but any appellate court dealing with the case is placed under similar obligations, subject to the same exceptions.

Custodial Sentences—Powers of Criminal Courts (Sentencing) Act 2000—Statutory Criteria

P.C.C.(S.)A. 2000, ss.79 to 83

References: Current Sentencing Practice A2–1

Note: these provisions apply only to offences committed before April 4, 2005.

The following sentences are "custodial sentences": imprisonment, detention in a young offenders institution, detention and training order, detention under P.C.C.(S.)A. 2000, s.91.

A committal for contempt is not a "custodial sentence".

All custodial sentences are subject to the same criteria. A custodial sentence may be imposed on an offender of any age only if one of three conditions is satisfied. These are:

(a) The offender has failed to express his willingness to comply with a requirement relating to psychiatric treatment, or treatment for drug or alcohol dependence, which the court proposes to include in a community rehabilitation order or supervision order, or a requirement to be included in a drug treatment and testing order, or a requirement to provide a sample in connection with a drug treatment and testing order;

(b) The offence is a violent or sexual offence and the court is of the opinion that only a custodial sentence would be adequate to protect the public from serious harm from him. (For definitions of "sexual offence", "violent offence" and "serious harm", see **Longer than Commensurate Sentences**);

(c) The offence or the combination of the offence and one or more offences associated with it is **so serious that only a custodial sentence can be justified for the offence**.

An "associated offence" is an offence of which the offender is convicted in the proceedings in which he is convicted of the other offence, or (although convicted of it in earlier proceedings) is sentenced for it at the same time as he is sentenced for that offence; or which the offender admits in the proceedings in which he is sentenced for the other offence and requests the court to take into consideration in sentencing him for that offence.

In determining the seriousness of an offence, the court must take into account information about the circumstances of the offence, but must not take into account information about the circumstances of the offender, except any previous convictions of the offender or any failure of his to respond to previous sentences.

The fact that an offence is "so serious" does not mean that a custodial sentence must be passed; the court may mitigate the sentence and pass a community order instead.

Procedural requirements

A pre-sentence report must be obtained and considered before the court forms the opinion that either condition (b) or condition (c) is satisfied unless the court considers a pre-sentence report unnecessary. If the offender is under 18 a report must be obtained unless a recent report is available.

Medical reports must normally be obtained if the offender is or appears to be mentally disordered.

In determining whether a custodial sentence is necessary for the protection of the public in the case of an offender convicted of a violent or sexual offence, the court may take into account any information about the offender which is before it.

The court must state which of the conditions justifying a custodial sentence is satisfied (unless the custodial sentence is passed under condition (a) above) and why the condition is satisfied, and in every case explain in ordinary language why it is passing a custodial sentence.

Length of sentence

Normally, the sentence must be for such a term as is **commensurate with the seriousness of the offence, or the combination of the offence and other offences associated with it**. A commensurate sentence may include a deterrent element.

If the offence is a **sexual offence or a violent offence**, and the court considers that a longer term than would be commensurate with the seriousness of the offences is necessary to protect the public from serious harm from the offender, the court may pass a **longer than commensurate sentence**.

Default Terms (Crown Court)

P.C.C.(S.)A. 2000, s.139

References: Current Sentencing Practice J1–1A01; Archbold 5–396

If the Crown Court imposes a fine or makes a confiscation order, the court must fix a term of imprisonment in default of payment of the fine.

The following table shows the default terms applicable to fines and confiscation orders.

Fine	*Term*
Not exceeding £200	7 days
More than £200, not exceeding £500	14 days
More than £500, not exceeding £1,000	28 days
More than £1,000, not exceeding £2,500	45 days
More than £2,500, not exceeding £5,000	3 months
More than £5,000, not exceeding £10,000	6 months
More than £10,000, not exceeding £20,000	12 months
More than £20,000, not exceeding £50,000	18 months
More than £50,000, not exceeding £100,000	2 years
More than £100,000, not exceeding £250,000	3 years
More than £250,000, not exceeding £1 million	5 years
Over £1 million	10 years

These terms are maximum terms for the sums in question; the court should exercise its discretion and fix an appropriate default term within the relevant maximum. The court may also allow time for payment and may fix instalments.

The Crown Court does not fix a default term when it makes a compensation order or orders the offender to pay the costs of the prosecution, but may enlarge the powers of the magistrates' court.

Deferment of Sentence

P.C.C.(S.)A. 2000, ss.1, 2

References: Current Sentencing Practice L8; Archbold 5–37

These provisions apply to all offences irrespective of the date on which the offence was committed.

Either the magistrates' court or the Crown Court may defer passing sentence on an offender for the purpose of enabling the court to have regard to his conduct after conviction (including the making by him of reparation for the offence) or any change to his circumstances.

The power may be exercised only if the offender **consents** and **undertakes to comply with any requirements** as to his conduct during the period of deferment that the court considers it appropriate to impose. *The court is not obliged to impose requirements on deferring sentence.* The court must also be satisfied that it would be in the interests of justice to defer sentence.

Sentence may be deferred for a period of **not more than six months**.

The requirements which the court may require the offender to comply with during the period of deferment are not specified, but it is provided that a residence requirement may be imposed and that the court may appoint an officer of a local probation board or other person to act as a supervisor. *The statutory power is not limited to the requirements which may be imposed in connection with a community order.* If the offender fails to comply with the requirements imposed during the period of deferment, he may be brought before the court and dealt with before the end of the period of deferment.

A court which has deferred sentence may deal with the offender before the end of the period of deferment if he is convicted of an offence during the deferment period. If the conviction for the later offence occurs in England and Wales, the court which sentences him for the later offence may deal with him for the offence or offences in respect of which sentence has been deferred, but a magistrates' court may not deal with an offender in respect of a sentence deferred by the Crown Court, and if the Crown Court deals with an offender in respect of a sentence deferred by a magistrates' court, the Crown Court may not pass a sentence which could not have been passed by a magistrates' court.

Deprivation Order

P.C.C.(S.)A. 2000, s.143

References: Current Sentencing Practice J4–1; Archbold 5–439

A court may order an offender to be deprived of his rights in property **which has been used, or was intended to be used, to commit or facilitate the commission of an offence, or in property of which he was unlawfully in possession**.

The power may be used in addition to any other sentence for the offence, or as the only sentence for the offence.

The power may be used by the Crown Court or by a magistrates' court on conviction for any offence.

The court must be satisfied that either:

(a) the property has been used for the purpose of committing or facilitating the commission of any offence; or

(b) the property was intended by the offender to be used for the purpose of committing or facilitating the commission of any offence; or

(c) that the offender has been convicted of unlawful possession of the property concerned; or

(d) that an offence of unlawfully possessing the property concerned has been taken into consideration.

The property must either:

(a) *have been lawfully seized from the offender; or*

(b) *have been in his possession or control at the time when he was apprehended for the offence; or*

(c) *have been in his possession or control at the time when a summons in respect of the offence was issued.*

"Facilitating the commission of an offence" includes *"the taking of any steps after it has been committed for the purpose of disposing of any property to which it relates or of avoiding apprehension or detection"*.

It is not necessary that the offence in relation to which the property has been used or was intended to be used should be the offence of which the offender has been convicted.

If a person commits an offence under the Road Traffic Act 1988 punishable with imprisonment, manslaughter, or wanton and furious driving contrary to Offences against the Person Act 1861, s.35 by driving, attempting to drive or being in charge of a vehicle, failing to provide a specimen for analysis or laboratory test, or failing to stop and give information or report an accident, the vehicle shall be regarded as used for the purpose of committing the offence and any offence of aiding the commission of the offence.

The power to make a deprivation order may not be used in relation to property taken from the offender, which has been used by another person to commit an offence.

Deprivation orders do not apply to land or buildings.

A deprivation order should not be made without a proper investigation of the grounds for making an order. A court considering whether to make an order under the section must have regard to the value of the property and must normally have evidence of the value of the property concerned before making a deprivation order.

A court considering whether to make a deprivation order must have regard to the likely financial and other effects on the offender of the order, taken together with any other order that the court contemplates making.

A deprivation order should be considered as part of the total sentence, and the court should bear in mind that the overall penalty, including the deprivation order, should be commensurate with the offence.

Where a deprivation order is to be made against one of a number of offenders, who are all equally responsible, there may be unjustifiable disparity.

A court which has made a deprivation order may order the proceeds arising from the sale of the property, not exceeding a figure specified by the court, to be paid to a person who has suffered loss, damage or personal injury as a result of the offence of which the offender has been convicted, or which he has asked the court to take into consideration, if the court would have made a compensation order in favour of the victim but was prevented from doing so by the inadequacy of the offender's means.

Detention under Powers of Criminal Courts (Sentencing) Act 2000, s.91

P.C.C.(S.)A. 2000, s.91

References: Current Sentencing Practice E4–1; Archbold 5–358

The power to award detention under the P.C.C.(S.)A. 2000, s.91, applies to:

(a) offenders aged at least 10 and under 18 who are convicted on indictment of any offence punishable in the case of an adult with imprisonment for 14 years or more (other than an offence the sentence for which is fixed by law), or an offence under ss.3, 13, 25 or 26 of the Sexual Offences Act 2003.

(b) offenders aged between 16 and 18 convicted of certain offences contrary to the Firearms Act 1968, s.5.

(c) offenders between the ages of 16 and 18 convicted of an offence under the Violent Crime Reduction Act 2006, s.28, involving a weapon to which the Firearms Act 1968, s.5, applies (with certain exceptions), unless there are exceptional circumstances.

A sentence of detention under the P.C.C.(S.)A. 2000, s.91 is a custodial sentence and may be imposed only if the general requirements for a custodial sentence are satisfied. (See **Custodial Sentences—Criminal Justice Act 2003— General Criteria.**)

If the offence was committed **before April 4, 2005**, the power may be exercised only if the court is of the opinion that *none of the other methods in which the case may legally be dealt with is suitable.*

If the offence was committed **on or after April 4, 2005**, the power may be exercised only if the court is of the opinion that *neither a community sentence nor a detention and training order is suitable.*

Where the power is available, the court may sentence the offender to be detained for such period not exceeding the maximum term of imprisonment for the offence as the court specifies. **There is no statutory minimum period.** A sentence of detention for life may be passed in an appropriate case. A sentence of detention for less than two years may be passed in appropriate circumstances.

Where the offender is to be sentenced for a number of associated offences, the court may pass a single sentence of detention which is commensurate with the seriousness of all the associated offences (including those for which detention under s.91 is not available) and impose no separate penalty for the other offences, provided that the other offences do not attract mandatory sentences.

The power may be exercised only where the offender is convicted on indictment.

An offender sentenced to detention under the P.C.C.(S.)A. 2000, s.91 is subject to the same provisions relating to early release as one sentenced to imprisonment.

Detention and Training Order

P.C.C.(S.)A. 2000, ss.100–107

References: Current Sentencing Practice E1–1; Archbold 5–348

A detention and training order may be made in the case of a child or young person convicted of an offence punishable with imprisonment.

A detention and training order is a custodial sentence and the criteria for the imposition of a custodial sentence must be satisfied. (See **Custodial Sentences—Criminal Justice Act 2003—General Criteria.**)

If the offender is **under 15**, in addition the court must be of the opinion that the offender is a **"persistent offender"**.

If the offender is **under 12**, in addition the court must be of the opinion that only a custodial sentence would be adequate to protect the public from further offending by the offender and the offence must have been committed on or after the appointed day. *No day had been appointed for this purpose by December 1, 2008.*

These conditions are cumulative.

The maximum term of a detention and training order is two years, or whatever sentence the Crown Court might impose for the offence, if less. The powers of the youth court to impose detention and training orders are not restricted to those of a magistrates' court. Any period in excess of 24 months is automatically remitted.

A detention and training order must be for 4, 6, 8, 10, 12, 18 or 24 months. No other period may be specified.

In determining the length of a detention and training order, the court must take account of any period for which the offender has been remanded in custody in connection with the offence. This includes time spent in police detention and in local authority secure accommodation. **Time in custody on remand is not deducted automatically.** The court must also make such allowance as is appropriate for a plea of guilty.

If the offender is convicted of more than one offence, or is convicted of offences while he is subject to an existing detention and training order, the court may pass consecutive detention and training orders, so long as the aggregate of the orders to which the offender is subject does not exceed two years. *The court may impose consecutive detention and training orders which amount in aggregate to a term which would not be lawful as a single detention and training order.*

A detention and training order may be ordered to run consecutively to a term of detention under the Powers of Criminal Courts (Sentencing) Act 2000, s.91 or an extended sentence of detention.

Offence committed after release

If an offender who has been released from a detention and training order commits an offence punishable with imprisonment during the period between his release and the end of the term of the order, the court which sentences him for that offence may order him to be detained for the whole or any part of a period equivalent to the period which remained of the original order on the date the offence was committed.

The period of detention must begin on the date when the order is made. Any sentence imposed for the new offence may run concurrently with the order for detention or consecutively to it, but the order for detention must not be ordered to run consecutively to any other sentence.

An order for renewed detention in respect of a detention and training order is not an order under the P.C.C.(S.)A. 2000, s.116.

Where a court makes a further detention and training order in respect of an offender who has been sentenced to a detention and training order from which he has been released, the length of the original detention and training order is disregarded for the purposes of the two year aggregate limit. It is uncertain whether a period of renewed detention counts against the aggregate for this purpose.

Breach of supervision requirement

If an offender fails to comply with a supervision requirement, he may be brought before the appropriate youth court who may order him to be detained for a period not exceeding the remainder of the order or three months, whichever is the less, or impose a fine.

Detention in a Young Offender Institution

P.C.C.(S.)A. 2000, s.96

References: Current Sentencing Practice E2–1; Archbold 5–344

Note: the sentence of detention in a young offender institution is abolished by Criminal Justice and Court Services Act 2000, s.61 with effect from a day to be appointed. No day had been appointed by December 1, 2008. The minimum age for imprisonment is reduced by the same Act to 18 (see Sch.7, para.180). That provision had not been brought into force on December 1, 2008. References in the Criminal Justice Act 2003 to sentences of imprisonment are for the most part to be read as references to imprisonment or detention in a young offender institution.

A sentence of detention in a young offender institution may be passed on an offender aged 18 and under 21 on the day of conviction.

The sentence is a custodial sentence and the general requirements for custodial sentences apply. (See **Custodial Sentences—Criminal Justice Act 2003—General Criteria.**)

The minimum term of a sentence of detention in a young offender institution is 21 days. The maximum term is the maximum term of imprisonment available to the court for the offence.

The sentence takes effect in the same way as a sentence of imprisonment.

A sentence of detention in a young offender institution passed for an offence committed on or after April 4, 2005, may be subject to a suspended sentence order. (See **Suspended Sentence Order.**)

Discount for Guilty Plea

CRIMINAL JUSTICE ACT 2003, s.144

References: Current Sentencing Practice A8–1; Archbold 5–78

Sentencing Guidelines Council Definitive Guideline: Reduction in Sentence for a Guilty Plea (Revised 2007).

As a general rule, a court which imposes a custodial sentence should reduce the length of the sentence to recognise the fact that the offender has pleaded guilty. The extent of the reduction is a matter for the discretion of the court.

It will not normally be appropriate to impose the maximum sentence for an offence on an offender who has pleaded guilty, unless there are grounds for refusing any discount.

A discount may be refused or reduced if the protection of the public requires a long sentence, or the offender has withheld his plea until a late stage in the case. A discount may be reduced if the defendant has unsuccessfully contested a Newton hearing. (See **Newton Hearings.**)

A court which passes a custodial sentence following a plea of guilty should always indicate that it has taken the plea into account.

There is a statutory duty in all cases to take into account the stage in the proceedings for the offence at which the offender indicated his intention to plead guilty, and the circumstances in which this indication was given.

Disparity of Sentence

References: Current Sentencing Practice A9–2; Archbold 5–101

As a general rule, when two or more offenders are convicted of the same offence, and their individual responsibility is the same, and there is no relevant difference in their personal circumstances, they should receive the same sentence.

There is no disparity if a difference in sentence reflects a difference in the respective responsibilities of the offenders, or a difference in their ages, previous convictions, or the existence of personal mitigating factors peculiar to one of them. Where one offender has the benefit of personal mitigation which is not available to other offenders, the other offenders should not be given the benefit of that mitigation.

There is no disparity if one offender who is likely to respond favourably to a community order is dealt with by means of a community order and the other offender is not.

A difference in sex is not in itself a reason for discriminating between offenders.

There may be objectionable disparity if one offender receives a more severe sentence than a co-defendant, and there are no relevant differences in their responsibility or personal mitigation; where two offenders receive the same sentence, despite a difference in their responsibility or personal mitigation; or where the difference in their sentences is either too large or too small to reflect the difference in their responsibility or personal mitigation.

There is no disparity where one offender has received an appropriate sentence and his co-defendant has received a lesser sentence as a result of statutory restrictions which apply only to him, or where an accomplice has been sentenced in a foreign jurisdiction where sentencing laws and practices are different from those of England and Wales.

There is no disparity where one offender who qualifies for a longer than commensurate sentence, or a sentence of imprisonment for public protection, receives such a sentence, and a co-defendant who does not qualify does not receive one.

Where an offender has already been sentenced by one judge, another judge who on a later occasion has to deal with his accomplice should pass the sentence on the accomplice which he considers appropriate, without regard to the sentence passed on the other offender.

Where there is an unjustified disparity in the sentences passed on two offenders, the Court of Appeal may reduce the more severe sentence if the disparity is so substantial as to create the appearance of injustice.

Disqualification from Directing Company

COMPANY DIRECTORS DISQUALIFICATION ACT 1986, s.2

References: Current Sentencing Practice H5–1; Archbold 5–851

The court may make a disqualification order under the Company Directors Disqualification Act 1986 if the offender has been convicted of any indictable offence committed in connection with the promotion, formation, management or liquidation of a company, or with the receivership of the company's property.

The offence concerned may relate to the internal management of the company, or the general conduct of its business.

It is not necessary in a criminal case for the court to consider the tests of fitness required for the purposes of an order under s.6 of the Act.

The period of a disqualification order is determined by the court in the exercise of its discretion. The maximum term is 15 years (where the order is made by a magistrates' court, five years). There is no minimum period.

If the offender is already subject to a disqualification order, any new order will run concurrently with the existing order.

The court should inform counsel of its intentions and invite him to mitigate on the question before making an order of disqualification.

Disqualification from Driving—General Power

P.C.C.(S.)A. 2000, s.146

References: Current Sentencing Practice H3A–1; Archbold 5–844

Any court may disqualify an offender from driving on conviction for any offence, either in addition to any other sentence or instead of any other sentence.

If the sentence for the offence is fixed by law, or the court is required to impose a mandatory custodial sentence, the court may impose a disqualification in addition to the sentence.

The power to disqualify may be used by the Crown Court or a magistrates' court.

It is not necessary that the offence should be connected in any way with the use of a motor vehicle.

The power may be used in respect of an offender who does not hold a driving licence.

Disqualification from Driving—Obligatory

ROAD TRAFFIC OFFENDERS ACT 1988, s.34

References: Current Sentencing Practice H1–1; Archbold 32–168

The following offences are subject to obligatory disqualification:

(a) causing death by dangerous driving;

(b) dangerous driving;

(c) causing death by careless driving while under the influence of drink or drugs;

(d) causing death by careless or inconsiderate driving;

(e) causing death by driving while unlicensed, disqualified or uninsured;

(f) driving or attempting to drive while unfit;

(g) driving or attempting to drive with excess alcohol;

(h) failing to provide a specimen for analysis (driving or attempting to drive);

(i) racing or speed trials;

(j) manslaughter;

(k) aggravated vehicle taking;

(l) furious driving committed in respect of a mechanically propelled vehicle (OAPA 1861, s.35)

(m) using vehicle in dangerous condition within three years of previous conviction for same offence.

The court **must disqualify unless there are special reasons for not disqualifying**, or for disqualifying for a shorter period. The obligation to establish special reasons lies on the defendant.

The existence of special reasons must be established by the defendant by calling evidence on the relevant matter, unless the prosecution are willing to admit the existence of the facts which are alleged to constitute special reasons. The defendant must establish the relevant facts on the balance of probabilities.

A special reason is an extenuating circumstance directly relating to the circumstances of the offence. Matters related to the effect of disqualification on the offender, or his employer or clients or patients, cannot constitute special reasons for this purpose.

The following matters have been held to be capable of amounting to special reasons in excess alcohol cases:

(a) the fact that the defendant consumed alcohol in the expectation that he would not be required to drive again that day, but was required to drive as a result of a sudden emergency;

(b) the fact that the defendant's consumption of excess alcohol was due to the act of another person who had laced his drink, or caused him to drink stronger liquor than he thought he was drinking;

(c) the fact that the defendant has driven an extremely short distance in circumstances where there was no risk to other road users.

Each of these matters may amount to a special reason in narrowly defined circumstances.

The following matters have been held not to be capable of amounting to special reasons:

(a) the fact that the defendant's alcohol level is only just over the relevant limit;

(b) the fact that the defendant's capacity to drive was not affected;

(c) the fact the defendant's peculiar metabolism caused him to retain the alcohol in his body for longer than the normal period;

(d) the fact that no other road user was endangered by the defendant's driving;

(e) the fact that the defendant had lost or destroyed part of his sample;

(f) the fact that the defendant had taken a test earlier on the same day which proved negative;

(g) the fact that the defendant had consumed the alcohol the day before he was tested and assumed that he had slept it off overnight.

If the court finds that special reasons exist, **it is not obliged to disqualify the defendant, but may do so in the exercise of its discretion**. Before disqualifying, where disqualification is discretionary, the court should inform counsel of its intention and invite submissions on the question of disqualification.

If the court finds that special reasons exist and does not disqualify, the court must award penalty points (within the range of 3 to 11) and follow the penalty points procedure. (See Disqualification from Driving—Penalty Points).

If the court finds no special reasons, it must disqualify for at least 12 months, unless either:

(a) the defendant is convicted of manslaughter, causing death by dangerous driving, or causing death by careless driving while under the influence of drink or drugs—minimum two years; or

(b) the defendant has been twice disqualified for 56 days or more in the three years before the commission of the present offence—minimum two years; or

(c) the defendant has been convicted of an excess alcohol offence and has been convicted of an excess alcohol offence within the last 10 years—minimum three years; or

(d) the defendant has been convicted of using a vehicle in a dangerous condition within three years of a conviction for a similar offence—six months.

The court may disqualify the offender for any period longer than the minimum.

If the defendant is convicted of manslaughter, causing death by dangerous driving, causing death by careless driving when affected by alcohol, committed on or after January 31, 2002 or dangerous driving, **the court must order him to take an extended driving test.**

If the defendant is convicted of any other offence involving obligatory disqualification the court may order him to take a further driving test.

If the court disqualifies the defendant, it does not award penalty points.

Disqualification from Driving—Penalty Points

ROAD TRAFFIC OFFENDERS ACT 1988, s.35

References: Current Sentencing Practice H2–1; Archbold 32–168

If the offender is convicted of an offence subject to obligatory endorsement, the court must determine the number of penalty points which are to be attributed to the offence from the table below. If the table shows a range of points, the court must determine a number within that range.

(For offences not shown below, see Road Traffic Offenders Act 1988, Sch.2.)

Offence	*Penalty*
Speeding	3–6
Careless driving	3–9
Being in charge of vehicle when unfit to drive	10
Being in charge of vehicle with excess alcohol level	10
Failing to provide breath specimen	4
Failing to provide specimen when disqualification not obligatory	10
Leaving vehicle in dangerous position	3
Failing to comply with directions or signs	3
Using vehicle in dangerous condition	3
Driving without licence	3
Driving with uncorrected eyesight	3
Driving while disqualified	6
Using vehicle without insurance	6–8
Failing to stop after accident	5–10
Failing to give information as to driver	6

(*if committed on or after September 24, 2007; otherwise 3*).

If the offender has committed more than one offence on the same occasion, the court must normally determine points only for the offence carrying the highest number of points, unless the court decides to determine points for other offences.

The court must add to these penalty points any other points on the offender's licence, except points for offences committed more than three years before the date of the commission of the offences for which points have just been awarded and points awarded before a disqualification imposed on the basis of penalty points.

If the total number of points is 12 or more, the defendant must be disqualified, unless there are grounds for mitigating the normal consequences of conviction.

The defendant must establish the mitigating grounds, normally by calling evidence.

The following matters may not constitute grounds for mitigating the normal consequences of conviction:

(a) circumstances alleged to make the offence or any of the offences not a serious one;

(b) hardship, other than exceptional hardship;

(c) any circumstances which have been taken into account as mitigating grounds within the last three years.

The fact that the offender has been sentenced to custody on this occasion may constitute a mitigating ground in an appropriate case.

If the court finds that there are mitigating grounds, the court may either disqualify for a shorter period than would otherwise be required, or refrain from disqualifying at all.

If the court does not disqualify, it should order the licence to be endorsed with the appropriate penalty points unless there are special reasons for not doing so. The offender may be ordered to take a further driving test.

If the defendant does not establish mitigating grounds, the court must disqualify him for at least the relevant minimum period; there is no maximum period.

The normal minimum period is six months. If there are previous disqualifications to be taken into account, the minimum period of disqualification may be 12 months or two years. The court may order the offender to take an extended driving test.

If the offender has been convicted of manslaughter, causing death by dangerous driving, or dangerous driving, and has been disqualified for a period less than the normal statutory minimum, the court must order him to take an extended driving test.

Disqualification from Driving—Vehicle used for Crime

P.C.C.(S.)A. 2000, s.147

References: Current Sentencing Practice H3–1; Archbold 5–845

The power to disqualify from driving where a vehicle has been used in connection with the commission of a crime may be exercised by the Crown Court where the offender has been convicted of any offence punishable with at least two years' imprisonment.

The power may be exercised by the Crown Court or by a magistrates' court where the offence consists of an assault committed by driving a vehicle.

The offender or an accomplice must have used the motor vehicle for the purpose of committing or facilitating the commission of the offence of which the offender has been convicted. This includes taking any steps after the offence has been committed to dispose of any property to which the offence relates, or to avoid apprehension or detection. It is not necessary that the offender should have been carried in the vehicle himself, or have driven the vehicle himself.

The power to disqualify may not be exercised on a conviction for conspiracy, if the only use of the vehicle is in the course of carrying out the conspiracy.

The court should inform counsel for the offender of its intentions and invite him to address the court on the question of disqualification.

The court should not impose a disqualification from driving if its effect will be to prevent the offender from obtaining employment on his release from any custodial sentence. This does not necessarily mean that the court should not impose a disqualification which will remain in force after the offender's release, if he has not previously been employed in a capacity in which driving is essential.

There is no minimum or maximum period of disqualification.

Disqualification Order

CRIMINAL JUSTICE AND COURT SERVICES ACT 2000, s.26

References: Current Sentencing Practice H7–1; Archbold 5–855

If an individual offender is convicted of an "**offence against a child**" committed when the offender was 18 or over and is sentenced by the Crown Court to a term of imprisonment of 12 months or more, or a hospital or guardianship order, the court **must** order the offender to be disqualified from working with children *unless it is satisfied having regard to all the circumstances that it is unlikely that the offender will commit any further offence against a child.* If the court does not make an order in these circumstances, it must state its reasons and cause them to be recorded.

If an individual offender is convicted of an "offence against a child" committed when he was under the age of 18 and is sentenced by the Crown Court to a term of imprisonment, detention under the P.C.C.(S.)A. 2000, s.91, or a detention and training order, of 12 months or more, or a sentence of detention during Her Majesty's Pleasure, or a sentence of detention for public protection, or an extended sentence of detention, or a hospital or guardianship order, the court **must** order the offender to be disqualified from working with children *if it is satisfied having regard to all the circumstances, that it is likely the offender will commit a further offence against a child.* If a court makes an order in these circumstances, it must state its reasons and order them to be recorded.

If the court does not impose a sentence of 12 months or more, or a hospital or guardianship order, **it may make a disqualification order if it is satisfied that it is likely that the offender will commit a further offence against a child.**

A disqualification order is for an indefinite period. An offender may appeal against the order as a sentence, or apply to the tribunal for a review of the order after the relevant period has expired.

The following offences are "offences against a child":

Common law offences:

> Murder of a person under 18;
>
> Manslaughter of a person under 18;
>
> Kidnapping of a person under 18;

False imprisonment of a person under 18.

Statutory offences:

An offence under:

Child Abduction Act 1984, s.1 (abduction of child by parent);

Children and Young Persons Act 1933, s.1 (cruelty to children);

Criminal Justice Act 1988, s.160 (possession of indecent photograph of child);

Criminal Law Act 1977, s.54 (inciting girl under 16 to incest)*;

Indecency with Children Act 1960, s.1 (indecent conduct towards young child)*;

Infanticide Act 1938, s.1 (infanticide);

Mental Health Act 1959, s.128 (intercourse with patient) committed with respect to a person under 18:

Misuse of Drugs Act 1971, s.4(3) (supplying etc., drugs) with respect to a person under 18.

Offences against the Person Act 1861:

Offences against the following sections are "offences against a child" when committed against or with respect to a person under 18:

Sections 16 (threats to kill), 18 (wounding with intent to cause grievous bodily harm), 20 (malicious wounding), 47 (assault occasioning actual bodily harm);

Protection of Children Act 1978, s.1 (indecent photographs of children);

Sexual Offences Act 1956*

Offences against the following sections are always an "offence against a child":

Sections 5 (intercourse with a girl under 13), 6 (intercourse with a girl under 16), 19 or 20 (abduction of girl under 18 or 16), 25 or 26 (permitting use of premises for intercourse), 28 (causing or encouraging prostitution).

Offences against the following sections are an "offence against a child" when committed against or with respect to a person under 18:

Sections 1 (rape), 2, 3 (procurement), 4 (administering drugs), 7 (intercourse with defective), 9 (procurement of defective), 10 and 11 (incest), 12

Disqualification from Driving—Discretionary

ROAD TRAFFIC OFFENDERS ACT 1988, S.34

References: Current Sentencing Practice H1–1; Archbold 32–168

The following offences are subject to discretionary disqualification but not endorsement:

(a) stealing or attempting to steal a motor vehicle;

(b) taking a motor vehicle without consent, or being carried;

(c) going equipped to steal a motor vehicle.

If an offender is convicted of any of these offences, the court may order the offender to be disqualified for such period as it thinks fit. There is no maximum or minimum period.

Most offences which are subject to obligatory endorsement, are also subject to discretionary disqualification. See Road Traffic Offenders Act 1988, Sch.2. The same principles apply in these cases.

If the court proposes to disqualify, the offender's advocate should be warned of the possibility of disqualification.

There is no obligation to disqualify. If the court does disqualify, the court does not award penalty points.

(buggery), 13 (gross indecency), 14 or15 (indecent assault), 16 (assault with intent to commit buggery), 17 (abduction), 21 (abduction of defective), 22 (causing prostitution), 23 (procuration), 24 (detention in brothel), 27 or 29 (offences in connection with defectives), 30 (living on earnings of prostitution), 31 (controlling prostitutes);

Sexual Offences Act 1967, ss.4 or 5 if committed against or with respect to a person under 18*;

Theft Act 1968, s.9(10)(a) (burglary with intent to rape) with respect to a person under 18;

Sexual Offences (Amendment) Act 2000, s.3 (abuse of trust)*;

Sexual Offences Act 2003;

Offences under ss.1 to 4, 5 to 26, 30 to 41, 47 to 50, 52, 53, 57 to 61, 62, 63, 66 and 67, where the offence is committed against or with reference to a person under 18.

*Note: references to these offences are deleted from the Schedule to the Criminal Justice and Court Services Act 2000, by the Sexual Offences Act 2003, Sch.7. The Sexual Offences Act 2003 does not contain any transitional provisions, but it is assumed that offences charged under these sections are still to be treated as offences against a child by virtue of the Interpretation Act 1978, s.16. See further, **Longer than Commensurate Sentences**.

Drink Banning Order

VIOLENT CRIME REDUCTION ACT 2006, s.6

Note: this provision was not in force on December 1, 2008.

A court may make a drink banning order against a person aged 16 or over who is convicted of an offence which was committed when he was under the influence of alcohol.

The court must consider whether the offender has engaged in **criminal or disorderly conduct while under the influence of alcohol** since the commencement of the Violent Crime Reduction Act 2006, s.3, and whether a drink banning order is necessary to protect other persons from further **criminal or disorderly conduct while he is under the influence of alcohol**.

If the court decides that the offender was under the influence of alcohol at the time of the offence, but that he has not engaged in criminal or disorderly conduct while under the influence of alcohol since the commencement of the Violent Crime Reduction Act 2006, s.3, or that a drink banning order is not necessary to protect other persons from further criminal or disorderly conduct while he is under the influence of alcohol, it **must state in open court that it has so decided** and give its reasons.

If the court decides that the offender was under the influence of alcohol at the time of the offence, and that he has engaged in criminal or disorderly conduct while under the influence of alcohol since the commencement of the Violent Crime Reduction Act 2006, s.3, and that a drink banning order is necessary to protect other persons from further criminal or disorderly conduct while he is under the influence of alcohol, but does not make a drink banning order, it **must give its reasons for not doing so in open court**.

A drink banning order prohibits the person against whom it is made from doing the things described in the order. It may impose *any prohibition which is necessary for the purpose of protecting other persons from criminal or disorderly conduct by the offender while he is under the influence of alcohol*.

The prohibitions must include such prohibitions as the court considers necessary on the offender's entering licenced premises or other premises where alcohol is available.

The order may not prohibit the offender from having access to a place where he resides, where he is required to attend for the purposes of work or employment, where he is expected to attend for the purposes of education or medical treatment, or where he is required to attend by any obligation imposed on him by any enactment or order of a court or tribunal.

A drink banning order lasts for **at least six months and not more than two years**. Different prohibitions may last for different periods, and the order may provide that the whole order, or any prohibition, may cease to have effect after a specified period, not less than half of the period specified in the original order, if the offender satisfactorily completes an approved course.

A drink banning order takes effect on the day on which it is made, or on the day on which the offender is released from custody.

A provision that the order or a prohibition in it may cease to have effect if the offender attends an approved course may be made only if a place on the specified approved course is available, and the offender has agreed to its inclusion in the order. The court must explain the effect of including the provision in the order, the requirements of the course and any fees which the offender will be liable to pay. If the court makes a drink banning order without a provision that the order or a prohibition in it may cease to have effect if the offender attends an approved course, it must **give its reasons for not including the provision in open court**.

A court considering whether to make a drink banning order may consider evidence led by the prosecution and by the defence, whether or not the evidence would have been admissible in the proceedings in which the offender was convicted.

A drink banning order may be made only in addition to a sentence or a conditional discharge.

Proceedings may be adjourned after sentence for the purpose of making a drink banning order. An interim drink banning order may be made.

A drink banning order may be varied, discharged or extended on application, so long as the order does not extend beyond two years.

Breach of a drink banning order is as **summary offence punishable with a fine at level 4**.

Drug Abstinence Order

P.C.C.(S.)A. 2000, s.58A

References: Current Sentencing Practice D5AA–1

Note: a drug abstinence order may be made only in respect of an offence committed before April 4, 2005.

A court may make a drug abstinence order if the offender is 18 or over when convicted and the court is of the opinion that he is dependent on or has a propensity to misuse specified Class A drugs, if either:

> the court is of the opinion that the offence for which the offender is to be sentenced was caused by the misuse of a specified Class A drug (or that such misuse contributed to the offence in question); or

> the offence for which he is to be sentenced is a "trigger offence." If the offence is a "trigger offence", it is not necessary for the court to be of the opinion that the offence was caused by the misuse of the specified Class A drug in question, or that the misuse of the drug contributed to the offence.

Specified Class A drugs are heroin and cocaine.

The following offences are "trigger offences": theft, robbery, burglary, aggravated burglary, taking a vehicle without consent, aggravated vehicle taking, obtaining property by deception, or going equipped for theft, and producing or supplying a controlled drug, possession of a controlled drug with intent to supply, or possession of a controlled drug committed in relation to specified Class A drugs.

A drug abstinence order requires the offender for the duration of the order to abstain from misusing specified Class A drugs and to provide when instructed a sample for the purpose of ascertaining whether he has any such drug in his body.

A court may not make a drug abstinence order unless it has been notified that arrangements for administering the order exist in the relevant area.

A person subject to a drug abstinence order is to be under the supervision of a person appointed for the purpose.

The drug abstinence order must be for a period of not less than six months and not more than three years.

A drug abstinence order is a community order and the general requirements for community orders must be satisfied before an order can be made. (See **Community Order—P.C.C.(S.)A. 2000—General Requirements.**)

Before making a drug abstinence order, the court must explain to the offender in ordinary language the effect of the order and its requirements, the consequences which may follow if he fails to comply with the requirements of the order, and the power of the court to review the order on application. It is not necessary for the offender to consent to the order or to express his willingness to comply with it.

Drug Treatment and Testing Order

P.C.C.(S.)A. 2000, s.52

References: Current Sentencing Practice D5A–1

A drug treatment and testing order may be made in the case of a person aged 18 or over convicted of an offence committed before April 4, 2005, or a person under the age of 18 but over the age of 16 convicted of an offence committed before April 4, 2009.

A drug treatment and testing order may be made only by a court which has been notified that arrangements for implementing the order have been made in the relevant area.

A court must not make a drug treatment and testing order unless it is satisfied that the offender is dependent on or has a propensity to misuse drugs; and that his dependency or propensity is such as requires and may be susceptible to treatment.

A drug treatment and testing order is a community order and the general requirements relating to community orders must be satisfied before a drug treatment and testing order can be made. A drug treatment and testing order may not be made if the offence is one for which the sentence is fixed by law, or falls to be imposed under P.C.C.(S.)A. 2000, ss.109, 110 or 111.

An order may not be made unless the offender expresses his willingness to comply with the requirements of the order.

The order must be for a period of between **six months and three years**.

A drug treatment and testing order must include a treatment requirement that the offender shall submit, during the whole of the treatment and testing period, to treatment by the treatment provider with a view to the reduction or elimination of the offender's dependency on or propensity to misuse drugs. The treatment may be treatment as a resident in a specified institution or place, treatment as a non-resident in a specified institution or place. The nature of the treatment is not specified in the order.

A drug treatment and testing order must include a testing requirement that, for the purpose of ascertaining whether he has any drug in his body during the treatment and testing period, the offender shall provide samples during that period, at such times and in circumstances determined by the treatment provider.

The order must also provide that the offender shall be under supervision during the treatment and testing period.

The court may order an offender to provide a sample to ascertain whether the offender has drugs in his body, provided that the offender expresses his willingness to comply with the requirements of the order. An offender who refuses to comply with the requirement of such an order may be sentenced to a custodial sentence for the offence.

A court must not make a drug treatment and testing order unless it is satisfied that arrangements have been or can be made for the treatment intended to be specified in the order.

A court which makes a drug treatment and testing order, must explain the effect of the order and its consequences.

A drug treatment and testing order must provide for the order to be reviewed periodically at intervals of not less than one month at a hearing held for the purpose by the court responsible for the order. The offender must attend each review hearing. At a review hearing the court, after considering the responsible officer's report, may amend any requirement or provision of the order. The court may not amend the treatment or testing requirement unless the offender expresses his willingness to comply with the amended requirement, and must not reduce the treatment and testing period below the minimum of six months, or increase it above three years. If the offender fails to express his willingness to comply with the amended order, the court may revoke the order, and deal with him, for the offence in respect of which the order was made, in any manner in which it could deal with him if he had just been convicted by the court of the offence.

If at a review hearing the court is of the opinion that the offender's progress under the order is satisfactory, the court may so amend the order as to provide for each subsequent review to be made by the court without a hearing, but this may be reversed.

Early Release—Criminal Justice Act 1991

CRIMINAL JUSTICE ACT 1991, ss.33–45

References: Current Sentencing Practice A7–1

Note: these provisions apply to sentences of less than 12 months, and sentences of any length imposed for offences committed before April 4, 2005, whatever date the sentence was imposed provided the sentence was imposed on or after October 1, 1992, and is not wholly or partly concurrent with, or consecutive to, a sentence imposed before October 1, 1992.

All offenders sentenced to imprisonment, detention in a young offender institution or determinate sentences of detention under P.C.C.(S.)A. 2000, serve at least half the term imposed by the court, less any time which is deducted from the sentence on account of time spent in custody on remand.

Offenders sentenced to less than four years are "short-term prisoners"; offenders sentenced to four years or more are "long-term prisoners".

These definitions apply to the total aggregate term which the offender is serving, whether or not the individual sentences were imposed on the same occasion.

Offenders sentenced to less than 12 months are released after serving half of the sentence; they are "at risk" for the remainder of the term of the sentence and may be returned to custody under P.C.C.(S.)A. 2000, s.116 if convicted of an offence committed during that period.

Offenders sentenced to 12 months and less than four years (more than 12 months and less than four years in the case of those under 18) are released after serving half of the sentence; they are on licence until the end of the third quarter of the sentence and "at risk" for the whole of the remainder of the term of the sentence, and may be returned to custody under s.116 if convicted of an offence committed during that period. Failure to comply with the requirement of a licence is a matter for the Parole Board.

Offenders sentenced to four years or more ("long-term prisoners") *for offences which are specified offences as defined by the Criminal Justice Act 2003, Sch.15 and certain other offences* serve at least half of the sentence; release is then at the discretion of the Secretary of State on the recommendation of the Parole Board. If they are still in custody when they have served two-thirds of the sentence, they are entitled to release. Irrespective of the time of release, they remain on licence until the end of the third quarter of the sentence. These offenders are "at risk" for the whole of the remainder of the term of the sentence and may be returned to custody under s.116 if convicted of an offence committed during that period. Failure to comply with the requirement of the licence is not a matter for the court.

Offenders sentenced to four years or more for offences which are not specified offences or are not otherwise excluded from the scope of the Criminal Justice Act 1991, s.33(1A), serve half of their sentence and are then released automatically; they remain on licence and liable to recall for the whole term of the sentence but are not liable to be returned to custody under the P.C.C.(S.)A. s.116.

In the case of an offender convicted of a **sexual offence** (but not a violent offence) **committed before September 30, 1998** the court may make an order under the P.C.C.(S.)A. 2000, s.86 **extending the licence to the end of the whole term of the sentence**. This order will apply to the whole of the sentence, if a combined sentence is passed for sexual and non-sexual offences. Such an order should not be made if the sentence is less than 12 months. An order under s.86 does not mean that the offender will spend longer in custody than he would otherwise do, unless his licence is suspended or revoked following his release.

A person committed to custody in default or for contempt will serve half of the term if the term is less than 12 months, or two-thirds of the term if the term is 12 months or more. The offender is then released automatically and not subject to licence.

The sentencer should take account of the actual period likely to be served when determining sentences.

Where the addition of a short consecutive sentence to a longer sentence will bring the aggregate up to four years, the status of the prisoner will be changed from that of a "short-term prisoner" to a "long-term prisoner". The addition of such a short consecutive term may result in the offender serving a longer period in custody than the length of the short additional term.

Where two offenders are before the court, and one offender, applying ordinary sentencing considerations, merits a sentence of less than four years, and the other a sentence of four years or more, the fact that one will be a short-term prisoner and the other a long-term prisoner does not constitute unjustified disparity.

The court should explain the effect of the sentence whenever a custodial sentence is passed.

Home detention curfew

An offender serving a sentence of not less than three months and less than four years may be released subject to a curfew condition if he has served the requisite period.

Early Release—Criminal Justice Act 2003

CRIMINAL JUSTICE ACT 2003, ss.237–268

References: Current Sentencing Practice A7A; Archbold 5–365

Note: the early release provisions of the Criminal Justice Act 2003 apply only to sentences of 12 months or more passed in respect of offences committed on or after April 4, 2005.

An offender sentenced to imprisonment, detention in a young offender institution or detention under the P.C.C.(S.)A. 2000, s.91, for a term of 12 months or more will be released on licence after serving half of the sentence imposed by the court (the "requisite custodial period") and will remain on licence until the end of the whole term of the sentence.

Home detention curfew

A prisoner who has served at least one half of the "requisite custodial period" (which is one half of the nominal sentence) may be released on home detention curfew provided that the requisite custodial period is at least six weeks and the prisoner has served at least four weeks. The effect of this limitation is that the home detention curfew scheme applies only to offenders sentenced to a custodial sentence of at least 12 weeks. Provided such a prisoner has served one quarter of the nominal sentence or four weeks, he may be released up to 135 days before the date on which he would be otherwise be entitled to be released (the half way point in his sentence).

The home detention curfew scheme does not apply to offenders sentenced to extended sentences of imprisonment or detention, or to certain categories of offenders listed in s.246(4).

An offender serving a sentence of 12 months or more who is released under this scheme must be subject to the standard licence conditions and to a curfew condition; he may also be subject to other conditions of a kind prescribed by the Secretary of State. The curfew condition remains in force until the day on which the offender would otherwise be entitled to be released from custody. It must require that the offender remains at a specified place for periods of not less than nine hours each day, and must provide for electronic monitoring of his whereabouts during the specified periods.

A person released on home detention curfew may have his licence revoked if he fails to comply with any condition of his licence, or if his whereabouts can no longer be monitored electronically. He must be informed of the reasons for the revocation and may make representations about the revocation to the Secretary of State, but he does not have the right to ask for his case to be reviewed by the Parole Board. If the Secretary of State does not reverse his decision to revoke the licence, the prisoner will remain in custody until the date on which he would otherwise have been released.

Licence conditions

Where a fixed term prisoner serving a sentence of 12 months or more is released on licence, the licence must include the standard conditions prescribed by the Secretary of State and such other conditions as may be specified. It may also include conditions relating to drug testing or electronic monitoring.

Recall

The Secretary of State may revoke the licence of a person who has been released on licence and recall him to custody. No particular conditions must be specified before this power is exercised.

On his return to custody, the prisoner must be informed of the reason for his recall and may make representations about his recall. His case must be referred to the Parole Board. If the Board does not recommend his immediate release, the Board must either fix a date for his release or fix a date for the next review of his case. The review must take place not later than one year after the decision to fix the date has been made. If the prisoner is not recommended for release at a later review, he will remain in custody until the end of the sentence.

Additional days

Prison rules may provide for the award of "additional days" for disciplinary offences committed while in custody. Such days must be added to the length of time which must be served before the prisoner becomes entitled to or eligible for release, and are carried forward into the licence period.

Concurrent and consecutive sentences

Where an offender is sentenced to terms of imprisonment which are wholly or partly concurrent, the offender does not become eligible for or entitled to be released from any of the sentences before the date on which he would be eligible for or entitled to be released from each of the other sentences.

Where an offender is sentenced to consecutive terms, whether they are imposed on the same occasion or different occasions, he is not entitled to be released until he has served half of the aggregate term, and will remain on licence until the end of the aggregate term.

Recommending licence conditions

When a court passes a sentence of imprisonment or detention in a young offender institution for 12 months or more (but not a sentence of detention under the P.C.C.(S.)A. 2000, s.91) it may "recommend . . . any particular conditions which in its view should be included in any licence granted to the offender." The recommendation is not binding on the Secretary of State and does not form part of the sentence "for any purpose". It is therefore not subject to appeal. The recommendation will be considered by the Secretary of State when the offender is released at the half way point in the sentence, or if he is released on licence at any other stage—under the home detention curfew scheme, or on compassionate grounds.

Exclusion Order

P.C.C.(S.)A. 2000, s.40A

References: Current Sentencing Practice D5AB

Note: the Powers of Criminal Courts (Sentencing) Act 2000, s.40A, was brought into force on September 2, 2004. There is nothing in either the Act or the Commencement Order which indicates that the power may be exercised retrospectively, and it appears to follow that it may not be used in respect of an offence committed before that date. Following the partial implementation of the Criminal Justice Act 2003, an exclusion order may be made in respect of a person aged 18 or over convicted of an offence committed on or after September 2, 2004 and before April 4, 2005, a person aged between 16 and 18 convicted of an offence committed before April 4, 2009, and a person under the age of 16 convicted of an offence committed on any date on or after September 2, 2004.

It is not necessary that the offence in respect of which the order is made should have been committed in or in the vicinity of the place or premises which are specified in the order.

An exclusion order is a community order and the general procedural requirements relating to community orders must be satisfied before an exclusion order may be made. (See **Community Orders—Powers of Criminal Courts (Sentencing) Act 2000—General Criteria.**)

The court must obtain and consider a pre-sentence report unless it considers it unnecessary to do so on the ground that the court has considered an earlier report.

The order prohibits the offender from entering any place specified in the order for a period not exceeding two years or, if the offender is under 16, three months.

The prohibition may operate continuously or only during specified periods, and different places may be specified in the order for different periods or days. The requirement of an exclusion order must so far as practical avoid conflict with the offender's religious beliefs or with the requirements of any other community order to which he may be subject, and any interference with his attendance at school or any other educational establishment.

The order must provide for monitoring the offender's whereabouts during the periods when the exclusion operates. **An exclusion order may**

be made only if the court has been notified that arrangements for monitoring the order are available.

Before making an exclusion order in respect of an offender under 16, the court must obtain and consider information about his family circumstances and the likely effect of such an order on those circumstances.

Exclusion Orders (Licensed Premises)

LICENSED PREMISES (EXCLUSION OF CERTAIN PERSONS) ACT 1980

References: Current Sentencing Practice H4–1; Archbold 5–841

If the offender has been convicted of an offence **committed on licensed premises** in the course of which he made **resort to violence**, the court may make an exclusion order. The order prohibits the offender from entering the **licensed premises specified** in the order without the express consent of the licensee or his servant or agent.

The order may be made in respect of any licensed premises, whether or not the offender has committed an offence in those premises, but **all the premises to which the order applies must be specified in the order**.

An exclusion order may be made in addition to any other form of sentence or order including a discharge. An exclusion order may not be made as the only sentence of order for the offence.

The court must fix the term of the order. The minimum term is three months; the maximum term is two years.

Extended Licence

P.C.C.(S.)A. 2000, s.86

References: Current Sentencing Practice A4A; Archbold 5–289

If the offender is sentenced to a determinate sentence of 12 months or more, and the whole or any part of his sentence was imposed for a **sexual offence, committed before September 30, 1998** the court may order that P.C.C.(S.)A. 2000, s.86 will apply to him.

The effect of the order is that when he is released on licence, he will remain on licence until the end of the whole of the sentence. The offender will not necessarily remain in custody any longer than would otherwise be the case, but he will be liable to supervision and recall throughout the whole of the sentence.

If the offender is sentenced to an aggregate of consecutive terms, some for sexual offences and some for offences which are not sexual offences, the order will relate to the whole of the sentence.

Before making an order, the court must have regard to the need to protect the public from serious harm and the desirability of preventing the commission of further offences.

For the definition of "sexual offence", see **Longer than Commensurate Sentences**.

Extended Sentence

P.C.C.(S.)A. 2000, s.85

References: Current Sentencing Practice A17–1; Archbold 5–288

Note: extended sentences passed under the P.C.C.(S.)A. 2000, s.85, should be distinguished from extended sentences of imprisonment or detention in a young offender institution passed under the Criminal Justice Act 2003, s.227 and extended sentences of detention passed under the Criminal Justice Act 2003, s.228. (See Specified Offences— Adult Offenders and Specified Offences—Young Offenders).

An extended sentence may be passed only for an offence committed on or after September 30, 1998 and not later than April 3, 2005.

An extended sentence may be passed on an offender convicted of a violent offence or a sexual offence.

For definitions of "violent offence" and "sexual offence," see **Longer than Commensurate Sentences**.

The court must be satisfied that the normal period of licence to which the offender would otherwise be subject would not be adequate to prevent the commission of further offences by the offender or secure his rehabilitation. (For normal licence periods, see **Early Release—Criminal Justice Act 1991.**)

An extended sentence consists of a "custodial term" and an "extension period."

The court must determine the length of the custodial term applying the normal legislation and principles of sentencing. The custodial term may be either a commensurate sentence or a longer than commensurate sentence. The offender will be released from this sentence under the normal procedures for custodial sentences.

The extension period is a period of licence beginning when the offender's normal period of licence expires, or when he is released from custody if he would not otherwise be on licence. The offender remains on licence until the end of the extension period, and is liable to be recalled to custody at any time up to the end of the extension period.

The combined total of the custodial term and the extension period must not exceed the maximum sentence for the offence.

If the offender is convicted of a **sexual offence**, the extension period must not exceed **10 years**.

If the offender is convicted of a **violent offence**, the extension period must not exceed **five years**. *An extended sentence may not be passed for a violent offence unless the custodial term is four years or more.*

An offender subject to an extended sentence may be recalled to custody at any time during the extension period. His case will normally be considered by the Parole Board when he is recalled, and the offender may require his case to be considered by the Parole Board at yearly intervals. If he is not released by direction of the Parole Board, he will remain in custody until the end of the extension period.

Extradited Offenders

CRIMINAL JUSTICE ACT 1991, s.47

References: Current Sentencing Practice A6–1

Note: this section applies only to sentences imposed for an offence committed before April 4, 2005. For offences committed on or after that date, see the Criminal Justice Act 2003, ss.240 and 243, summarised in **Time on Remand—Criminal Justice Act 2003**.

If the offender has been sentenced after having been extradited to the United Kingdom and without having first been restored or had an opportunity of leaving the United Kingdom, and he was kept in custody while awaiting his extradition for any period, the court by which he is sentenced **may** order that that period shall be treated as a "relevant period" for the purposes of Criminal Justice Act 1967, s.67.

The effect of such an order is that that period will be treated as having been served as part of his sentence.

The court may specify such period as in the opinion of the court is just in all the circumstances. The period specified must not exceed the period spent in custody awaiting extradition.

The court is not bound to specify the whole of the period concerned, particularly when the offender has prolonged the period spent in custody abroad by resisting extradition.

Financial Circumstances Order

CRIMINAL JUSTICE ACT 2003, s.162

References: Current Sentencing Practice J1–1; Archbold 5–392

Where an individual has been convicted of an offence, the court may, before sentencing him, make a financial circumstances order with respect to him, requiring him to give to the court, within such period as may be specified in the order, such a statement of his financial circumstances as the court may require.

A financial circumstances order may also be made by a magistrates' court which has been notified that an individual desires to plead guilty without appearing before the court, or by a court considering whether to make an order against the parent or guardian of a child or young person who has been convicted of an offence.

Failure to comply with a financial circumstances order, or making a false statement in response to a financial circumstances order, is a summary offence.

A court may make a financial circumstances order irrespective of the kind of sentence that it has in mind.

Financial Reporting Order

SERIOUS ORGANISED CRIME AND POLICE ACT 2005, s.76

References: Current Sentencing Practice J16–1; Archbold 5–886a

A court may make a financial reporting order when sentencing or otherwise dealing with a person for the following offences:

Obtaining by deception (Theft Act 1968, s.15);

Obtaining a money transfer by deception (Theft Act 1968, s.15A);

Obtaining a pecuniary advantage by deception (Theft Act 1968, s.17);

Procuring a valuable security by deception (Theft Act 1968, s.20(2));

Obtaining services by deception (Theft Act 1978, s.1);

Evasion of liability by deception (Theft Act 1978, s.2);

Any offence specified in the Proceeds of Crime Act 2002, Sch.2;

Fraud (Fraud Act 2006, s.1);

Obtaining services dishonestly (Fraud Act 2006, s.11);

Conspiracy to defraud*;

False accounting (Theft Act 1968, s.17)*;

Bribery (common law)*;

Corruption (Public Bodies Corrupt Practices Act 1889, s.1)*;

Bribes obtained by or given to agents (Prevention of Corruption Act 1906, s.1)*;

Assisting another to retain the benefit of criminal conduct (Criminal Justice Act 1988, s.93A)*;

Acquisition, possession or use of proceeds of criminal conduct ((Criminal Justice Act 1988, s.93B)*;

Concealing or transferring proceeds of criminal conduct ((Criminal Justice Act 1988, s.93C)*;

Concealing or transferring proceeds of drug trafficking (Drug Trafficking Act 1994, s.49)*;

Assisting another person to retain the benefit of drug trafficking (Drug Trafficking Act 1994, s.50)*;

Acquisition, possession or use of proceeds of drug trafficking (Drug Trafficking Act 1994, s.51)*;

Fund-raising for purposes of terrorism (Terrorism Act 2000, s.15)*;

Use and possession of money etc. for purposes of terrorism (Terrorism Act 2000, s.16)*;

Funding arrangements for purposes of terrorism (Terrorism Act 2000, s.17)*;

Money laundering in connection with terrorism (Terrorism Act 2000, s.18)*;

Acquisition, use and possession of criminal property (Proceeds of Crime Act 2002, s.329)*;

Cheating in relation to the public revenue*;

Fraudulent evasion of duty (Customs and Excise Management Act 1979, s.170)*;

VAT offences (Value Added Tax Act 1994, 72) (c.23) (offences relating to VAT)*;

Fraudulent evasion of income tax (Finance Act 2000, s.144)*;

Tax credit fraud (Tax Credits Act 2002, s.35)*;

Attempting, conspiring in or inciting the commission of, or aiding, abetting, counselling or procuring or any of these offences*.

Note: the section as originally enacted contained references to obtaining by deception (Theft Act 1968, s.15), obtaining a money transfer by deception (Theft Act 1968, s.15A) and obtaining a pecuniary advantage by deception (Theft Act 1968, s.17). References to these offences were repealed and replaced by references to offences of fraud and obtaining services dishonestly by the Fraud Act 2006, Sch.1, with effect from January 15, 2007. No express provision is made dealing with the question whether an order may be made after that date in respect of one of the offences specified in the repealed paragraphs committed before that date. The list of offences was extended to as to apply to attempts, conspiracies, incitements, and aiding and abetting of the offences listed. These provisions do not apply to the offences of obtaining by deception, obtaining a money transfer by deception, and obtaining a pecuniary advantage by deception.

*Offences marked with an asterisk were added to the list by the Serious Organised Crime and Police Act 2006 (Amendment of Section 76(3)) Order, 2007. This order came into force on May 4, 2007. It is uncertain whether an order may be made in respect of the offences added to the list by this order if the offence was committed before that date.

The court must be satisfied that *the risk of the offender committing another such offence is sufficiently high as to justify the making of a financial reporting order.*

The order has effect for the period specified, which must not exceed five years if the order is made by a magistrates' court, 20 years if the offender is sentenced to life imprisonment, or otherwise 15 years.

The effect of a financial reporting order is that the offender must make a report to a person specified by the court of such particulars of his financial affairs as may be specified, within the specified number of days at the end of the period or periods specified.

A person who fails to comply with a financial reporting order is guilty of an offence.

Fines

CRIMINAL JUSTICE ACT 2003, s.163

References: Current Sentencing Practice J1–1; Archbold 5–391

Crown Court

The Crown Court may impose a fine in lieu of or in addition to any other form of sentence, except a discharge, for any offence other than murder.

A fine may not be imposed in place of a sentence required to be imposed by the P.C.C.(S.)A. 2000, ss.109, 110, 111, or by the Criminal Justice Act 2003, ss.225 to 228.

There is no limit to the amount of the fine.

Before fixing the amount, the court must inquire into the offender's financial circumstances.

The court may make a financial circumstances order. (See **Financial Circumstances Order.**)

The amount of any fine must reflect the seriousness of the offence, and the court must take into account the circumstances of the case including, among other things, the financial circumstances of the offender, so far as they are known.

In the case of a corporation, the court is not obliged to inquire into the means of the offender but must take them into account as far as they are known.

Where the Crown Court imposes a fine it may allow time for payment and direct payment by instalments. Time for payment must be allowed unless the offender appears to have sufficient means to pay the fine immediately, or is unlikely to remain long enough at a fixed address to allow the fine to be enforced, or is simultaneously sentenced to, or is already serving, a custodial sentence.

The court must fix a term of imprisonment to be served in default of payment. (See **Default Terms—Crown Court.**) The default term is fixed in relation to the whole amount of the fine, not to individual instalments.

Magistrates' court

A magistrates' court may impose a fine not exceeding £5,000 for any one either-way offence unless special provision is made for a larger fine. There is no limit on the amount of the aggregate fine imposed for a number of different offences.

A magistrates' court may impose a fine for a summary offence subject to the maximum fine provided for the offence by reference to the standard scale. There is no limit to the aggregate amount which may be imposed for a number of separate offences.

The standard scale is:

Level 1 £200
Level 2 £500
Level 3 £1,000
Level 4 £2,500
Level 5 £5,000

The maximum fine which a magistrates' court may impose on an offender under 14 is £250, and on a person between 14 and 18 is £1,000.

A magistrates' court may allow time for payment and direct payment by instalments. Time for payment must be allowed unless the offender appears to have sufficient means to pay the fine immediately, or is unlikely to remain long enough at a fixed address to allow the fine to be enforced, or is simultaneously sentenced to, or is already serving, a custodial sentence.

A magistrates' court does not fix a term to be served in default on the occasion when a fine is imposed, unless the offender appears to have sufficient means to pay the fine immediately, or is unlikely to remain long enough at a fixed address to allow the fine to be enforced, or is simultaneously sentenced to, or is already serving, a custodial sentence.

The default terms for fines imposed by magistrates' courts are the same as for the Crown Court (see **Default Terms—Crown Court**) except that the maximum default term which may be fixed is 12 months.

Forfeiture Orders—Misuse of Drugs Act 1971

MISUSE OF DRUGS ACT 1971, s.27

References: Current Sentencing Practice J4–1; Archbold 27–118

The offender must be convicted of a drug trafficking offence (as defined in the Proceeds of Crime Act 2002 Sch.2) or an offence under the Misuse of Drugs Act 1971.

The court may order forfeiture of anything **shown to the satisfaction of the court to relate to the offence**. The offender may give evidence to show that the property is not related to the offence.

The court may not order forfeiture of intangible property or land or buildings.

If anyone claims to be the owner of the property or otherwise interested in it, he must be given the chance to show cause why the forfeiture order should not be made.

The court may order the property concerned to be destroyed, or dealt with in such manner as the court may order.

Property may not be forfeited on the grounds that it is the proceeds of offences of which the offender has not been convicted, or is intended to be used to facilitate the commission of future offences.

Guardianship Order

MENTAL HEALTH ACT 1983, s.37

References: Current Sentencing Practice F2–1; Archbold 5–887

The court may make a guardianship order provided that the offender is 16 or older and the court is satisfied on the written or oral evidence of two medical practitioners that the offender is suffering from mental disorder and the court is satisfied that the mental disorder from which he is suffering is of a nature or degree which warrants his reception into guardianship.

The court must be of the opinion, having regard to all the circumstances, including the nature of the offence and the character and antecedents of the offender that the most suitable method of disposing of the case is by means of a guardianship order.

A guardianship order may not be made unless the court is satisfied that the local authority or other person concerned is willing to receive the offender into guardianship.

The order must specify the form or forms of mental disorder from which the offender is suffering. At least two practitioners must agree that the offender is suffering from the same form of mental disorder.

The court may not impose a sentence of imprisonment, impose a fine or make a community order but may make such other forms of order as may be appropriate.

A guardianship order may be made despite the fact that the offender would otherwise qualify for a required minimum sentence under the Firearms Act 1968, s.51A, a prescribed custodial sentence under the P.C.C.(S.)A. 2000, ss.110 or 111, or a sentence of life imprisonment, imprisonment for public protection or an extended sentence under the Criminal Justice Act 2003, ss.225 to 228. **This exception does not apply to an automatic life sentence**.

Hospital and Limitation Direction

MENTAL HEALTH ACT 1983, ss.45A, 45B

References: Current Sentencing Practice F2–1; Archbold 5–907

A court which passes a sentence of imprisonment for an offence other than murder on an offender may make a hospital and limitation direction, if the court is satisfied on the evidence of two medical practitioners (one of whom must give evidence orally) that:

(a) the offender is suffering from a mental disorder;

(b) the disorder is of a nature or degree which makes it appropriate for him to be detained in a hospital for medical treatment; or

(c) the treatment is likely to *alleviate or prevent a deterioration in his condition*.

The order must direct that the offender be removed to a hospital, and be subject to the restrictions set out in Mental Health Act 1983, s.41.

The hospital must be specified in the direction, and the court must be satisfied that the offender will be admitted to the hospital within 28 days of the making of the order.

An offender subject to a hospital and limitation direction will be treated as if he had been sentenced to imprisonment and transferred to hospital by order of the Secretary of State.

If the offender ceases to be in need of treatment before the expiration of the sentence, he will be liable to be returned to prison. If he is still in hospital when the period during which he is liable to be detained under the sentence expires, he will be liable to be detained in hospital as an unrestricted patient.

A hospital and limitation direction may be made in conjunction with a determinate sentence of imprisonment, a longer than commensurate sentence of imprisonment, a discretionary sentence of life imprisonment or an automatic sentence of life imprisonment. It may not be made in conjunction with a sentence of detention under P.C.C.(S.)A. 2000, s.91, or a

sentence of detention in a young offender institution, or a mandatory life
sentence imposed for murder.

Hospital Order

MENTAL HEALTH ACT 1983, S.37

References: Current Sentencing Practice F2–1; Archbold 5–887

The court may make a hospital order provided that it is satisfied on the written or oral evidence of two medical practitioners that the offender is suffering from mental disorder and the court is satisfied that the mental disorder from which he is suffering is of a nature or degree which makes it appropriate for him to be *detained in a hospital for medical treatment*.

The court must be of the opinion, having regard to all the circumstances including the nature of the offence and the character and antecedents of the offender, and to the other means of dealing with him that the most suitable means of dealing with the case is by means of a hospital order.

A hospital order may not be made unless the court is satisfied that arrangements have been made for his admission to a hospital within 28 days of the making of the order.

The court may request any regional health authority to furnish such information as the authority has or can reasonably obtain with respect to hospitals in its region or elsewhere at which arrangements could be made for the admission of the offender.

The order must specify the hospital to which the offender is to be admitted and the form or forms of mental disorder from which the offender is suffering.

At least two practitioners must agree that the offender is suffering from the same form of disorder.

A hospital order may be made despite the fact that the offender would otherwise qualify for a required minimum sentence under the Firearms Act 1968, s.51A, a prescribed custodial sentence under the P.C.C.(S.)A. 2000, ss.110 or111, or a sentence of life imprisonment, imprisonment for public protection or an extended sentence under the Criminal Justice Act 2003, ss.225 to 228. **This exception does not apply to an automatic life sentence**.

Interim Hospital Order

MENTAL HEALTH ACT 1983, s.38

References: Current Sentencing Practice F2–1; Archbold 5–893

The court may make an interim hospital order provided that it is satisfied on the written or oral evidence of two medical practitioners that the offender is suffering from mental disorder and there is reason to suppose that the mental disorder from which he is suffering is such that it may be appropriate for a hospital order to be made in his case.

An interim hospital order may be made only if a hospital place is available.

One of the practitioners on whose evidence the order is based must be employed at the hospital to be specified in the order.

An order may not be made unless the court is satisfied that arrangements have been made for the offender's admission to the hospital specified within 28 days of the making of the order.

An interim hospital order may be made for any period not exceeding 12 weeks in the first instance. The order may be renewed for further periods of 28 days at a time, if the court is satisfied that the continuation of the order is warranted. The order may not continue for more than 12 months in all.

An interim hospital order may be renewed in the absence of the offender provided that he is represented by counsel or solicitor and his counsel or solicitor is given the opportunity to be heard. At the conclusion of the interim order the offender must be sentenced or dealt with by means of a hospital order or otherwise.

The court must give directions for the conveyance of the offender and his detention in a place of safety pending his admission to hospital.

The order must be terminated if the court makes a hospital order or decides after considering the evidence of the responsible medical officer to deal with the case in some other way.

A court may make a hospital order in the case of an offender subject to an interim hospital order in the absence of the offender, provided that he is represented by counsel or solicitor and his counsel or solicitor is given the opportunity to be heard.

Legal Representation

P.C.C.(S).A. 2000, s.83

References: Current Sentencing Practice L6–1; Archbold 5–12

Statutory requirements relating to legal representation apply in the following cases:

(a) a sentence of imprisonment passed on a person who has not previously been sentenced to a sentence of imprisonment (for this purpose, a previous committal for contempt or in default, a suspended sentence, a sentence of detention in a young offender institution or detention under Children and Young Persons Act 1933, ss.53(2) and(3) or under P.C.C.(S.)A. 2000, s.91, does not count);

(b) a sentence of detention under P.C.C.(S.)A. 2000, s.91 passed on any offender, irrespective of previous sentences;

(c) a local authority residence requirement or a foster parent residence requirement in a supervision order. (See **Supervision Order**);

(d) a detention and training order;

(e) a sentence of detention in a young offender institution;

(f) a youth rehabilitation order containing either a local authority residence requirement or a fostering requirement.

A court must not pass such a sentence on a person who is not legally represented unless he has applied for legal representation and his application has been refused on the ground that his means are adequate, or he has refused or failed to apply for legal representation after being told of his right to do so.

A person is legally represented only if he has the assistance of counsel or a solicitor at some time after he has been found guilty and before he has been sentenced. It is not sufficient that the offender was represented at the trial, or when he pleaded guilty.

An offender who has dismissed his representatives after having advice between conviction and sentence may be sentenced while unrepresented, but the court must first withdraw any legal representation order.

A sentence passed in breach of these requirements is unlawful, but the Court of Appeal on an appeal against such a sentence may substitute a lawful sentence.

Life Imprisonment

P.C.C.(S.)A. 2000, s.82A

References: Current Sentencing Practice F3–1

Note: this section summarises the practice relating to discretionary life sentences imposed for offences committed before April 4, 2005. For offences committed on or after April 4, 2005, see **Specified Offences—Adult Offenders.**

Before a discretionary sentence of life imprisonment may be passed:

(a) all the rules relating to the imposition of a sentence of imprisonment must be satisfied;

(b) the court must be entitled to pass a sentence which is longer than would be commensurate with the seriousness of the offences concerned. (See **Longer than Commensurate Sentences**);

(c) the offence must be punishable with imprisonment for life; and

(d) the offender must be eligible for a sentence of life imprisonment under the criteria established in the case law.

The criteria for a discretionary life sentence are:

(a) the offence for which the sentence is passed is sufficiently serious to justify a long sentence;

(b) it is apparent from the nature of the offender's offences and history that he is a person of unstable character likely to commit similar offences in the future or is otherwise dangerous;

(c) the offences which he is likely to commit, are likely to be specially injurious to others.

Normally the court will consider psychiatric evidence before deciding that the conditions for the imposition of a life sentence are present, but it is not necessary that the offender should be suffering from mental illness.

In exceptional cases the court may conclude that the conditions for the imposition of a life sentence are satisfied without considering medical evidence.

A life sentence may be passed even though there is no prospect of improvement in the offender's condition, but a life sentence should not be passed if the safety of the public can be secured by a shorter sentence.

A court should not impose a sentence of life imprisonment without indicating its intention to counsel for the defendant and offering counsel the opportunity to make submissions on the question whether the defendant satisfies the conditions for a sentence of life imprisonment.

In addition to passing the sentence, the court must normally specify a period for the purposes of P.C.C.(S.)A. s.82A. This period is the minimum period during which the offender will be required to remain in prison before becoming eligible for consideration before the Parole Board with a view to release. (See **Minimum Terms**.)

Longer than Commensurate Sentences

P.C.C.(S.)A. s.80(2)(B)

References: Current Sentencing Practice A4–1

A longer than commensurate sentence may be passed only if the offender has been convicted of a violent offence or a sexual offence **committed before April 4, 2005**.

A **violent offence** is one which leads, or is intended or likely to lead, to a person's **death or to physical injury to a person**, and includes an offence which is required to be charged as **arson** (whether or not it would otherwise fall within this definition). Whether or not a particular offence is a violent offence depends on the facts of the individual case, except in the case of arson or attempted arson. *An offence which is likely to lead to psychological injury but not physical injury is not a "violent offence" for this purpose.*

A **sexual offence** is any of the following:

(a) an offence under any provision of Pt 1 of the Sexual Offences Act 2003 except ss.52, 53, or 71;

(b) an offence under the Protection of Children Act 1978;

(c) an offence of conspiracy to commit any of the offences mentioned above;

(d) an offence of attempting to commit any of those offences;

(e) an offence of inciting another to commit any of those offences.

The definition of "sexual offence" in the P.C.C.(S.)A. s.161, was amended by the Sexual Offences Act 2003. That Act contains no transitional or saving provisions, and is assumed to apply only to offences committed on or after its commencement date, May 1, 2004. The liability of an offender to be sentenced for a sexual offence committed before that date depends on the Interpretation Act 1978, s.16, which provides:

"(1) Without prejudice to section 15, where an Act repeals an enactment, the repeal does not, unless the contrary intention appears . . .
(d) affect any penalty, forfeiture or punishment incurred in respect of any offence committed against that enactment . . .
and any such investigation, legal proceeding or remedy may be instituted, continued or enforced, and any such penalty, forfeiture or punishment may be imposed, as if the repealing Act had not been passed."

It is assumed that s.16 preserves the liability to a longer than commensurate sentence of an offender convicted of a sexual offence under the repealed legislation which would have been a "sexual offence" for the purposes of s.161 prior to its amendment by the Sexual Offences Act 2003. The earlier form of the definition applied to the following offences:

(a) an offence under the Sexual Offences Act 1956, other than an offence under ss.30, 31, or 33 to 36 of that Act;

(b) an offence under s.128 of the Mental Health Act 1959;

(c) an offence under the Indecency with Children Act 1960;

(d) an offence under s.9 of the Theft Act 1968 of burglary with intent to commit rape;

(e) an offence under s.54 of the Criminal Law Act 1977;

(f) an offence under the Protection of Children Act 1978;

(g) an offence of conspiracy to commit any of the offences mentioned above;

(h) an offence of attempting to commit any of those offences;

(i) an offence of inciting another to commit any of those offences.

This definition does not include child abduction, contrary to the Child Abduction Act 1984, or indecent exposure. It is uncertain whether an offence contrary to the Sexual Offences (Amendment) Act 2000, s.3 (abuse of trust) is a "sexual offence" for this purpose. See s.6(1) of that Act, purporting to amend Criminal Justice Act 1991, s.31(1) (repealed).

The fact that the offender has committed such an offence is not normally in itself sufficient to justify the imposition of a longer than normal sentence. There must usually be some further basis for the inference that the offender will commit further offences in the future which will themselves be violent or sexual offences, and which will result in serious harm to members of the public in the form of death or serious personal injury, whether physical or psychological. The inference of dangerousness will often be based in part on psychiatric evidence and in part on the offender's previous convictions.

The anticipated harm likely to be produced by the expected future offences may be either physical or psychological, but it must be "serious". The offence which is expected to produce the harm, must itself be a violent or sexual offence.

An offender may qualify for a longer than commensurate sentence even though the members of the public who are risk from him are a very small group, or possibly a single individual. Where the offender's behaviour is directed at a small group of people, who can be protected from him by other means, a longer than commensurate sentence may not be justified.

A longer than commensurate sentence may be passed to run consecutively to a sentence which the offender is already serving, or to a period which he is ordered to serve under the P.C.C.(S.)A. 2000, s.116, but it should not be ordered to be served consecutively to a sentence passed on the same occasion.

Where a long sentence would be justifiable as a commensurate sentence under P.C.C.(S.)A. 2000, s.80(2)(a), the extent to which the commensurate sentence is extended under s.80(2)(b) will not be so great as in other cases.

There is no disparity in a case where a longer than commensurate sentence is passed on one offender and a commensurate sentence on the other, provided that there is evidence of continuing dangerousness on the part of one offender and not in the case of the other.

A longer than commensurate sentence may be imposed on an offender even though he does not qualify for a sentence of life imprisonment under the criteria established for that form of sentence.

Where a sentencer has in mind the possibility of passing a longer than commensurate sentence, he should warn counsel for the defendant of his intentions and invite submissions on the question. Where a court passes a longer than commensurate sentence it must state in open court that it is of the opinion that s.80(2)(b) applies and why it is of that opinion, and explain to the offender in open court and in ordinary language why the sentence is for such a term.

Where a court fails to pass a longer than commensurate sentence where such a sentence should be passed, the resulting sentence may be "unduly lenient" and may be the subject of a reference by the Attorney General.

Where a person sentenced to a longer than commensurate sentence appeals against the sentence and persuades the Court of Appeal that the case is not one in which a longer than commensurate sentence should have been passed, the Court of Appeal is not bound to substitute a shorter sentence.

Magistrates' Courts' Powers—Custodial Sentence

MAGISTRATES' COURTS ACT 1980, ss.132 AND 133, P.C.C.(S.)A. 2000, s.78

References: Current Sentencing Practice A10–1

Note: substantial amendments to the provisions summarised below are made by the Criminal Justice Act 2003. The amendments were not in force on December 1, 2008.

The following limitations apply to sentences of imprisonment. They do not apply to detention and training orders.

Summary offences

The maximum for any one offence is six months, or the maximum provided for the offence in question, if that is less. The maximum aggregate term for more than one summary offence is six months.

Either-way offences

The maximum term for any one offence is six months. The maximum aggregate term for more than one either-way offence is 12 months. The minimum term of imprisonment which a magistrates' court may impose is five days.

The restrictions on aggregate terms do not include activation of suspended sentences or orders for return to custody under P.C.C.(S.)A. 2000, s.116.

The restrictions do not apply to default terms fixed in respect of fines imposed on the same occasion as a custodial sentence is imposed, but they do apply where an offender is sentenced to a custodial sentence and committed in default on the same occasion.

The restrictions must be observed by the Crown Court when dealing with an offender in respect of the following matters:

(a) an offence for which he has been committed for sentence under P.C.C.(S.)A. 2000, s.6;

(b) an offence in respect of which the offender has been committed which a view to a restriction order under Mental Health Act 1983, s.43 and in respect of whom the Crown Court does not make a hospital order;

(c) an offence in respect of which a magistrates' court has made a community order which the Crown Court has revoked;

(d) an offence for which the Crown Court has power to deal with the offender under Criminal Justice Act 1988, ss.40 or 41;

(e) an offence in respect of which the offender has appealed against his conviction or sentence;

(f) an offence for which the offender is sentenced under P.C.C.(S.)A. 2000, s.4(5).

Maximum Sentence

References: Current Sentencing Practice A1–1; Archbold 5–280

The maximum sentence for an offence should normally be reserved for the most serious examples of that offence which are likely to be encountered in practice.

The maximum sentence should not normally be imposed for an attempt to commit an offence, or where the offender has pleaded guilty, or where there is substantial mitigation.

Consecutive maximum sentences may be properly imposed provided that each individual offence is one of the most serious examples of the type of offence, and the sentences are properly made consecutive. (See **Consecutive Sentences.**)

Where the maximum sentence for an offence is increased, the new maximum sentence will normally apply only to offences committed after the increase has taken effect. Where an offender has been convicted of an offence committed on a date unknown between two dates, and the maximum sentence has been increased between those two dates, the lower maximum sentence applies.

Where the offender has been convicted of an offence of a general nature, but the facts fall within the scope of a more narrowly defined offence for which a lower maximum sentence has been provided, the court should have regard to the lower maximum sentence, but is not necessarily bound by it.

Minimum Term

P.C.C.(S.)A. s.82A

References: Current Sentencing Practice A18–1K; Archbold 5–310

These provisions apply where the court passes any of the following sentences:

(a) a discretionary life sentence;

(b) a statutory life sentence under the Criminal Justice Act 2003, s.225;

(c) an automatic life sentence under the P.C.C.(S.)A. 2000, s.109;

(d) a sentence of custody for life (otherwise on conviction for murder);

(e) a sentence of detention under the P.C.C.(S.)A. 2000, for life;

(f) a sentence of imprisonment or detention in a young offender institution for public protection;

(g) a sentence of detention for public protection.

They do not apply where the court passes a mandatory life sentence on a person convicted of murder.

In addition to passing the sentence, the court must normally specify the minimum period during which the offender will be required to remain in prison before becoming eligible for consideration by the Parole Board with a view to release.

The period is calculated by deciding what determinate term of imprisonment would have been appropriate if a sentence of life imprisonment had not been passed (the notional determinate sentence) and then specifying a period equal to between one-half and one-third of that term. Normally, the period should be equal to one-half of the term. *In certain exceptional cases the period may be more than one-half of the notional determinate sentence*.

In fixing the specified period, the court should give appropriate credit for a guilty plea.

If the offender has been convicted of more than one offence, the period should reflect the gravity of all of the offences of which he has been convicted, including those for which a sentence of life imprisonment is not passed.

If the offender has spent **time in custody on remand**, or awaiting extradition, the sentencer should deduct an appropriate amount of time from the specified period. The time deducted should not exceed the actual period spent in custody on remand.

If the offender was **over 21 when the offence was committed** and is sentenced to life imprisonment, the court need not specify a period if it is of the opinion that no period should be specified because of seriousness of the offence or offences concerned. *This does not apply to sentences of imprisonment for public protection.*

If an offender who is serving the minimum term of an indeterminate sentence falls to be sentenced for another offence, the court may impose a determinate sentence to begin at the expiry of the minimum term of the indeterminate sentence.

Murder

CRIMINAL JUSTICE ACT 2003, s.269

References: Current Sentencing Practice B0–1; Archbold 5–236

A person convicted of murder who is aged 21 on the date of conviction must be sentenced to imprisonment for life, unless he was under 18 on the date when the offence was committed.

A person convicted of murder who is aged under 21 and over 18 on the date of conviction, must be sentenced to custody for life, unless he was under 18 on the date when the offence was committed.

A person convicted of murder who was under 18 on the date when the offence was committed must be sentenced to be detained during Her Majesty's Pleasure, *irrespective of his age on the date of conviction*.

In all cases, a court which imposes a mandatory life sentence on a person convicted of murder must order that the early release provisions shall apply to him after he has served a part of the sentence specified by the court, unless the offender is over 21 and the seriousness of the offence or offences concerned is such that a "whole life order" must be made.

In deciding what part of the life sentence to specify, the court must have regard to the general principles set out in the Criminal Justice Act 2003, Sch.21, and any guidelines relating to offences in general which are relevant to the case and are not incompatible with the provisions of Sch.21.

Having identified an appropriate starting point in accordance with Sch.21, the court must take into account any aggravating or mitigating factors, to the extent that it has not allowed for them in its choice of starting point, and specify a minimum term which it considers appropriate to the seriousness of the offence or offences concerned. The minimum term may be of any length (whatever the starting point).

In the case of a person sentenced to custody for life or imprisonment for life (but not detention during Her Majesty's Pleasure) for an offence committed before December 18, 2003, the minimum term must not be greater than the term which under the practice followed by the Secretary of State before December 2002, the Secretary of State would have been likely to have specified.

On passing sentence, the court must state in open court, in ordinary language, its reasons for deciding on the order made, and in particular must state which of the starting points in Sch.21 it has chosen and its reasons for doing so, and why it has departed from that starting point.

Newton Hearings

References: Current Sentencing Practice L2–2; Archbold 5–72

The purpose of a Newton hearing is to determine factual issues which are relevant to the sentence and which have not been resolved by the offender's plea of guilty to the charges in the indictment.

If the defendant intends to plead guilty to a charge on a basis of facts that differs significantly from that on which the prosecution will rely, the defendant's representatives must inform the prosecution and where the plea is entered, the judge must be informed of the basis of the plea.

Where the prosecution agree that a plea will be accepted on a particular basis of fact, it is desirable that the basis on which the plea is entered should be recorded in writing.

The judge is not bound to accept a plea offered by a defendant on a particular basis, even though the prosecution have agreed to accept the plea on that basis. The judge may direct that a hearing should take place. If this occurs the defendant is not entitled to withdraw his plea and counsel for the prosecution must present the evidence to the court.

Where the defendant offers a plea on a basis which is not acceptable to the prosecution, and the issue cannot be resolved by amending the indictment, the judge must either hear evidence and determine the issue of fact, or sentence on the basis put forward by the defendant.

Such a hearing is limited to the determination of matters which are consistent with the terms of the counts in the indictment to which the defendant has pleaded guilty. It is not open to the prosecution to allege that the defendant is guilty of more offences than are charged in the indictment or taken into consideration, or that the offence committed was more serious than the offence charged in the indictment.

The hearing is conducted in the form of a trial without a jury. Evidence is adduced and witnesses are examined in the normal way. The judge should not intervene in the examination of witnesses.

The judge should direct himself that the prosecution must establish their version of the facts to the criminal standard of proof.

It is not necessary for the judge to hear evidence if the matter in issue is not relevant to sentence, or the defendant's story can be considered wholly false or manifestly implausible, or where the matters put forward by the defendant relate to personal mitigation only.

If a defendant puts forward a plea on a particular basis of fact, but that basis is rejected by the judge after hearing evidence, the defendant may lose some of the discount that he would otherwise expect for his plea.

Offences taken into Consideration

References: Current Sentencing Practice L3–1; Archbold 5–107

Where an offender admits an offence with which he has not been charged and asks the court to take it into consideration, the court may take account of that offence when passing sentence for the offence of which the offender has been convicted, but there is no conviction for the offence taken into consideration and the powers of the court depend on the offences of which the offender has been convicted, except as indicated below.

An offence which has been taken into consideration is an "associated offence" for the purposes of the P.C.C.(S.)A. 2000, s.161. A compensation order or confiscation order may be made in relation to an offence that is taken into consideration.

An offence should not normally be taken into consideration if the court would not have power to deal with the offender for the offence, or if the offence would result in a mandatory sentence.

The offender should be shown a list of all the offences which he wishes to have taken into consideration; if he does not wish to have all the offences taken into consideration, he should be asked to indicate personally and specifically which offences he does wish to have taken into consideration.

Where an offender is committed to the Crown Court for sentence, the Crown Court may take offences into consideration only if the defendant admits the offences and asks for them to be taken into consideration when he appears before the Crown Court.

Where an offender admits that the offences to which he has pleaded guilty are specimen offences representing a larger number of offences which are not separately identified, those other offences are not "offences taken into consideration".

Parenting Order

CRIME AND DISORDER ACT 1998, s.8

References: Current Sentencing Practice E8A–1; Archbold 5–933

A parenting order may be made only if the court has been notified that arrangements for implementing the order are available in the relevant area.

A parenting order may be made against the parent or guardian of a child or young person convicted of an offence or in certain other cases.

"Guardian" includes any person who in the opinion of the court has for the time being the charge of or control over the child or young person.

The order must require the parent or guardian to comply, for a period not exceeding 12 months, with such requirements as the court may consider desirable in the interests of preventing the commission of a further offence. The order must also include a requirement to attend for a period, not exceeding three months, counselling or guidance sessions, unless the parent has previously been the subject of a parenting order.

Unless the court makes a referral order, a court must make a parenting order in respect of a child or young person under the age of 16 who is convicted of an offence, or state in open court that a parenting order would not be desirable in the interests of preventing the commission of any further offence by the child or young person, and why not. The court may make both a referral order and a parenting order after considering a report from an appropriate officer.

The court must explain the effect of the order, the consequences that may follow a failure to comply with the requirements of the order, and the power of the court to review the order.

The consent of the parent or guardian is not required.

Parents and Guardians

P.C.C.(S.)A. 2000, ss.136–138, 150

References: Current Sentencing Practice E8–1; Archbold 5–927

Where a person **under 16** is found guilty of an offence, and the court considers that the matter should be dealt with by means of a fine, costs or compensation order, the court **must** order the fine, costs or compensation order to be paid by the offender's parent or guardian, unless the parent or guardian cannot be found or it would be **unreasonable to make an order for payment**.

Where a person **over 16 but under 18** is found guilty of an offence, and the court considers that the matter should be dealt with by means of a fine, costs or compensation order, the court **may** order the fine, costs or compensation order to be paid by the offender's parent or guardian, unless the parent or guardian cannot be found or it would be **unreasonable to make an order for payment**.

The parent or guardian must be given the opportunity to be heard before the order is made.

In considering the means of the offender for the purpose of such an order, the court should consider the means of the parent or guardian, rather than the means of the offender.

A court should not make an order against a parent or guardian on the basis that the offender has been neglected unless there is evidence of such neglect. The court should not base a finding adverse to a parent or guardian on information disclosed by the parent or guardian for the purposes of a pre-sentence report.

Where the offender is in the care of a local authority, or living in local authority accommodation, and the local authority has parental responsibility, the court may make an order against the local authority. An order should not be made against a local authority unless the local authority has failed to do everything that it reasonably could have done to protect the public from the offender, and there is a causative link between the failure and the offence.

Where the offender is living in local authority accommodation on a voluntary basis, it will normally be unreasonable to make an order against the parent or guardian.

Where an offender under the age of 18 is found guilty of an offence, the court may (and if the offender is under 16, **must**) bind over the parent or guardian to take proper care and control of the offender, if it is satisfied that this would be desirable in the interests of preventing further offences by the offender. **If the court fails to exercise this power, it must state in open court that it is not satisfied that this would be desirable in the interests of preventing further offences by the offender**.

The recognisance may be in an amount not exceeding £1,000 and for a period not exceeding three years, or until the offender's 18th birthday, whichever is the shorter.

Before fixing the amount of the recognisance, the court must take into account the means of the parent or guardian, so far as they appear or are known.

If the parent or guardian refuses to be bound over, the court may impose a fine of £1,000. (See also **Parenting Order.**)

Prescribed Custodial Sentence—Burglary

P.C.C.(S.)A. 2000, s.111

References: Current Sentencing Practice A15–1; Archbold 5–253

A court which sentences an offender for a domestic burglary must impose a sentence of at least three years' imprisonment or detention in a young offender institution if:

(a) the burglary was committed on or after December 1, 1999;

(b) at the time when the burglary was committed the offender was 18 or over;

(c) at the time when the burglary was committed the offender had been convicted of two other domestic burglaries;

(d) each of the earlier domestic burglaries was committed on or after December 1, 1999;

(e) the offender had been convicted of the first domestic burglary before he committed the second.

A domestic burglary is a burglary committed in respect of a building or part of a building which is a dwelling. It is submitted that a burglary may not be treated as a domestic burglary for this purpose unless the fact that it was committed in respect of a dwelling is alleged in the indictment or information.

A conviction which has been followed by a conditional or absolute discharge does not count for these purposes. A conviction by a magistrates' court does count. A finding of guilt by a youth court does count.

Burglaries committed before December 1, 1999 do not count for the purposes of prescribed custodial sentences.

The offender must have been 18 or over at the time of the third burglary, but it is not necessary that he should have been 18 at the time of either of the earlier burglaries.

The court is not obliged to impose a sentence of three years if there are *particular circumstances which relate to any of the offences and which would make it unjust to do so in all the circumstances.* Where the court does not impose the prescribed sentence, it must state in open court what the circumstances are.

If the offender has pleaded guilty, the court may pass a sentence which is not less than 80 per cent of three years (876 days, slightly less than two years and five months).

If the offender qualifies for a hospital order under Mental Health Act 1983, the court may make a hospital order.

A burglary committed in circumstances in which the obligation to pass a minimum sentence applies is triable only on indictment.

Prescribed Custodial Sentence—Drug Trafficking Offences

P.C.C.(S.)A. 2000, s.110

References: Current Sentencing Practice A15–1; Archbold 5–252

A court which sentences an offender for a Class A drug trafficking offence must pass a sentence of **at least seven years' imprisonment** or detention in a young offender institution, if:

(a) the offence was committed on or after October 1, 1997;

(b) the offender was 18 or over when he committed the offence;

(c) he has been convicted on at least two separate previous occasions of a Class A drug trafficking offence.

It is not necessary that the two earlier offences should have been committed after the commencement of this section.

The following offences are "drug trafficking offences":

(i) producing, supplying or possessing with intent to supply controlled drugs (Misuse of Drugs Act 1971, ss.4(2), 4(3) and 5(3)). (NB. simple possession is not included);

(ii) assisting in or inducing the commission outside the United Kingdom of an offence punishable under a corresponding law (Misuse of Drugs Act 1971, s.20);

(iii) improper importation, exportation, or fraudulently evading the rohibition or restriction on importation or exportation of controlled substances whose importation or exportation is prohibited by Misuse of Drugs Act 1971 (Customs and Excise Management Act 1979, ss.50(2), 68(2) or 170);

(iv) manufacturing or supplying a scheduled substance, knowing or suspecting that it is to be used in the production of a controlled drug (Criminal Justice (International Cooperation) Act 1990, s.12);

(v) having possession of a controlled drug on a ship, or being concerned in carrying or concealing a controlled drug on a ship, knowing it is intended to be unlawfully imported or has been exported (Criminal Justice (International Cooperation) Act 1990, s.19);

(vi) inciting, attempting or conspiring to commit any of these offences or aiding, abetting, counselling or procuring the commission of any of them.

A conviction which has been followed by a conditional or absolute discharge does not count for these purposes. A conviction which has been followed by a probation order made before October 1, 1992 does not count. A conviction by a magistrates' court does count. A finding of guilt by a youth court does count.

The court need not pass a sentence of seven years if there are "particular circumstances" which would make it "unjust to do so". If the court does not impose a sentence of seven years, the circumstances which make the sentence unjust must be stated in open court.

If the defendant has pleaded guilty the court may pass a sentence which is not less than 80 per cent of the seven years (2045 days, slightly less than five years and eight months).

If the offender qualifies for a hospital order under Mental Health Act 1983, the court may make a hospital order.

A drug trafficking offence committed in circumstances in which the obligation to pass a minimum sentence applies is triable only on indictment.

Pre-sentence Drug Testing

P.C.C.(S.)A. 2000, ss.36A, 52(4)

References: Current Sentencing Practice D1–1, D5A–1

Note: on December 1, 2008, the Criminal Justice Act 2003, s.161, had not been brought into force, but the P.C.C.(S.)A. 2000, s.36A (as inserted by the Criminal Justice and Court Services Act 2000, s.48) had been repealed.

The P.C.C.(S.)A. 2000, s.52(4), which relates to drug treatment and testing orders, is repealed by the Criminal Justice Act 2003 but saved in respect of those cases where the power to make a drug treatment and testing order is still available.

A court which is considering making a drug treatment and testing order against an offender aged 16 or over may order the offender to provide samples of such description as it may specify for the purpose of ascertaining whether the offender has any drug in his body, in order to satisfy itself whether the offender is dependent on or has a propensity to misuse drugs and that his dependency or propensity is such as requires and may be susceptible to treatment.

This power is not limited to any particular kind of drug.

The court may not make such an order unless the offender expresses his willingness to comply with the order; if an offender refuses to express his willingness to comply, he will qualify for a custodial sentence.

Pre-Sentence Reports

CRIMINAL JUSTICE ACT 2003, s.159

References: Current Sentencing Practice A2–1; D1–1B01

A pre-sentence report is a report made by probation officer or other appropriate officer to assist the court in determining the most suitable method of dealing with the offender. *A pre-sentence report need not be in writing, unless it is required before a court passes a custodial sentence on an offender under the age of 18 or is required to be in writing by rules made by the Secretary of State.*

The pre-sentence report must be disclosed to the offender or his representative, and to the prosecutor, if the prosecutor is a Crown Prosecutor, or represents the CPS, the Customs and Excise, the DSS, the Inland Revenue or the Serious Fraud Office. If the prosecutor is not of such a description (such as a local authority or private prosecutor), a copy of the report need not be given to the prosecutor if the court considers that it would be inappropriate for him to be given one.

If the offender is under 18, the court must give a copy of the report to any *parent or guardian* of the offender who is present in court, even though a copy has been given to the offender or his counsel or solicitor. If the disclosure to the offender or any parent or guardian of the information contained in the report would be likely to create a risk of significant harm to the offender, a complete copy of the report need not be given to the offender or his parents or guardians, but a full copy of the report must be given to the offender's counsel or solicitor.

Previous Convictions

CRIMINAL JUSTICE ACT 2003, s.143

References: Current Sentencing Practice A0–1; Archbold 5–54

This section applies irrespective of the date on which the offence was committed.

If the offender has one or more previous convictions, the court must treat each previous conviction as an aggravating factor if (in the case of that conviction) the court considers that it can reasonably be treated as an aggravating factor, having regard to the nature of the offence to which the conviction relates and its relevance to the current offence, and the time that has elapsed since the conviction.

"Previous conviction" does not include convictions which are deemed not to be convictions by provisions dealing with discharges and probation orders. Under the P.C.C.(S.)A. 2000, s.14(1), a conviction which results in a discharge is deemed not to be a conviction, subject to the qualifications set out in subss.(2) and (3). A conviction before October 1, 1992 which led to a probation order is also deemed not to have been a conviction (see the P.C.C.(S.)A. 2000, s.13). A finding of guilt in service disciplinary proceedings amounts to a conviction.

A court is not required to treat convictions by a court outside the United Kingdom as aggravating factors, but may take them into account and treat them as aggravating factors if it considers it appropriate to do so.

Prosecution Costs

PROSECUTION OF OFFENCES ACT 1985, S.18

References: Current Sentencing Practice J6–1; Archbold 6–27

Where a person has been convicted, or the Crown Court has dismissed an appeal, the court may order him to pay such costs to the prosecutor as it considers to be just and reasonable. *The amount to be paid must be specified in the order.*

An offender should not be ordered to pay costs unless the court is satisfied that he has the means to pay the costs ordered, or will have the means within a reasonable time. An offender who is sentenced to custody should not be ordered to pay costs unless he has the means to pay immediately, or good prospects of employment on release.

The fact that an offender has pleaded guilty is a material factor in considering whether to order him to pay the costs of the prosecution, but it does not necessarily mean that an order is inappropriate. An offender should not be ordered to pay costs simply because he has refused to consent to summary trial.

The fact that the amount of costs is greater than the amount of a fine imposed for the offence is not necessarily a ground for objecting to the order, but the court should consider the overall effect of any combination of financial penalties.

The court does not fix any term of imprisonment in default, but may allow time for payment or fix payment by instalments.

If the amount of the order exceeds £20,000, the Crown Court has the power to enlarge the powers of the magistrates' court responsible for enforcing the order if it considers that the maximum default term of 12 months is inadequate. The court should make an order that the maximum term of imprisonment in default should be a figure taken from the following table:

Amount not exceeding	Maximum term
£50,000	18 months
£100,000	24 months
£250,000	36 months
£1 million	60 months
Over £1 million	120 months

Racially or Religiously Aggravated Crimes

CRIMINAL JUSTICE ACT 2003, s.145

References: Current Sentencing Practice A16–1; Archbold 5–84

A crime is racially or religiously aggravated if at the time of committing the offence, or immediately before or after doing so, the offender demonstrates towards the victim of the offence hostility based on the victim's membership (or presumed membership) of a racial or religious group or the offence is motivated (wholly or partly) by hostility towards members of a racial or religious group based on their membership of that group.

A "racial group" means a group of persons defined by reference to race, colour, nationality (including citizenship) or ethnic or national origins.

A "religious group" is a group of persons defined by reference to religious belief or lack of religious belief.

If the offence was racially or religiously aggravated, the court must treat that fact as an aggravating factor and must state in open court that the offence was so aggravated.

If an offender is convicted of a racially or religiously aggravated offence under Crime and Disorder Act 1998, ss.29, 30, 31 or 32, the court may in its discretion treat the racial or religious aggravation as an aggravating factor, but it is not bound to do so by s.145. The court is not bound to make the statement required by s.145(2)(b).

If the offender is convicted of an offence which could have been charged as a racially or religiously aggravated offence under Crime and Disorder Act 1998, ss.29 to 32 (such as unlawful wounding or assault occasioning actual bodily harm), but he has not been charged with the racially or religiously aggravated offence, or he has been acquitted of the racially or religiously aggravated offence, the court must not treat the offence as racially or religiously aggravated for the purposes of s.145.

References in this paragraph to religious aggravation apply only to offences committed on or after December 14, 2001.

Reasons for Sentence

CRIMINAL JUSTICE ACT 2003, s.174

References: Current Sentencing Practice L9–1; Archbold 5–111

Note: this section applies to all sentences passed on or after April 4, 2005, irrespective of the date on which the offence was committed.

The court must state in open court, in ordinary language and in general terms, its reasons for deciding on the sentence passed.

This duty does not apply where the sentence is fixed by law, or is a required minimum sentence imposed under the P.C.C.(S.)A. 2000, ss.110 or 111, or the Firearms Act 1968, s.51A, although it may be appropriate for the court to explain that the sentence is passed under one of those provisions. Specific obligations to explain the choice of a minimum term in a case of murder are imposed by s.270.

In explaining the reasons for a custodial sentence, the court must:

(a) state that it is of the opinion that the offence or the combination of the offence and one or more offences associated with it was so serious that neither a fine alone nor a community sentence can be justified for the offence, and why it is of that opinion (this does not apply where the offender has refused to express his willingness to comply with a requirement of a proposed community order);

(b) if the court decides on a sentence which falls outside the range or kind of sentence indicated by a definitive guideline published by the Sentencing Guidelines Council, state its reasons for deciding on that sentence;

(c) if the court has reduced the sentence as a result of taking into account the offender's guilty plea, state the fact that it has done so;

(d) mention any aggravating factors or mitigating factors which the court has regarded as being of particular importance;

(e) if the offence is racially or religiously aggravated, state that that has been treated as an aggravating factor;

(f) if the offence has been aggravated by reference to the victim's sexual orientation or disability, state that that has been treated as an aggravating factor.

If the court passes a community sentence, the court must:

(a) state that the offence or the combination of the offence and one or more offences associated with it was serious enough to warrant a community sentence;

(b) if the court decides on a sentence which falls outside the range or kind of sentence indicated by a definitive guideline published by the Sentencing Guidelines Council, state its reasons for deciding on that sentence;

(c) if the court has reduced the sentence as a result of taking into account the offender's guilty plea, state the fact that it has done so;

(d) mention any aggravating factors or mitigating factors which the court has regarded as being of particular importance;

(e) if the offence is racially or religiously aggravated, state that that has been treated as an aggravating factor;

(f) if the offence has been aggravated by reference to the victim's sexual orientation or disability, state that that has been treated as an aggravating factor.

If the court imposes a fine, discharge or any other sentence, it must:

(a) if the court decides on a sentence which falls outside the range or kind of sentence indicated by a definitive guideline published by the Sentencing Guidelines Council, state its reasons for deciding on that sentence;

(b) if the court has reduced the sentence as a result of taking into account the offender's guilty plea, state the fact that it has done so;

(c) mention any aggravating factors or mitigating factors which the court has regarded as being of particular importance;

(d) if the offence is racially or religiously aggravated, state that that has been treated as an aggravating factor;

(e) if the offence has been aggravated by reference to the victim's sexual orientation or disability, state that that has been treated as an aggravating factor.

Explaining the effect of the sentence

The duty to explain the effect of the sentence applies to all sentences, including sentences fixed by law and required minimum sentences.

In the case of a custodial sentence, the court must explain "the effect of the sentence". This appears to require an explanation of the relevant provisions governing release and licence, which will vary according to the nature of the sentence imposed (life imprisonment, imprisonment or detention for public protection, extended sentence, fixed-term sentence).

In the case of a community order, the court must explain the requirements of the order, the effects of non-compliance, and the power of the court on application to vary the order.

In the case of a fine, the court must explain the effect of the order and the effect of failure to pay the fine.

In the case of other orders, (such as football banning orders, orders under the Crime and Disorder Act 1998, s.1C, sexual offence prevention orders, disqualification orders, disqualification from driving, etc.) the court must explain the effect of the order, the effect of non-compliance with the order, and any power of the court to vary the order.

Reasons for not making particular orders

In certain cases a court is required to explain in open court why it has **not** made an order of a particular kind, where it has power to do so.

These include:

> Failure to make a **compensation order**;
>
> Failure to impose an obligatory disqualification from driving;
>
> Failure to make a disqualification order;
>
> Failure to make a drink banning order;
>
> Failure to make a football banning order;
>
> Failure to impose an automatic life sentence;
>
> Failure to activate a suspended sentence in full;
>
> Failure to activate in full a sentence subject to a suspended sentence order;
>
> Failure to bind over parents of a child under the age of 16 convicted of an offence.

Recommendation for Deportation

IMMIGRATION ACT 1971, S.6 AND SCH.3

References: Current Sentencing Practice K1–1; Archbold 5–910

A court may recommend for deportation an offender aged 17 on the day of conviction if he is not a British citizen and has been convicted of an offence punishable with imprisonment.

The court may not recommend the offender for deportation unless he has been given seven days' notice in writing setting out the definition of a British citizen and explaining the exemptions from liability to be recommended for deportation. The court may adjourn to enable the required notice to be served. Failure to comply with this requirement does not necessarily mean that any recommendation will be quashed on appeal.

The court must not make a recommendation without a full inquiry into the relevant circumstances.

Counsel for the offender must be specifically invited to address the court on the question of a recommendation.

The court must give reasons for making a recommendation for deportation, if it does so.

The offender must be 17 years old by the day of his conviction. The offender is deemed to have attained the age of 17 at the date of his conviction if on considering any evidence he appears to have done so to the court.

If any question arises as to whether any person is a British citizen, or is entitled to any exemption, the person claiming to be a British citizen or to be entitled to any exemption must prove that he is.

The principal classes of persons exempted from liability to deportation are Commonwealth citizens and citizens of the Republic of Ireland who:

(a) had that status in 1973; and

(b) were then ordinarily resident in the United Kingdom; and

(c) had been ordinarily resident in the United Kingdom during the five years prior to the conviction.

If the offender is an EC citizen, he may be entitled to the protection of the EC Treaty. If this is so, the court must not recommend him for deportation unless it is satisfied that his continued presence in the United Kingdom involves a genuine and sufficiently serious threat affecting one of the fundamental interests of society. In determining whether this condition is satisfied the court must consider the likely future behaviour of the offender, but his past behaviour may be considered as evidence of this. Previous convictions do not in themselves constitute grounds for a recommendation.

It is not sufficient that the offender has committed a serious offence or has a record of offending in the United Kingdom, if there is no basis for anticipating further offences.

The following principles are found in the cases:

(a) The principal criterion for recommending deportation is the extent to which the offender will represent a **potential detriment** to the United Kingdom if he remains in the country;

(b) The court is primarily concerned with his **expected future behaviour**, as evidenced by his offence and previous record;

(c) The court is not concerned with the political situation or conditions in the offender's home country;

(d) *The fact that the offender is living on social security benefit is not a relevant consideration;*

(e) The fact that the offender is not lawfully in the United Kingdom is not a relevant consideration, except in cases where he has secured admission to the United Kingdom by fraudulent means.

If the court makes a recommendation for deportation, the court should consider whether to give a direction relating to the offender's custody or release pending the decision of the Secretary of State whether to make a deportation order on the basis of the recommendation.

If the court gives no direction for the release of the offender, he will remain in custody until this matter has been decided, irrespective of the type of sentence imposed by the court for the offence. The court may direct that the offender be released pending the decision of the Secretary of State, or released subject to such conditions as to residence or reporting to the police as the court may direct.

Thank you for purchasing **Sentencing Referencer 2009**.

 Don't miss important updates

So that you have all the latest information, **Sentencing Referencer** is published annually. Sign up today for a Standing Order to ensure you receive the updating copies as soon as they publish. Setting up a Standing Order with Sweet & Maxwell is hassle-free, simply tick, complete and return this FREEPOST card and we'll do the rest.

You may cancel your Standing Order at any time by writing to us at Sweet & Maxwell, PO Box 2000, Andover, SP10 9AH stating the Standing Order you wish to cancel.

Alternatively, if you have purchased your copy of **Sentencing Referencer** from a bookshop or other trade supplier, please ask your supplier to ensure that you are registered to receive the new editions.

All goods are subject to our 30 day Satisfaction Guarantee (applicable to EU customers only)

Yes, please send me new editions of **Sentencing Referencer** to be invoiced on publication, until I cancel the standing order in writing.

☐ **All new editions**

Title   **Name**

Organisation

Job title

Address

Postcode

Telephone

Email

S&M account number (if known)

PO number

All orders are accepted subject to the terms of this order form and our Terms of Trading. (see www.sweetandmaxwell.co.uk). By submitting this order form I confirm that I accept these terms and I am authorised to sign on behalf of the customer.

Signed   **Job Title**

Print Name   **Date**

(LBU007) V7 (12.2008) JG / KS

SWEET & MAXWELL

SWEET & MAXWELL

FREEPOST

PO BOX 2000

ANDOVER

SP10 9AH

UNITED KINGDOM

Referral Orders

P.C.C.(S.)A. 2000, ss.16–32

References: Current Sentencing Practice E14–1; Archbold 5–924

Where a defendant under the age of 18 appears for sentence before a youth court or magistrates' court for an offence **punishable with imprisonment** the court **must** make a referral order if:

(a) none of the offences is one for which the sentence is fixed by law;

(b) the court is not proposing to impose a custodial sentence or make a hospital order, or to grant an absolute discharge;

(c) the defendant has pleaded guilty to all the offences for which he is to be sentenced;

(d) the defendant has never been convicted by a court in the United Kingdom of any other offence;

(e) the defendant has never been bound over to keep the peace.

If the offender appears to qualify for a sentence of detention for public protection or an extended sentence of detention, he must be committed to the Crown Court for sentence. (See **Committal for Sentence.**)

Where a defendant pleads guilty to the offences with which he has been charged, and asks the court to take other offences into consideration, it is uncertain whether these conditions are satisfied.

The court **may** make a referral order if the following conditions are satisfied:

(a) the offence concerned is not punishable with imprisonment;

(b) the court is not proposing to impose a custodial sentence or make a hospital order, or to grant an absolute discharge;

(c) the defendant has pleaded guilty to all the offences for which he is to be sentenced;

(d) the defendant has never been convicted by a court in the United Kingdom of any other offence;

(e) the defendant has never been bound over to keep the peace.

The court **may** also make a referral order if the following conditions are satisfied:

(a) the offender is being dealt with by the court for the offence and one or more connected offences (whether or not any of them is punishable with imprisonment);

(b) although he pleaded guilty to at least one of the offences, he also pleaded not guilty to at least one of them;

(c) he has never been convicted by or before a court in the United Kingdom of any other offence;

(d) he has never been bound over in criminal proceedings in England and Wales or Northern Ireland to keep the peace or to be of good behaviour.

Where the court makes a referral order, the court must not make a community order, impose a fine, grant a conditional discharge or make a reparation order for that offence. The court may make a compensation order. The court may not bind the offender over to keep the peace, or order his parents or guardians to be bound over. The court may make a parenting order after considering a report from an appropriate officer.

A referral order must specify the youth offending team responsible for implementing the order, require the offender to attend meetings of the panel established by the team, and specify the period (not less than three months and not more than 12 months) during which the contract is to have effect.

The court must explain the effect of the order and the consequences of non-compliance or breach.

The court may order the offender's parent or a representative of the local authority to attend meetings of the panel.

The offender must attend meetings of the panel and reach an agreement on a programme of behaviour aimed at preventing re-offending by the offender. The agreement takes effect as a "youth offender contract".

If the offender does not agree with the panel within a reasonable time, or fails to sign the contract, or fails to comply with the contract, or if there is a change in the offender's circumstances, the panel may refer the offender back to the court.

If the offender is referred back to the court, and the court is satisfied that the panel was entitled to make any finding of fact that it did make, and that the panel reasonably exercised its discretion, the court may revoke the order and deal with the offender in any manner in which the court which made the order could have dealt with him. The court which deals with the offender, must have regard to the circumstances of his referral back to the court, and the extent to which he has complied with the contract if one has been made. The court may decline to revoke the referral order, or may declare that the referral order is discharged.

If the offender is convicted of an offence committed after the referral order was made, the court may revoke the referral order and deal with the offender in any manner in which the court which made the order, could have dealt with him. Alternatively, the court may extend the compliance period if it is satisfied that there are exceptional circumstances which indicate that extending his compliance period is likely to help prevent further re-offending by him. The compliance period must not be extended so as to exceed a total period of 12 months.

If the offender is convicted by a youth court or magistrates' court of an offence committed before the referral order was made, the court may impose a custodial sentence, make a hospital order, grant an absolute discharge, or extend the compliance period. If the offender is convicted of such an offence by the Crown Court the offender may be sentenced in the normal way.

If an offender subject to a referral order is sentenced for another offence otherwise than by means of an order extending the compliance period or an absolute discharge, the referral order is revoked and the court may deal with the offender for the offence for which the order was made in any manner in which he could have been dealt with by the court which made the order.

Remand to Hospital for Psychiatric Reports

MENTAL HEALTH ACT 1983, s.35

References: Current Sentencing Practice L7–1; Archbold 5–891

The Crown Court may remand an accused person to a specified hospital for a report on his mental condition, at any time before he is sentenced or otherwise dealt with for the offence. The accused may be remanded before or after arraignment.

The court must be satisfied on the written or oral report of one medical practitioner that there is reason to suspect that the accused person is suffering from mental disorder and the court must be of the opinion that it would be impracticable for a report to be made if he were remanded on bail.

The power may be used in the case of a person awaiting trial for murder, but not after a person has been convicted of murder.

The court may remand a person to a hospital only if it is satisfied that arrangements have been made for the accused person to be admitted to the hospital within seven days of the beginning of the remand period.

The accused may be further remanded without appearing in court if he is represented by counsel or solicitor and the court is satisfied that a further remand is necessary for the assessment of the accused person's mental condition.

The accused person may not be remanded or further remanded for a period exceeding 28 days at a time, or for a total period exceeding 12 weeks.

The court must give directions for the conveyance and detention in a place of safety of the accused pending his admission to hospital.

Remand to Hospital for Psychiatric Treatment

MENTAL HEALTH ACT 1983, S.36

References: Current Sentencing Practice L7–1; Archbold 5–892

The Crown Court may remand an accused person who is in custody awaiting trial or sentence to a specified hospital for medical treatment at any time before he is sentenced or otherwise dealt with for the offence. The power may not be used in the case of a person awaiting trial for murder.

The accused may be remanded before or after arraignment. The court must be satisfied on the written or oral evidence of two medical practitioners that the accused is suffering from mental disorder of a nature or degree which makes it appropriate for him to be detained in a hospital for treatment.

The accused may be further remanded without appearing in court if he is represented by counsel or solicitor and the court is satisfied that a further remand is warranted.

The accused person may not be remanded or further remanded for a period exceeding 28 days at a time or for a total period exceeding 12 weeks. The court may terminate the remand at any time if it appears to the court to be appropriate to do so.

The court must give directions for the conveyance and detention in a place of safety of the accused pending his admission to hospital.

Remitting a Juvenile

P.C.C.(S.)A. 2000, ss.8–10

References: Current Sentencing Practice L13–1; Archbold 5–35

Where a child or young person is found guilty before the Crown Court of an offence other than homicide, the Crown Court must remit the offender to the youth court, unless it is satisfied that it would be undesirable to do so. It will be undesirable to remit if the judge who presided over the trial will be better informed as to the facts and circumstances, or if there would be a risk of disparity if defendants were sentenced by different courts, or if there would be delay, duplication of proceedings or unnecessary expense.

Where a child or young person is found guilty before a magistrates' court which is not a youth court, the magistrates' court must remit the offender to a youth court unless it proposes to deal with the offender by means of a discharge, a fine, or an order binding over his parents or guardians to take proper care and exercise proper control. This applies also to an offender who was a young person when the proceedings began.

Reparation Order

P.C.C.(S.)A. 2000, s.73

References: Current Sentencing Practice E11–1; Archbold 5–435

A reparation order may be made only by a court which has been notified that arrangements for implementing such orders have been made.

A reparation order is an order requiring an offender to make reparation for the offence otherwise than by the payment of compensation.

The restrictions on liberty imposed by a reparation order should be commensurate with the seriousness of the offence, or the combination of the offence and associated offences.

A reparation order may be made against an offender under 18.

A reparation order may not be made in respect of an offence committed before April 4, 2005, if the court proposes to pass a custodial sentence or to make a community punishment order, a community punishment and rehabilitation order, or a supervision order which includes requirements under P.C.C.(S.)A. 2000, Sch.6, an action plan order or a referral order.

A reparation order may not be made in respect of an offence committed on or after April 4, 2005, if the court proposes to pass a custodial sentence or to make a community order under the Criminal Justice Act 2003, or a supervision order which includes requirements under P.C.C.(S.)A. 2000, Sch.6, an action plan order or a referral order.

A reparation order may be combined with a fine, a restitution order, or a compensation order, or a supervision order without additional requirements.

A reparation order may not require the offender to work for more than 24 hours in all, or to make reparation to any person without the consent of that person.

The requirements of the order must so far as possible, avoid conflict with the offender's religious beliefs or any community order to which he is subject, and with the times at which he normally works or attends school.

The reparation must be made within three months of the making of the order.

Before making a reparation order the court must obtain and consider a report indicating the type of work that is suitable for the offender and the attitude of the victim or victims to the requirements proposed to be included in the order.

The consent of the offender is not required.

Required Minimum Sentence—Possessing Prohibited Weapon

FIREARMS ACT 1968, s.51A

References: Current Sentencing Practice A15A–1; Archbold 5–258

A court dealing with an offender for an offence under the Firearms Act 1968, s.5 **must** impose **the required minimum sentence** "unless the court is of the opinion that there are exceptional circumstances relating to the offence or to the offender which justify its not doing so".

The section applies to offences committed on or after January 22, 2004.

The section applies to all prohibited weapons except weapons designed to discharge noxious gas, liquids or other things, and various types of rockets as specified in s.5(1A)(c)–(g).

The duty to impose a required minimum sentence applies to offences under the Firearms Act 1968, ss.16 (possession of a firearm with intent), 16A (possession of a firearm with intent to cause fear), 17 (possession or use of a firearm to resist arrest or when arrested for a Scheduled offence), 18 (carrying a firearm with intent to commit an offence), 19 (carrying a firearm in a public place), and 20 (trespassing in a building with a firearm), where the firearm is a prohibited weapon to which s.51A applies, **if the offence was committed on or after April 6, 2007.**

The **required minimum sentence** is at least five years in the case of an offender aged 18 or over when offence was committed, or three years detention under the P.C.C.(S.)A. 2000, s.91, if the offender was over 16 but under the age of 18 when the offence was committed.

The court may not allow a discount for a plea of guilty if the effect of doing so would be to reduce the length of the sentence below the required minimum term.

If a person between the ages of 18 and 21 is convicted of one of the offences to which the requirement to impose a minimum sentence applies, **committed on or after May 28, 2007**, he must be sentenced to five years' detention in a young offender institution, unless there are "exceptional circumstances". If the offence was committed before that date, the obligation to impose the required minimum sentence does not apply. The obligation to impose the required minimum sentence of three years' detention does apply to an offender aged between 16 and 18 convicted of an offence committed before that date.

A person over 18 convicted of an offence under the **Violent Crime Reduction Act 2006, s.28**, must be sentenced to a minimum term of five years if the weapon concerned is one to which s.51A applies, subject to the same exceptions. A person over 16 and under 18 must be sentenced to a minimum term of three years.

Restitution Order

P.C.C.(S.)A., s.148

References: Current Sentencing Practice J3–1; Archbold 5–431

The court has power to make a restitution order if goods have been stolen and the offender has been convicted of any offence with reference to the theft. "Stolen" for this purpose includes obtained by deception or blackmail, or by fraud contrary to the Fraud Act 2006.

The court may order the offender to restore the stolen goods to any person entitled to recover them from him.

On the application of the person entitled to recover the goods, the court may order the offender to deliver or transfer to that person any other goods which directly or indirectly represent the stolen goods.

The court may order a sum not exceeding the value of the stolen goods to be paid to the owner of those goods from money taken out of the possession of the offender on his apprehension.

If any third party has possession of the stolen goods, the court may order him to restore them to the person entitled to recover them. If the third party has bought the goods in good faith from the person convicted, or lent money to him on the security of them, the court may order payment to that person of a sum not exceeding the purchase price of the goods, or the amount of the loan, out of money taken out of the possession of the offender on his apprehension.

The court may not make a restitution order unless all the relevant facts are admitted or appear from the evidence given at the trial and the witness statements or depositions. The court may not embark on its own investigations with a view to making a restitution order.

Failure to comply with a restitution order is a contempt of court; the court does not make any order dealing with failure to comply.

Restraining Order

PROTECTION FROM HARRASSMENT ACT 1997, s.5

Where a court is sentencing an offender for any offences against s.2 or s.4 of the Protection from Harrassment Act 1997 it may make an order prohibiting the defendant from doing anything described in the order, for the purpose of protecting the victim of the offence, or any other person mentioned in the order, from further conduct which amounts to harassment, or will cause fear of violence.

The order may be for a specified period or until further order.

The prosecutor, the defendant or any other person mentioned in the order may apply to the court which made the order for it to be varied or discharged by a further order.

Note: provisions of the Domestic Violence, Crime and Victims Act 2004 extending the scope of the power to make restraining orders were not in force on December 1, 2008.

Restriction Orders (Mental Health Act 1983)

Mental Health Act 1983, s.41

References: Current Sentencing Practice F2–1; Archbold 5–898

A restriction order may be made only in conjunction with a hospital order. (See **Hospital Order**.)

The Crown Court may make a restriction order if it makes a hospital order in respect of the offender and it appears to the court, having regard to the nature of the offence, the antecedents of the offender and the risk of his committing further offences if set at large, that is necessary for the protection of the public from **serious harm** to do so.

A restriction order may be made only if at least one of the medical practitioners whose evidence has been taken into account has given evidence orally before the court.

In deciding whether to make a restriction order, the court is concerned with the seriousness of the harm which will result if the offender reoffends, rather than with the risk of reoffending.

The seriousness of the offence committed by the offender is not necessarily important for this purpose. An offender convicted of a relatively minor offence may properly be subjected to a restriction order if he is mentally disordered and dangerous. An offender convicted of a serious offence should not be subjected to a restriction order unless he is likely to commit further offences which will involve a risk of serious harm to the public.

It is not necessary that the offender should be dangerous to the public as a whole; it is sufficient if he is dangerous to a particular section of the public, or to a particular person.

The harm to which the public would be exposed if the offender were at large need not necessarily be personal injury.

It is the responsibility of the court, and not that of the medical witnesses, to determine whether a restriction order is appropriate.

A restriction order should normally be without limit of time.

Return to Custody

P.C.C.(S.)A., s.116

References: Current Sentencing Practice A7–3

The power to order return to custody applies to offenders sentenced to determinate custodial sentences on or after October 1, 1992 who have been released under Pt 2 of the Criminal Justice Act 1991 and who are convicted of an offence committed after release but before the whole period of the sentence has expired.

The power does not apply to offenders who have been released in accordance with the Criminal Justice Act 2003, s.244, from sentences of 12 months or more imposed for offences committed on or after April 4, 2005. The power does apply to persons released from sentences of less than 12 months imposed for offences committed on or after April 4, 2005.

The power does not apply to offenders who have been released under the Criminal Justice Act 1991, s.33(1A) (long term prisoners sentenced for non-specified offences committed before April 4, 2005, and released on or after June 9, 2008).

The power applies to persons sentenced to determinate sentences of imprisonment, detention in a young offender institution or detention under P.C.C.(S.)A. 2000, s.91.

The power does not apply to persons committed in default or for contempt, or sentenced to detention and training orders.

The subsequent offence must be punishable with imprisonment, and committed within the full term of the original sentence.

The court may order the offender to return to custody for a period equal to the part of the original sentence which remained on the day when the offence was committed. The date of conviction does not matter; the power is available when the offender is convicted after the original sentence has expired.

The power is discretionary; the court is not obliged to make an order under the section, and may order the offender to serve less than the full remaining period of the sentence.

The period ordered to be served must be served before any new sentence or concurrently with it, but not consecutively to it.

The period ordered to be served must be disregarded in determining the length of the new sentence. There is no statutory restriction on reducing the period to allow for the length of the new sentence.

In deciding whether the later offence was committed within the full term of the original sentence, and how much of the original sentence remained on the date of the offence, the court should allow for time spent in custody on remand.

If the offender is convicted of the later offence by a magistrates' court, and the relevant period exceeds six months, the magistrates' court may order him to return to prison for a period not exceeding six months, or commit him to the Crown Court.

The magistrates' court should either commit the whole matter to the Crown Court, or deal with the whole matter itself. It should not sentence the offender for the latest offence and commit him to the Crown Court to be dealt with under s.116. An order under s.116 made by a magistrates' court does not count as part of the permissible aggregate sentence of imprisonment available to the court. If the magistrates' court commits the offender to the Crown Court to be dealt with under s.116, it should commit him for sentence for the later offence under either P.C.C.(S.)A., s.3 or s.6.

The fact that the offender has been recalled to custody following the revocation of his licence by the Secretary of State or the Parole Board does not prevent the court from ordering his return to custody, but the court should adjust the period of return to take account of any period served following the revocation of the licence, and to allow for the fact that time spent in custody on remand during which the offender was also in custody by reason of the revocation of the licence will not be deducted from the sentence for the new offence.

Sentencing Guidelines

CRIMINAL JUSTICE ACT 2003, s.172

References: Current Sentencing Practice G; Archbold 5–100

If the Sentencing Guidelines Council has issued a "**definitive guideline**" every court in sentencing an offender must "**have regard to**" any definitive guidelines which are relevant to the case.

The Act does not require courts to follow a "definitive guideline" without regard to the detailed circumstances of the individual case. The court has a **discretion** to depart from a guideline in any case where it considers it to be appropriate or just to do so, provided that the court can give **reasons for the departure**.

If the court decides that the appropriate sentence in a particular case is not one which is indicated by a relevant definitive guideline, the court must **state its reasons for deciding that the appropriate sentence is of a different kind or outside the range of sentences indicated by the guideline**. Where the court imposes a sentence which is consistent with a "definitive guideline," the general duty imposed by s.174(1)(a) to state the reasons for deciding on the sentence passed appears to include by implication a duty to refer to the guideline to which the court has had regard.

A court is not obliged to have regard to draft guidelines issued by the Council as a preliminary stage in the process of consultation, or to any views expressed by the Sentencing Advisory Panel.

Where a definitive guideline is published by the Sentencing Guidelines after an offence is committed, but before the offender is sentenced, there is no breach of Art.7 of the European Convention on Human Rights if the sentencing judge takes the guideline into account.

Serious Crime Prevention Order

SERIOUS CRIME ACT 2007, ss.1–43

References: Current Sentencing Practice H13; Archbold 5–873d

These provisions came into force on April 6, 2008. They do not apply where an offender is sentenced after that date for an offence of which he has been convicted before that date, but it appears that they do apply where an offender is convicted after that date of an offence committed before that date.

The Crown Court may make a serious crime prevention order where person **aged 18 or over** is convicted of a **"serious offence"** or has been convicted of a "serious offence" by a magistrates court and committed to the Crown Court to be dealt with for the offence.

A serious crime order may also be made on application by the High Court in the case of a person who has been involved in serious crime.

An order may be made only in addition to the sentence is respect of the offence concerned, or in addition to a conditional discharge or absolute discharge.

An order may be made if the court has *reasonable grounds to believe that the order would protect the public by preventing, restricting or disrupting involvement by the person in serious crime in England and Wales*. The order may contain such prohibitions, restrictions or requirements as the court considers appropriate for protecting the public by preventing, restricting or disrupting involvement by the person concerned in serious crime.

A serious crime prevention order may be made **only on an application** by the Director of Public Prosecutions, the Director of Revenue and Customs prosecutions, or the Director of the Serious Fraud Office. *The Crown Court must give an opportunity to a person other than the offender to make representations,* if that person applies to do so, if it considers that the making of a serious crime prevention order would be likely to have a significant adverse effect on that person.

Proceedings in the Crown Court in relation to serious crime prevention orders are civil proceedings and *the standard of proof to be applied is the civil standard of proof.* The court is not restricted to considering evidence that would have been admissible in the criminal proceedings in which the person concerned was convicted and may adjourn any proceedings in relation to a serious crime prevention order even after sentencing the person concerned.

A serious crime prevention order is binding on a person only if he is present or represented at the proceedings at which the order is made, or a notice setting out the terms of the order has been served on him.

A serious crime prevention order may not require a person to answer questions or provide information orally or to answer any privileged question, or provide any privileged information or documents. An order may not require a person to produce any excluded material (Police and Criminal evidence Act 1984, s.11). An order may not require a person to produce information or documents in respect of which he owes an obligation of confidence by virtue of carrying on a banking business unless the person to whom the obligation of confidence is owed consents to the disclosure or production or the order contains a requirement to disclose information or produce documents of this kind. An order may not require a person to answer any question, provide any information or produce any document if the disclosure concerned is prohibited under any other enactment.

A serious crime prevention order must specify when it is to come into force and when it is to cease to be in force. An order may not be in force for **more than five years** beginning with the date on which it comes into force. Different provisions of the order may come into force or cease to be in force on different dates.

A person who is subject to a serious crime prevention order, or an authority who has applied for an order, may appeal to the Court of Appeal in relation to a decision in relation to a serious crime prevention order. A person who has been given the opportunity to make representations in respect of an order may also appeal to the Court of Appeal.

If a person who is subject to a serious crime prevention order is convicted by the Crown Court of a serious offence, or is convicted by a magistrates' court of such an offence and committed to the Crown Court to be dealt with, the Crown Court may vary the order if the court has reasonable grounds to believe that the terms of the order as varied would protect the public by preventing , restricting or disrupting involvement by the person in serious crime in England and Wales. The Crown Court may vary a serious crime prevention order which has been made by the High Court.

If a person is convicted of an offence of failing without reasonable excuse to comply with a serious crime prevention order, the Crown Court may vary the order if it has reasonable grounds to believe that the terms of the order as varied would protect the public by preventing, restricting or disrupting involvement by the person in serious crime in England and Wales.

A serious crime prevention order may be made against an individual, a body corporate, a partnership or an unincorporated association.

Offences against the following provisions are **serious offences** for the purposes of serious crime prevention orders:

The court may treat any other offence as if it were a specified offence if it considers the offence to be sufficiently serious to be treated as if it were a specified offence.

> **Asylum and Immigration (Treatment of Claimants, etc) Act 2004**, s.4;
>
> **Common law offences**;
>
> Assault with intent to rob (where the assault involves a firearm, imitation firearm or an offensive weapon); conspiracy to defraud; cheating the public revenue; bribery;
>
> **Control of Trade in Endangered Species (Enforcement) Regulations 1997,** reg.8;
>
> **Copyright, Designs and Patents Act 1988**, ss.107(1)(a), (b), (d)(iv) or (e), 198(1)(a), (b) or (d)(iii), 297A;
>
> **Criminal Justice (International co-operation) Act 1990**, ss.12, 19;
>
> **Customs and Excise Management Act 1979**, ss.15(2), 15(3), 68(2) (if the offence is committed in connection with the prohibition or restriction on the importation of controlled drugs, or if committed in connection with firearms or ammunition), 170;
>
> **Environmental Protection Act 1990**, s.33;
>
> **Finance Act 2000**, s.144;
>
> **Firearms Act 1968**, s.3(1);
>
> **Forgery and Counterfeiting Act 1981**, ss.14, 15, 16, 17;
>
> **Fraud Act 2006**, ss.1, 6, 7, 9, 11;
>
> **Gangmasters (Licensing) Act 2004**, s.12(1), 12(2);
>
> **Immigration Act 1971**, ss.25, 25A or 25B;
>
> **Misuse of Drugs Act 1971**, ss.4(2), 4(3), 5(3), 8, 20;
>
> **Prevention of Corruption Act 1906**, s.1(1) (first or second offence only);
>
> **Proceeds of Crime Act 2002**, ss.327, 328 and 329;
>
> **Public Bodies Corrupt Practices Act 1889**, s.1;

Salmon and Freshwater Fisheries Act 1975, s.1;

Sexual Offences Act 1956, s.33A;

Sexual Offences Act 2003, ss.14, 48, 49, 50, 52, 53, 57, 58, 59;

Tax Credits Act 2002, s.35;

Theft Act 1968, s.8(1) (where the offence involves the use or threat to use a firearm, an imitation firearm or an offensive weapon), 17, 21;

Trademarks Act 1994, ss.92(1), 92(2), 92(3).

Value Added Tax Act 1994, s.72;

Wildlife and Countryside Act 1981, s.14;

Any offence of **attempting or conspiring** to commit any scheduled offence (other than conspiracy to defraud), or any offence under the Serious Crime Prevention Act 2007 with reference to a scheduled offence.

In relation to conduct before the passing of the Serious Crime Act 2007, the scheduled offences include any corresponding offences under the law in force at the time of the conduct.

Sexual Offences Prevention Order

SEXUAL OFFENCES ACT 2003, s.104

References: Current Sentencing Practice H11–1A; Archbold 20–323

A court dealing with an offender for one of the offences listed in Sch.3 or Sch.5 of the Sexual Offences Act 2003 may make a sexual offences prevention order if it is satisfied that *it is necessary to make such an order, for the purpose of protecting the public or any particular members of the public from serious sexual harm from the defendant.*

Where an offence is included in Sch.3 of the Act subject to conditions relating to the age of the offender or the victim, or the sentence imposed on the offender, those conditions may be disregarded in making a sexual offences prevention order.

The power may be exercised in relation to an offence committed before the commencement of the Act. "Protecting the public or any particular members of the public from serious sexual harm from the defendant" means protecting the public in the United Kingdom or any particular members of that public from *serious physical or psychological harm, caused by the defendant committing one or more offences listed in Sch.3.*

A court may make a sexual offences prevention order in respect of a person convicted of an offence which is a specified offence for the purposes of the Criminal Justice Act 2003 (see Specified Offences—Adult Offenders) notwithstanding that it has decided that the offender does not present a significant risk or serious harm from future specified offences and that accordingly a sentence of life imprisonment, imprisonment for public protection or an extended sentence is not required.

A sexual offences prevention order may prohibit the defendant from doing anything described in the order. The only prohibitions that may be included in the order are those necessary for the purpose of protecting the public or any particular members of the public from serious sexual harm from the defendant.

The order may have effect for a fixed period **(not less than five years)** specified in the order or until further order.

Sexual Offenders—Notification Requirements

SEXUAL OFFENCES ACT 2003, S.80

References: Archbold 20–263

A person is subject to the notification requirements of the Sexual Offences Act 2003 if:

(a) he is convicted of an offence listed in Sch.3;

(b) he is found not guilty of such an offence by reason of insanity;

(c) he is found to be under a disability and to have done the act charged against him in respect of such an offence; or

(d) he is cautioned in respect of such an offence.

The periods during which the offender is liable to the notification requirements are as follows:

A person who, in respect of the offence, is or has been sentenced to imprisonment for life or for a term of 30 months or more	**An indefinite period beginning with the relevant date**
A person who, in respect of the offence or finding, is or has been admitted to a hospital subject to a restriction order	**An indefinite period beginning with that date**
A person who, in respect of the offence, is or has been sentenced to imprisonment for a term of more than 6 months but less than 30 months	**10 years beginning with that date**
A person who, in respect of the offence, is or has been sentenced to imprisonment for a term of 6 months or less	**7 years beginning with that date**
A person who, in respect of the offence or finding, is or has been admitted to a hospital without being subject to a restriction order	**7 years beginning with that date**
A person who has been cautioned	**2 years beginning with that date**
A person in whose case an order for conditional discharge is made in respect of the offence	**The period of conditional discharge**
A person of any other description	**5 years beginning with the relevant date**

Where a person is under 18 on the relevant date, the periods are one half of those specified as fixed length periods. If an offender under 18 is sentenced to a detention and training order, the relevant period for the purpose of determining his liability to the notification requirements is the custodial part of the order (normally half of the term of the order). A person sentenced to a detention and training order with a term of more than 12 months is liable to the requirements for a period of five years; if the order is for any period not exceeding 12 months, the period of liability is three-and-a-half years.

Where the offender is sentenced to terms which are wholly or partly consecutive, the table applies to the effective length of the aggregate terms.

Where an offender under 18 is convicted of an offence within the scope of Sch.3 and sentenced in a manner which results in an obligation to notify, the court may direct that obligation shall be treated as an obligation of the parent.

The only function of the court is to state that the offender has been convicted of a sexual offence to which the Sexual Offences Act 2003 applies, and to certify those facts.

This is not a mandatory obligation, and failure to make a statement does not affect the offender's liability under the Act. The court is not obliged to inform the offender of his liability, or of the period during which it will continue.

The obligation to notify imposed by the Sexual Offences Act 2003 is not a relevant consideration in determining the sentence for the offence.

Sexual Orientation or Disability

CRIMINAL JUSTICE ACT 2003, s.146

References: Current Sentencing Practice A16A; Archbold 5–84

Note: this section does not apply to offences committed before April 4, 2005.

If at the time of committing the offence, or immediately before or after doing so, the offender demonstrated towards the victim of the offence hostility based on either the sexual orientation (or presumed sexual orientation) of the victim, or a disability (or presumed disability) of the victim, the court must treat that as an aggravating factor.

The same applies where the offence was motivated (wholly or partly) by hostility towards persons who are of a particular sexual orientation, or by hostility towards persons who have a disability or a particular disability.

In either case, the court must state in open court that the offence was aggravated in this way.

Specified Offences—Adult Offenders

CRIMINAL JUSTICE ACT 2003, ss.225–229

References: Current Sentencing Practice A18; Archbold 5–292

If an offender aged 18 or over on the date of conviction is convicted of a "**specified offence**" committed **on or after April 4, 2005**, and the court considers that there is **a significant risk to members of the public of serious harm occasioned by the commission by him of further specified offences,** the court may impose a sentence of life imprisonment (custody for life if the offender is under 21), imprisonment for public protection (detention in a young offender institution for public protection if the offender is under 21) or an extended sentence of imprisonment (extended sentence of detention in a young offender institution if the offender is under 21).

If the offence is charged as having been committed on a day unknown within a period beginning before April 4, 2005, and ending after that date, these provisions do not apply, unless the court finds that the offence was in fact committed on or after April 4, 2005.

For specified offences, see **Maximum Sentence**.

"**Serious harm**" means "death or serious personal injury, whether physical or psychological".

A sentence of **life imprisonment** (or custody for life) must be imposed if the offence is punishable with life imprisonment and the court considers that the seriousness of the offence, or of the offence and one or more offences associated with it, is such as "to justify the imposition of a sentence of imprisonment for life".

A sentence of **imprisonment for public protection** (or detention in a young offender institution for public protection) **may** be imposed if the offence is **punishable by 10 years' imprisonment or more**, but either it is not punishable with imprisonment for life or the seriousness of the offence does not justify a sentence of life imprisonment.

A sentence of imprisonment for public protection (or detention in a young offender institution for public protection) may be imposed only if the offender had been convicted of an offence listed in the Criminal Justice Act 2003, Sch.15A before committing the latest offence, or the notional minimum term (the minimum term which

the court would impose under the P.C.C.(S.)A. s.82A, before the deduction of time spent in custody on remand) would be at least two years.

Alternatively, the court may pass an extended sentence of imprisonment or detention in a young offender institution.

A sentence of imprisonment (or detention in a young offender institution) for public protection is an indeterminate sentence. Offenders sentenced to imprisonment or detention in a young offender institution for public protection may be detained in custody for a period of longer than the maximum term normally permissible for the offence of which they have been convicted, if the Parole Board considers that their continued detention is necessary for the protection of the public.

A court which imposes a sentence either of imprisonment (or custody) for life or imprisonment (or detention in a young offender institution) for public protection must fix a minimum term in accordance with the P.C.C.(S.)A. 2000, s.82A. The offender may not be released until he has served the minimum term. See **Minimum Term**.

If an offender who was **21 when the offence was committed** is sentenced to **life imprisonment**, the court may decline to fix a minimum term if it is of the opinion that, because of the seriousness of the offence or of the combination of the offence and one or more offences associated with it, no order fixing a minimum term should be made.

An offender sentenced to life imprisonment (or custody for life) will remain on licence for the rest of his life. An offender sentenced to imprisonment or detention in a young offender institution for public protection will remain on licence for a minimum of 10 years. After this period has expired, the Parole Board may direct that his licence shall cease to have effect. If the Board does not give such a direction, he will remain on licence for the rest of his life.

The only difference in practice between the sentence of life imprisonment (or custody for life) and a sentence of imprisonment or detention in a young offender institution for public protection, is the power of the Parole Board in the case of a sentence of imprisonment or detention in a young offender institution for public protection to direct that the licence shall cease to have effect after a period of 10 years following release from custody.

Extended Sentences

The court may impose an extended sentence of imprisonment or detention in a young offender institution on a person convicted of any specified offence (whether or not it is punishable with 10 years' imprisonment), if the court considers that there is a significant risk to members of the public of serious harm occasioned by the commission by him of further specified offences.

An extended sentence of imprisonment (or detention in a young offender institution) may be imposed only if the offender had been convicted of an offence listed in the Criminal Justice Act 2003, Sch.15A before committing the latest offence, or the appropriate custodial term would be at least four years.

An extended sentence consists of two components: the "appropriate custodial term" and "the extension period." *The combined length of the two components must not exceed the maximum sentence for the offence*.

The appropriate custodial term is the determinate custodial sentence which would have been imposed if the case had not required an extended sentence. In determining this term, the court must comply with the general provisions governing the use of imprisonment, in particular s.153(2), which requires that the custodial term must be the "shortest term" that in the opinion of the court is commensurate with the seriousness of the offence or the combination of the offence and one or more offences associated with it. **If the offender has a previous conviction for an offence in Sch.15A of the Criminal Justice Act 2003, and the custodial term would be less than 12 months, a term of 12 months must be imposed**. The custodial term may not otherwise be increased beyond what is the shortest term which would be commensurate with the offence, on account of the offender's dangerousness.

The extension period is a period of licence, which is *"of such length as the court considers necessary for the purpose of protecting members of the public from serious harm occasioned by the commission by him of further specified offences."* It must not be more than **five years in the case of a specified violent offence or eight years in the case of a specified sexual offence**.

An offender serving an extended sentence will be released on licence automatically after he has served one half of the appropriate custodial term.

Assessing dangerousness (s.229)

In assessing whether there is a significant risk of serious harm from future specified offences, the court must take into account all such information as is available to it about the nature and circumstances of the offence, and may take into account all such information as is available about the nature and circumstances of any other offences of which the offender has been convicted by a court anywhere in the world. The court may take into account any information which is before it about any pattern of behaviour of which any of the offences of which the offender has been convicted forms part, and may take into account any information about the offender which is before it.

If an offender qualifies for a hospital order under the Mental Health Act 1983, s.37, the court may make such an order even though the offender otherwise qualifies for a sentence of life imprisonment, custody for life, imprisonment or detention in a young offender institution for public protection or an extended sentence of imprisonment or detention in a young offender institution.

The following offences are listed in the Criminal Justice Act 2003, Sch.15A:

Part 1 Offences under the law of England and Wales

1 Murder.

2 Manslaughter.

3 An offence under s.4 of the Offences against the Person Act 1861 (c.100) (soliciting murder).

4 An offence under s.18 of that Act (wounding with intent to cause grievous bodily harm).

5 An offence under s.1 of the Sexual Offences Act 1956 (c.69) (rape).

6 An offence under s.5 of that Act (intercourse with a girl under 13).

7 An offence under s.16 of the Firearms Act 1968 (c.27) (possession of firearm with intent to endanger life).

8 An offence under s.17(1) of that Act (use of a firearm to resist arrest).

9 An offence under s.18 of that Act (carrying a firearm with criminal intent).

10 An offence of robbery under s.8 of the Theft Act 1968 (c.60) where, at some time during the commission of the offence, the offender had in his possession a firearm or an imitation firearm within the meaning of the Firearms Act 1968.

11 An offence under s.1 of the Sexual Offences Act 2003 (c.42) (rape).

12 An offence under s.2 of that Act (assault by penetration).

13 An offence under s.4 of that Act (causing a person to engage in sexual activity without consent) if the offender was liable on conviction on indictment to imprisonment for life.

14 An offence under s.5 of that Act (rape of a child under 13).

15 An offence under s.6 of that Act (assault of a child under 13 by penetration).

16 An offence under s.8 of that Act (causing or inciting a child under 13 to engage in sexual activity) if the offender was liable on conviction on indictment to imprisonment for life.

17 An offence under s.30 of that Act (sexual activity with a person with a mental disorder impeding choice) if the offender was liable on conviction on indictment to imprisonment for life.

18 An offence under s.31 of that Act (causing or inciting a person with a mental disorder to engage in sexual activity) if the offender was liable on conviction on indictment to imprisonment for life.

19 An offence under s.34 of that Act (inducement, threat or deception to procure sexual activity with a person with a mental disorder) if the offender was liable on conviction on indictment to imprisonment for life.

20 An offence under s.35 of that Act (causing a person with a mental disorder to engage in or agree to engage in sexual activity by inducement etc.) if the offender was liable on conviction on indictment to imprisonment for life.

21 An offence under s.47 of that Act (paying for sexual services of a child) if the offender was liable on conviction on indictment to imprisonment for life.

22 An offence under s.62 of that Act (committing an offence with intent to commit a sexual offence) if the offender was liable on conviction on indictment to imprisonment for life.

23 (1) An attempt to commit an offence specified in the preceding paragraphs of this Part of this Schedule ("a listed offence").
   (2) Conspiracy to commit a listed offence.
   (3) Incitement to commit a listed offence.
   (4) An offence under Part 2 of the Serious Crime Act 2007 in relation to which a listed offence is the offence (or one of the offences) which the person intended or believed would be committed.
   (5) Aiding, abetting, counselling or procuring the commission of a listed offence.

Part 2 Offences under the law of Scotland

24 Murder.

25 Culpable homicide.

26 Rape.

27 Assault where the assault—

    (a) is aggravated because it caused severe injury or endangered the victim's life, or

    (b) was carried out with intent to rape or ravish the victim.

28 Sodomy where the person against whom the offence was committed did not consent.

29 Lewd, indecent or libidinous behaviour or practices.

30 Robbery, where, at some time during the commission of the offence, the offender had in his possession a firearm or an imitation firearm within the meaning of the Firearms Act 1968 (c.27).

31 An offence under s.16 of the Firearms Act 1968 (possession of firearm with intent to endanger life).

32 An offence under s.17(1) of that Act (use of a firearm to resist arrest).

33 An offence under s.18 of that Act (carrying a firearm with criminal intent).

34 An offence under s.5(1) of the Criminal Law (Consolidation) (Scotland) Act 1995 (c.39) (unlawful intercourse with a girl under 13).

35 (1) An attempt to commit an offence specified in the preceding paragraphs of this Part of this Schedule ("a listed offence").

    (2) Conspiracy to commit a listed offence.

    (3) Incitement to commit a listed offence.

    (4) Aiding, abetting, counselling or procuring the commission of a listed offence.

Part 3 Offences under the law of Northern Ireland

36 Murder.

37 Manslaughter.

38 Rape.

39 An offence under s.4 of the Offences against the Person Act 1861 (c.100) (soliciting murder).

40 An offence under s.18 of that Act (wounding with intent to cause grievous bodily harm).

41 An offence under s.4 of the Criminal Law Amendment Act 1885 (c.69) (intercourse with a girl under 14).

42 An offence of robbery under s.8 of the Theft Act (Northern Ireland) 1969 (c.16) where, at some time during the commission of the offence, the offender had in his possession a firearm or an imitation firearm within the meaning of the Firearms (Northern Ireland) Order 2004 (S.I. 2004/702 (N.I.3)).

43 An offence under Art.17 of the Firearms (Northern Ireland) Order 1981 (S.I. 1981/155 (N.I.2)) (possession of firearm with intent to endanger life).

44 An offence under Art.18(1) of that Order (use of a firearm to resist arrest).

45 An offence under Art.19 of that Order (carrying a firearm with criminal intent).

46 An offence under Art.58 of the Firearms (Northern Ireland) Order 2004 (possession of firearm with intent to endanger life).

47 An offence under Art.59 of that Order (use of a firearm to resist arrest).

48 An offence under Art.60 of that Order (carrying a firearm with criminal intent).

49 An offence under s.47 of the Sexual Offences Act 2003 (paying for sexual services of a child) if the offender was liable on conviction on indictment to imprisonment for life.

50 (1) An attempt to commit an offence specified in the preceding paragraphs of this Part of this Schedule ("a listed offence").
   (2) Conspiracy to commit a listed offence.
   (3) Incitement to commit a listed offence.
   (4) An offence under Pt 2 of the Serious Crime Act 2007 in relation to which a listed offence is the offence (or one of the offences) which the person intended or believed would be committed.
   (5) Aiding, abetting, counselling or procuring the commission of a listed offence.

Part 4 Offences under service law

51 An offence under s.70 of the Army Act 1955, s.70 of the Air Force Act 1955 or s.42 of the Naval Discipline Act 1957 as respects which the corresponding civil offence (within the meaning of the Act in question) is an offence specified in Pt 1 of this Schedule.

52 (1) An offence under s.42 of the Armed Forces Act 2006 as respects which the corresponding offence under the law of England and Wales (within the meaning given by that section) is an offence specified in Pt 1 of this Schedule.

(2) Section 48 of the Armed Forces Act 2006 (attempts, conspiracy, etc.) applies for the purposes of this paragraph as if the reference in subs.(3)(b) of that section to any of the following provisions of that Act were a reference to this paragraph.

Specified Offences—Young Offenders

CRIMINAL JUSTICE ACT 2003, ss.226, 228

References: Current Sentencing Practice E5; Archbold 5–292

If an offender aged **under 18** on the date of conviction is convicted of a "specified offence" committed on or after April 4, 2005, and the court considers that there is a **significant risk to members of the public of serious harm occasioned by the commission by him of further specified offences**, the court **may** impose a sentence of detention for life, detention for public protection, or an extended sentence of detention.

For specified offences, see **Maximum Sentence**.

If the offender is convicted by a youth court or magistrates' court, and it appears to the court that the criteria for the imposition of a sentence of detention for life, detention for public protection, or an extended sentence of detention would be met, the court must commit the offender to the Crown Court. (See **Committal for Sentence**.)

A sentence of **detention for life** must be imposed if the offence is punishable with detention for life and the court considers that the seriousness of the offence, or of the offence and one or more offences associated with it, is such as "to justify the imposition of a sentence of detention for life."

A sentence of detention for public protection may be imposed if the offence is punishable by 10 years' imprisonment or more, but either it is not punishable with imprisonment for life or the seriousness of the offence does not justify a sentence of life imprisonment.

A sentence of detention for public protection may be imposed only if the notional minimum term (the minimum term which the court would impose under the P.C.C.(S.)A., s.82A, before the deduction of time spent in custody on remand) would be at least two years. The fact that the offender had been convicted of an offence listed in the Criminal Justice Act 2003, Sch.15A before committing the latest offence is not a qualifying condition for a sentence of detention for public protection.

A sentence of **detention for public protection** is an indeterminate sentence. Offenders sentenced to detention for public protection may be detained in custody for a period longer than the maximum term normally permissible for the offence of which they have been convicted, if the Parole Board considers that their continued detention is necessary for the protection of the public.

A court which imposes a sentence either of detention for life or detention for public protection must fix a minimum term in accordance with the P.C.C.(S.)A., s.82A. The offender may not be released until he has served the minimum term.

An offender sentenced to detention for life will remain on licence for the rest of his life. An offender sentenced to detention for public protection will remain on licence for a minimum of 10 years. After this period has expired, the Parole Board may direct that his licence shall cease to have effect. If the Board does not give such a direction, he will remain on licence for the rest of his life.

Extended sentence of detention

The court may impose an extended sentence of detention on a person convicted of any specified offence (whether or not it is punishable with 10 years' imprisonment), if the court considers that there is a significant risk to members of the public of serious harm occasioned by the commission by him of further specified offences.

An extended sentence of detention may be imposed only if the appropriate custodial term would be at least four years. The fact that the offender had been convicted of an offence listed in the Criminal Justice Act 2003, Sch.15A before committing the latest offence is not a qualifying condition for an extended sentence of detention.

An extended sentence of detention consists of two components: the "appropriate custodial term" and "the extension period." *The combined length of the two components must not exceed the maximum sentence for the offence.*

The appropriate custodial term is the term which the court considers appropriate and which does not exceed the maximum term of imprisonment for the offence. **The custodial term must never be less than four years**. An extended sentence may be passed even though no other form of custodial sentence would be permissible in the circumstances of the case.

The extension period is a period of licence which is "**of such length as the court considers necessary for the purpose of protecting members of the public from serious harm occasioned by the commission by him of further specified offences.**" It must not be more than **five years in the case of a specified violent offence or eight years in the case of a specified sexual offence.**

An offender serving an extended sentence of detention will be released automatically on licence after he has served one-half of the appropriate custodial term.

If an offender qualifies for a hospital order under the Mental Health Act 1983, s.37, the court may make such an order even though the offender otherwise qualifies for a sentence of detention for life, detention for public protection or an extended sentence of detention.

Supervision Order

P.C.C.(S.)A. 2000, ss.63–66

References: Current Sentencing Practice E6–1; Archbold 5–164

Where an offender under 18 is found guilty of an offence, the court which deals with him may make a supervision order.

A supervision order may not be made unless the general requirements for a community order are satisfied. (See **Community Orders—Criminal Justice Act 2003—General Criteria.**)

The court must obtain and consider a pre-sentence report unless it considers it unnecessary to do so on the ground that the court has considered an earlier report.

A supervision order lasts for the period specified by the court, or three years, whichever is the shorter.

A supervision order places the offender under the supervision of a local authority or of an officer of a local probation board.

A local authority must not be designated as a supervisor unless it agrees and the offender resides or will reside in the local authority area.

An officer of a local probation board must not be designated as the supervisor of an offender under the age of 14 unless the relevant local authority agrees and the probation officer is already supervising a member of the offender's household.

The consent of the offender is not necessary except where the order contains requirements relating to psychiatric treatment.

The following types of requirements may be included in a supervision order:

Residence with individual

A supervision order may require the offender to reside with a named individual. The individual concerned must agree to the requirement.

Directions of supervisor

A supervision order may require the offender to comply with the directions of the supervisor to live at a specified place, to present himself to a specified person or to participate in specified activities.

Reparation requirements

A supervision order may include a requirement that the offender make reparation to the person or persons specified or to the community at large. A requirement to make reparation to a specified individual may not be made unless the person concerned is a victim of the offence or is otherwise affected by it, and consents to the inclusion of the requirement in the order.

Residence requirement (local authority)

If the offender:

(a) is subject to an existing supervision order which contains either a requirement to live at a specified place, to present himself to a specified person to participate in specified activities, to remain overnight in a place, to refrain from specified activities, or a residence requirement; and

(b) has been found guilty of an offence committed while the existing supervision order was in force or has been found to be in breach of the order; and

(c) the court is satisfied that the failure to comply with the requirement or the behaviour which constituted the offence, was due to a significant extent to the circumstances in which the offender was living, and that the imposition of a residence requirement will assist in his rehabilitation.

The court may make a residence requirement requiring the offender to live in local authority accommodation. The local authority who are to receive the offender must be designated in the order and must be consulted before the residence requirement is made.

The maximum period which may be specified in a residence requirement is six months.

The offender must be legally represented at the time the question of a local authority residence requirement is considered, unless he has been refused legal representation on the ground that he appears to have sufficient resources or has declined to apply for legal representation.

Foster parent residence requirement

If the offence is sufficiently serious to warrant a custodial sentence (apart from restrictions related to age) and the court is satisfied that the behaviour which constituted the offence was due to a significant extent to the circumstances in which the offender was living, and that the imposition of a foster parent residence requirement will assist in his rehabilitation, the court may a make a foster parent residence requirement for a period of not more than 12 months.

The offender must be legally represented at the time the question of a residence requirement is considered, unless he has been refused legal representation on the ground that he appears to have sufficient resources or has declined to apply for legal representation.

A foster parent residence requirement may not be made unless the court has been notified that suitable arrangements are available.

Specified activities, etc.

A supervision order may require the offender to present himself to a person specified in the order at a place specified in the order or to participate in activities specified in the order on a day or days specified in the order.

The court must consider that the requirements are necessary for securing the good conduct of the offender or for preventing the commission by him of further offences. Such a requirement may not be included in a supervision order unless the court has consulted the supervisor and is satisfied that it is feasible to secure compliance with the requirement and any person whose co-operation is involved in the requirement has consented.

The offender may be required to comply with such requirements for not more than 90 days.

Negative requirements

A supervision order may require the offender to refrain from participating in activities specified in the order on a day or days specified in the order or during the period of the order, or such portion of it as may be specified.

Such a requirement may not be included in a supervision order unless the court has consulted the supervisor and is satisfied that it is feasible to secure compliance with the requirement and any person whose co-operation is involved in the requirement has consented.

The court must be of the opinion that the requirement is necessary for securing the good conduct of the offender or for preventing the commission by him of further offences.

School attendance

If the offender is of compulsory school age, the supervision order may require the offender to comply with such arrangements for his education as may be made by his parents and approved by the local authority.

The court may not include such a requirement unless it has consulted the local authority and is satisfied that arrangements exist under which the offender will receive efficient full-time education suitable to his age, ability and aptitude and special educational needs.

Such a requirement may not be included in a supervision order unless the court has consulted the supervisor and considers that the requirement is necessary for securing the good conduct of the offender or for preventing the commission by him of further offences.

Psychiatric treatment

A supervision order may include a requirement that the offender submit to treatment under the direction of a qualified medical practitioner with a view to the improvement of his mental condition.

A requirement of this kind may not be included in a supervision order in respect of an offender who has attained the age of 14 unless he consents to the inclusion of the requirement.

Before including such a requirement, the court must be satisfied on the evidence of an approved medical practitioner that the mental condition of the offender is such as requires and is susceptible to treatment but does not warrant his detention under a hospital order.

The requirement relating to treatment may be for the whole period of the supervision order, or for any part of the supervision order. The treatment required by the order may be either treatment as a resident patient in a mental hospital or mental nursing home, other than a special hospital, or treatment as a non-resident patient at such institution or place as may be specified in the order, or treatment by or under the direction of a practitioner specified in the order.

The court may not make a supervision order including a requirement for psychiatric treatment unless it is satisfied that arrangements have been made or can be made for the proposed treatment, including arrangements for his reception as a resident patient where such treatment is proposed. The medical nature of the treatment is not specified in the order.

218 *Sentencing Referencer*

Drug treatment and testing requirements may be included if they are recommended, suitable arrangements are available, and the offender consents.

Surcharge Order

CRIMINAL JUSTICE ACT 2003, s.161A

References: Current Sentencing Practice J17; Archbold 5–948

Where a court deals with an offender for an offence **committed on or after April 1, 2007,** by means of a **fine** (whether or not any other sentence is imposed), the court must order the offender to pay a **surcharge of £15**. The obligation to make a surcharge order does not apply were the court deals with the offender by means of a compensation order alone, without a fine.

If the court considers that it would be appropriate to make a compensation order in addition to a fine, but that the offender has insufficient means to pay both the surcharge and the appropriate compensation, the court must reduce the surcharge accordingly.

A court may reduce the amount fine if it finds that the offender has insufficient means to pay both the appropriate fine and the surcharge.

A surcharge is enforceable as a fine imposed on summary conviction.

Suspended Sentence

P.C.C.(S.)A. 2000, s.118

References: Current Sentencing Practice A11–1

Note: these provisions apply to sentences imposed for offences committed before April 4, 2005.

Where a court passes a sentence of imprisonment for a term not exceeding two years, the court may suspend the operation of the sentence for a period of not less than one year or more than two years.

A court may not suspend a sentence of imprisonment unless the case is one in which a sentence of imprisonment would have been appropriate even without the power to suspend the sentence and the exercise of the power to suspend the sentence can be **justified by the exceptional circumstances of the case**.

All the statutory requirements for a custodial sentence must be satisfied before a suspended sentence is passed.

The court should decide the length of sentence, before deciding whether to suspend it; the fact that the sentence is suspended does not justify a sentence longer than the sentence that would have been passed if the sentence were to be served immediately.

Where a suspended sentence is passed, the court must consider whether the circumstances of the case warrant in addition the imposition of a fine or the making of a compensation order.

A court which passes a suspended sentence may not make a community order in respect of the offender for another offence of which he is convicted by or before the court or for which he is dealt with by the court.

The court must explain to the offender in ordinary language his liability to be ordered to serve the sentence if he commits an offence punishable with imprisonment during the operational period of the suspended sentence.

Where an offender is sentenced to a number of consecutive sentences of imprisonment, the court may suspend the sentences only if the aggregate term does not exceed two years.

Where an offender has spent time in custody on remand, the court should make an appropriate allowance for that time in fixing the term of the suspended sentence. If the time spent in custody on remand is equivalent to a sentence of imprisonment of appropriate length, the court should not suspend the sentence.

Where a number of suspended sentences are imposed on the same occasion, the court suspending the sentences should say whether they will be served concurrently or consecutively if enforced. Where a suspended sentence is imposed on an offender who is already subject to an existing suspended sentence, the court should not decide whether the sentences should be served consecutively or concurrently if enforced.

A suspended sentence should not be imposed at the same time as a sentence of imprisonment, or on a person serving a sentence of imprisonment.

Suspended Sentence—Activation

P.C.C.(S.)A. 2000, s.119

References: Current Sentencing Practice A13–1

Note: these provisions apply only to suspended sentences passed for offences committed before April 4, 2005.

The appropriate court has power to deal with a suspended sentence if the offender has been convicted of an offence punishable with imprisonment committed during the operational period of the suspended sentence. If the court has power to deal with a suspended sentence, it must do so.

If the offence was committed before the suspended sentence was imposed, but after the commission of the offence for which the suspended sentence was imposed, there is no power to activate the suspended sentence.

The offender must have been convicted of the relevant offence. If that offence was taken into consideration, there is no power to deal with the suspended sentence.

If the court which deals with the offender for the latest offence grants a discharge, it must still deal with the suspended sentence.

An offence under Bail Act 1976 which is dealt with as a contempt, is an offence for this purpose.

A court dealing with a suspended sentence must make one of four orders:

(a) the court may order that the suspended sentence will take effect with the term unaltered;

(b) the court may order that the suspended sentence will take effect with the term reduced;

(c) the court may extend the operational period by substituting a further period of suspension not exceeding two years from the date of the extension;

(d) the court may make no order with respect to the suspended sentence.

The court must order the sentence to take effect with the term unaltered unless it would be unjust to do so in all the circumstances, including the facts of the latest offence.

The suspended sentence should normally be ordered to run consecutively to any new sentence imposed for the later offence.

The court should review the totality of the activated suspended sentence and the sentence imposed for the later offence. If the aggregate sentence is excessive in all the circumstances, the court should adjust the total sentence, usually by ordering the suspended sentence to take effect with the term reduced.

If the offender is subject to a number of different suspended sentences imposed on separate occasions, the court should deal with all of them, deciding whether to activate them concurrently or consecutively. The court should not activate a series of suspended sentences so that the offender is ordered to serve more than two years in respect of all the suspended sentences.

If the court does not activate the suspended sentence in full, it must state the reasons for its opinion that activation of the sentence in full would be unjust.

The following matters have been held not to be reasons for deciding not to activate the suspended sentence:

(a) the fact that the later offence is of a different kind from the earlier offence;

(b) the fact that the offence is committed at a late stage in the operational period (although this may justify activation with a reduced term).

The gravity of the latest offence is a significant factor. If the latest offence would not justify a custodial sentence itself, this may be a reason for not activating the suspended sentence, particularly if the court has dealt with the offender for the later offence with a community sentence.

If the court has imposed a custodial sentence for the latest offence, it should not leave the suspended sentence in existence so that it will hang over the offender on his release from custody.

Suspended Sentence—Supervision Orders

P.C.C.(S.)A. 2000, s.122

References: Current Sentencing Practice A11

Note: these provisions apply only to offences committed before April 4, 2005.

A suspended sentence supervision order may be made only where a court passes a suspended sentence for a term of more than six months for a single offence.

If the offender is sentenced to a total term of imprisonment exceeding six months, and the whole term is suspended, but no individual term exceeds six months, there is no power to make a supervision order.

The effect of making a supervision order is to place the offender under the supervision of a supervising officer for the period specified in the order. The supervision order may not include any additional requirements.

If the offender fails to keep in touch with the supervising officer in accordance with his instructions, or fails to notify him of any change of address, he may be fined up to £1,000. Failure to comply with a supervision order does not lead to the activation of the suspended sentence.

The court must explain the effect of the supervision order to the offender in ordinary language.

Suspended Sentence Order

CRIMINAL JUSTICE ACT 2003, ss.189–193

References: Current Sentencing Practice A13A; Archbold 5–321

Note: the sections of the Criminal Justice Act 2003 mentioned above are subject to temporary modifications. They apply only to sentences imposed for offences committed on or after April 4, 2005.

A court which passes a sentence of imprisonment or detention in a young offender institution for a term of **at least 14 days but not more than 12 months** (or *six months in the case of a magistrates' court*) may order that the sentence of imprisonment is not to take effect unless either the offender fails to comply with a requirement imposed by the court or commits another offence during the period specified in the order.

In making a suspended sentence order the court must order the offender to comply with such requirements (known as **"community requirements"**) as may be specified during the **"supervision period"**, and fix the **"operational period."** If the offender commits an offence during the operational period, he will be liable to serve the custodial period of the sentence.

The supervision and operational periods must each be at least six months and not more than two years; the supervision period may not extend beyond the operational period, but the operational period may extend beyond the end of the supervision period. *If the court passes a suspended sentence, it may not impose a community sentence in respect of that offence or any other offence for which the offender is sentenced by the court.*

The community requirements which may be included in a suspended sentence order, are all of those which may be included in a community order, subject to the same conditions as apply to a community order. (See **Community Order—Criminal Justice Act 2003—Requirements.**)

If a court imposes two sentences to be served consecutively, the power to suspend the sentence is available only if the aggregate term **does not exceed 12 months**, or *six months if the sentences are imposed by a magistrates' court*.

The court may not simply suspend a sentence, without imposing any community requirements, but it may impose a suspended sentence with a very modest or nominal community requirement (such as a supervision requirement or a prohibited activity requirement).

A suspended sentence order may provide for periodic review of the order by the court which made the order, except where the requirement is a drug rehabilitation requirement, in which case periodic reviews are provided for in the provisions governing the requirement itself.

Where a suspended sentence order is made by the Crown Court, the Crown Court should consider whether to direct that any failure to comply with a community requirement of the sentence should be dealt with by the magistrates' court. If no such direction is given, any alleged breach of the community requirement will be brought before the Crown Court.

Breach of suspended sentence order (Sch.12)

A "breach" of a suspended sentence order may occur either by a failure to comply with a community requirement during the supervision period, or by the commission of an offence during the operational period. *As these two periods may be different in any particular case, it will be important to ensure that the relevant event took place during the relevant period.*

Where it is alleged that an offender has **failed to comply with a community requirement**, the offender will be brought before the appropriate court. If it is proved to the satisfaction of the court that the offender has failed to comply with any of the community requirements of the order without reasonable excuse, the court **may order the sentence to take effect with the original term unaltered**, or may order the sentence to take effect with the term reduced. Alternatively the court may **impose more onerous community requirements**, or extend either the supervision period or the operational period. (It is assumed that any extension or reduction of a relevant period must result in a sentence which could have been passed in that form.)

The court **must order the sentence to take effect**, either in its original form or with a reduction of the term of the sentence, unless it would be **"unjust to do so in all the circumstances"**. If the court considers that it would be unjust to do so, it must state its reasons.

If the offender is **convicted of an offence** committed during the operational period of a suspended sentence, he may be dealt with in respect of the suspended sentence by a magistrates' court only if the suspended sentence was passed by a magistrates' court. If the suspended sentence was passed by the Crown Court and the offender is convicted by a magistrates' court of the later offence, the magistrates' court may commit him to the Crown Court to be dealt with. If the magistrates' court does not commit the offender to the Crown Court, it must notify the Crown Court, and the Crown Court may issue process to secure his appearance before the Crown Court.

If the offender is convicted by the Crown Court of an offence committed during the operational period of a suspended sentence, the Crown Court may deal with the suspended sentence whether the suspended sentence was passed by the Crown Court or by a magistrates' court.

It is not necessary that the later offence should be punishable with imprisonment.

Where the court has power to deal with the suspended sentence, it may exercise the same powers as in the case of a breach of a community requirement. The court must order the sentence to take effect, either in its original form or with a reduction of the term of the sentence, unless it would be "unjust to do so in all the circumstances". If the court considers that it would be unjust to do so, it must state its reasons.

The court may not revoke the order and impose a custodial sentence of greater length than the sentence which was suspended.

Time on Remand

CRIMINAL JUSTICE ACT 1967, s.67

References: Current Sentencing Practice A6–1

Note: the Criminal Justice Act 2003, s.240, makes provision for courts to give directions relating to the treatment of time spent in custody on remand. These provisions apply only to sentences imposed for offences committed on or after April 4, 2005. Their effect is summarised below. (See **Time on Remand—Criminal Justice Act 2003.**) *The provisions summarised below apply only to sentences imposed for offences committed before April 4, 2005.*

A sentence of imprisonment, detention in a young offender institution or detention under P.C.C.(S.)A. 2000, s.91, is reduced by any "relevant period" spent by the offender in custody in proceedings related to the offence or sentence.

A relevant period is any period during which the offender was in police detention in connection with the offence for which the sentence was passed, or any period during which he was in custody by reason only of the proceedings related to the offence in question.

Time which the offender would have spent in custody as a result of some other matter (such as another sentence or a committal in default) does not count. Time which the offender spent in custody otherwise than by order of a court does count.

Time spent in custody on remand does not count in the following cases:

(a) time spent in custody in connection for an offence which is subsequently taken into consideration;

(b) time spent in custody before a suspended sentence is passed;

(c) time spent in custody before the court makes a community rehabilitation order, a community punishment order, a community punishment and rehabilitation order or a conditional discharge;

(d) time spent in local authority care in accommodation which is not "secure accommodation";

(e) time spent in custody before a discretionary life sentence is imposed;

(f) time spent in custody before a detention and training order is made.

Where an offender is sentenced to life imprisonment (in any form), custody for life, detention during Her Majesty's Pleasure, imprisonment for public protection, detention for public protection, time spent in custody on remand does not count against the minimum term fixed by the court and an appropriate allowance should be made in the length of the term.

Time spent in custody before the imposition of a community order other than those mentioned in (c) does count.

Where time has been spent in custody and does not count, the court should make an appropriate allowance in the length of the sentence.

Time spent in custody abroad pending extradition does not count unless the court makes an order under Criminal Justice Act 1991, s.47: see **Extradited Offenders**.

Where time spent in custody on remand counts towards the sentence, it is taken into account in determining whether the offender has served half or two-thirds of the sentence for the purpose of early release, and for the purpose of determining the whole term of the sentence for the purposes of return to prison under the P.C.C.(S.)A. 2000, s.116.

Time on Remand—Criminal Justice Act 2003

CRIMINAL JUSTICE ACT 2003, s.240

References: Current Sentencing Practice A6A; Archbold 5–368

Note: this section applies only to offences committed on or after April 4, 2005.

Where a court imposes a term of imprisonment, detention in a young offender institution or detention under the P.C.C.(S.)A. 2000, s.91 **for offences committed on or after April 4, 2005**, the court should make an order dealing with the treatment of any time spent by the offender in custody on remand.

The power applies to extended sentences of imprisonment or extended terms of detention. *It does not apply to sentences of life imprisonment or imprisonment for public protection, or to detention and training orders.*

Time spent in custody on remand includes time spent in custody following a remand or committal by a court, time spent in local authority secure accommodation or a secure training centre following a committal or remand, and time spent in hospital following a remand, admission or removal under the Mental Health Act 1983. *It does not include time spent in police detention.*

The court may make an order in respect of time spent on remand in connection with the offence or a "related offence". A "related offence" is an offence "founded on the same facts or evidence" as the offence for which the sentence is imposed.

In the normal case, **the court must give a direction that the number of days which the offender has spent remanded in custody shall count as part of the sentence.** *The court must state the number of days which the offender has spent in custody on remand, and the number of days in respect of which the direction is given.*

The court may not direct that time spent in custody on remand shall count as part of the sentence **if the offender was serving another sentence while he was on remand,** or the *sentence is to run consecutively to a sentence from which the same time is deducted automatically under the 1967 Act,* or **"it is the opinion of the court just in all the circumstances not to give a direction".** If the court decides that a direction that the whole number of days spent in custody on remand shall count as part of the sentence should not be made, it may either give no direction at all (in which case none of the days will count), or a direction that a number of days less than the total should count. In either case, it **must state in open court either**:

(a) that the decision not to make a direction, or to make a direction for less than the total number of days, is made in accordance with the rules made by the Secretary of State (which relate to days which were spent in custody on remand when the offender was also serving a sentence, and to time which is deducted automatically from another sentence to which the sentence concerned is consecutive); or

(b) that it was made because the court considered that it was just in all the circumstances to make the decision not to direct that all the remand days would count, and *indicate what were the circumstances which made that decision "just in all the circumstances"*.

The statute does not require the court in either of these cases to state the number of days which have been spent in custody on remand (as is required where a full direction is given), but it may be that such a statement should be made for the sake of clarity. The grounds on which a limited direction may be made will be matters for the court's discretion.

If the offender is sentenced to a **suspended sentence order under the Criminal Justice Act 2003**, any order in relation to time spent in custody on remand is to be made by the court which orders the sentence to take effect, not by the court which passes the original sentence.

Where time has been spent in custody before a community order is made, which is subsequently revoked and replaced by a custodial sentence, the court which revokes the community order and replaces it with a custodial sentence may make an appropriate order in relation to the time spent in custody before the community order was made. It is a matter for the court's discretion whether the fact that the offender has been found to be in breach of the community order, or has committed a further offence while subject to the order, amounts to a circumstance in which is just not to direct that all the time spent in custody before the community order was made shall count as part of the eventual sentence. **A court which imposes a community order under the Criminal Justice Act 2003 on an offender who has spent time in custody on remand may take that time into account in determining the restrictions on liberty to be imposed by the order**. The extent to which such time has been taken into account at that stage may be a relevant consideration in determining whether to take it into account at this stage.

In the case of **extradited prisoners** who have been kept in custody outside the United Kingdom before being returned, time spent in custody abroad is treated as time spent in custody on remand, and the court must make an appropriate direction under the section as if the time had been spent in custody in the United Kingdom. The court may decline to make a direction, or may make a less than full direction, in the exercise of its discretion, if it considers such a course to be "just in all the circumstances". It may be that this will apply in particular to cases where offenders have prolonged the period of custody by resisting extradition.

Where a direction is given under the section, the number of days specified in the direction must be treated as having been served when determining whether the offender has served a particular proportion of his sentence.

A direction under s.240(3) that all of the days shall count, or a direction under s.240(6) that none of the days shall count, or that less than the whole number of days shall count, is "an order made on conviction when dealing with an offender" for the purposes of the Criminal Appeal Act 1968 s.50, and thus subject to an appeal by the offender or a reference by the Attorney General.

If a defendant appears before the Crown Court for sentence, but it is uncertain how many days he has spent in custody on remand, the court may pass sentence and adjourn the order under s.240 until the matter has been clarified.

Time Spent on Remand on Bail Subject to Qualifying Curfew Condition

CRIMINAL JUSTICE ACT 240A

References: Current Sentencing Practice A6B; Archbold 5–368a

These provisions apply where a court sentences an offender to imprisonment, a determinate sentence of detention under s.91 of the P.C.C.(S.)A. 2000, an extended sentence of detention, a sentence of detention in a young offender institution or an extended sentence of detention in a young offender institution, in respect of an offence **committed on or after April 4, 2005**, *and the offender was remanded on bail by a court in course of or in connection with proceedings for the offence, or any related offence,* **on or after November 3, 2008**. *The section does not apply to a detention and training order or the minimum term of an indeterminate sentence.*

If the sentence is imposed for an offence **committed before April 4, 2005**, *the court must* **specify** *the credit period, subject to the same conditions and exceptions as apply to giving a direction. The credit period specified is treated as a "relevant period" for the purposes of the Criminal Justice Act 1967, s.67, and deducted from the sentence automatically.*

If the offender is subject to a suspended sentence or suspended sentence order, the provisions apply to the court which activates the sentence, not the court which imposes the sentence.

If the offender's bail was subject to *a qualifying curfew condition and an electronic monitoring condition*, the court must direct that the credit period is to count as time served by the offender as part of the sentence. The "credit period" is the number of days represented by half of the sum of the day on which the offender's bail was first subject to conditions that would have been relevant conditions, and the number of other days on which the offender's bail was subject to those conditions (excluding the last day), rounded up to the nearest whole number.

An **"electronic monitoring condition"** is any electronic monitoring requirement imposed under the Bail Act 1976 for the purpose of securing the electronic monitoring of a person's compliance with a qualifying curfew condition.

A **"qualifying curfew condition"** means a condition of bail which requires the person granted bail to remain at one or more specified places *for a total of not less than nine hours in any given day*.

"Related offence" means an offence, other than the offence for which the sentence is imposed, with which the offender was charged and *the charge for which was founded on the same facts or evidence* as the offence for which the sentence is imposed.

The court is not obliged to give a direction if in the opinion of the court it is just in all the circumstances not to give a direction. In considering whether it is just in all the circumstances not to give a direction, the court must, in particular, *take into account whether or not the offender has, at any time whilst on bail subject to the relevant conditions, broken either or both of them.* The court may not give a direction if the The Remand on Bail (Disapplication of Credit Period) Rules 2008 apply.

The court may give a direction that a period of days which is less than the credit period is to count as time served by the offender as part of the sentence.

Where the court gives a direction that time spent on remand subject to qualifying conditions is to count, it **must** state in open court the number of days on which the offender was subject to the relevant conditions, and the number of days in relation to which the direction is given.

If the court directs that a period of days which is less than the credit period is to count, or that no days are to count, the court **must** state in open court that it is of the opinion that it is just in all the circumstances not to give a direction, or a direction that the whole of the credit period shall count, and what the circumstances are, or that the decision not to give a direction, or a full direction, is made in accordance with the The Remand on Bail (Disapplication of Credit Period) Rules 2008.

The rules provide that if the court has included a particular day in calculating a credit period which has been directed to count as time served by the offender as part of one sentence, the same day may not be counted as part of the credit period for the purposes of any other sentence to which that sentence is ordered to run consecutively, or with which it is ordered to run wholly or partly concurrently.

The rules provide that a court may not give a direction in respect of a day when the offender was also subject to requirements imposed *for the purpose of securing the electronic monitoring* of the offender's compliance with—

(1) a curfew condition imposed in connection with early release from custody;

(2) a requirement to remain at one or more specified places for a specified number of hours in any given day following release from a detention and training order under section before the half way point of the term of the detention and training order;

(3) a licence condition imposed following release from prison;

(4) a curfew requirement imposed as part of a suspended sentence order or as part of a community order;

(5) a curfew order;

(6) any other requirement to remain at one or more specified places for a specified number of hours in any given day, provided that the requirement is imposed by a court or the Secretary of State as a result of a conviction.

A direction may not be given in respect of any day when the offender was on temporary release from prison, a young offender institution, or a secure training centre, whether or not he was subject to electronic monitoring in connection with that release.

Travel Restriction Order

CRIMINAL JUSTICE AND POLICE ACT 2001, s.33

References: Current Sentencing Practice H9–1; Archbold 5–867

Where a court convicts an offender of a drug trafficking offence **as defined in s.34 of the Act committed on or after April 1, 2002**, and determines that it would be appropriate to impose a sentence of imprisonment of four years or more, the court must make such travel restriction order in relation to the offender as the court thinks suitable in all the circumstances unless it determines that it is not appropriate to do so.

The following offences are "drug trafficking offences" for this purpose: offences under the Misuse of Drugs Act 1971, ss.4(2), 4(3), 19 and 20; offences under the Customs and Excise Management Act 1979, ss.50(2), 50(3), 68(2), 170 (in relation to prohibited drugs), and attempts, conspiracies or incitements in relation to these offences.

Possession with intent to supply, and money laundering offences, are not included.

A travel restriction order must be for at least two years.

If the court determines that it is not appropriate to make an order where there is power to do so, the court must **state its reasons** for not making a travel restriction order.

A travel restriction order prohibits the offender from leaving the United Kingdom at any time during the period beginning with his release from custody and continuing to the end of the period specified by the court. *A travel restriction order may contain a direction to the offender to deliver up to the court any UK passport held by him.*

A court which has made a travel restriction order may revoke or suspend the order on an application made by the offender at any time which after the end of the minimum period, and not less than three months after the making of any previous application for the revocation of the prohibition.

The minimum period in the case of an order for four years or less is a period of two years, in the case of an order for more than four years but less than ten years is a period of four years, and in any other case is a period of five years.

A court must not revoke a travel restriction order unless it considers that it is appropriate to do so in all the circumstances of the case and having regard, in particular the offender's character, his conduct since the making of the order, and the offences of which he was convicted on the occasion on which the order was made.

A court must not suspend a travel restriction order for any period unless it is satisfied that there are exceptional circumstances that justify the suspension on compassionate grounds. A court must not suspend a travel restriction order unless it considers that it is appropriate to do so in all the circumstances of the case and having regard, in particular the offender's character, his conduct since the making of the order, the offences of which he was convicted on the occasion on which the order was made and any other circumstances of the case that the court considers relevant.

Youth Community Orders

The following orders are youth community orders:

A curfew order;

An exclusion order;

An attendance centre order;

A supervision order;

An action plan order.

A court must not make a youth community order, or pass a sentence which includes one or more youth community orders, unless the general requirements for passing a community order are satisfied. (See **Community orders—Criminal Justice Act 2003—General Criteria.**)

The court must obtain and consider a presentence report unless it considers it unnecessary to do so on the ground that the court has considered an earlier report.

Breaches of youth community orders are not subject to the general provisions relating to breaches of community orders provided by the Criminal Justice Act 2003, Sch.8. (See Community Orders—Criminal Justice Act 2003—Breaches of Orders and Re-offending.)

For breaches of **curfew orders and exclusion orders**, see P.C.C.(S.)A. 2000, Sch.3 (as substituted by the Criminal Justice Act 2003, Sch.32, para.125, with reference to orders made for offences committed on or after April 4, 2007.

For breaches of **attendance centre orders**, see P.C.C.(S.)A. 2000, Sch.5 (Current Sentencing Practice E7–1; Archbold 5–211.

For breaches of **supervision orders**, see P.C.C.(S.)A. 2000, Sch.7 (Current Sentencing Practice E6–1; Archbold 5–217); summarised under **Breach of Supervision Order.**

For breaches of **action plan** orders see P.C.C.(S.)A. 2000, Sch.8 (Current Sentencing Practice E13.

Youth Rehabilitation Order

These provisions were not in force on December 1, 2008.

Where a person **under 18** is convicted of an offence, the court may make a youth rehabilitation order containing specified requirements. *A youth rehabilitation order may be made only if the court is of the opinion that the offence or the combination of the offence and one or more offences associated with it was serious enough to warrant a youth rehabilitation order, the particular requirements forming part of the order are the most suitable for the offender and the restrictions on liberty imposed by the order are commensurate with the seriousness of the offence or the combination of the offence and one or more offences associated with it.*

A youth rehabilitation order may not be made where the court is required to impose a mandatory custodial sentence.

Before making a youth rehabilitation order, the court must obtain and consider information about the offender's family circumstances and the likely effect of the order on those circumstances. Before making an order with two or more requirements, or two or more orders in respect of associated offences, the court must consider whether the requirements are compatible with each other. The requirements must so far as is practicable avoid conflict with the offender's religious beliefs, avoid any interference with the times at which the offender normally works or attends any school or educational establishment, and avoid any conflict with the requirements of any other youth rehabilitation order to which the offender is subject.

A youth rehabilitation order takes effect on the day after the day on which it is made. If the offender is subject to a detention and training order, the court may order the youth rehabilitation order to take effect when the offender is released from custody under supervision, or at the expiry of the term of the detention and training order.

A youth rehabilitation order must specify a date, **not more than three years** after the date on which the order takes effect, by which all the requirements in it must have been complied with. An order which imposes two or more different requirements may also specify an earlier date or dates in relation to compliance with any one or more of them. In the case of a youth rehabilitation order with intensive supervision and surveillance, the date specified must not be earlier than 6 months after the date on which the order takes effect.

Where the Crown Court makes a youth rehabilitation order, it may give a direction that further proceedings relating to the order should be in a youth court or other magistrates' court.

The following requirements may be included in a youth rehabilitation order:

Activity requirement. An activity requirement is a requirement that the offender must participate in specified activities at a specified place or places, or participate in one or more residential exercises for a continuous period or periods of the number or numbers of days to be specified in the order, or engage in activities in accordance with instructions of the responsible officer on the number of days specified in the order. The total number of days specified in an activity requirement must not in aggregate exceed 90.

Supervision requirement. A supervision requirement is a requirement that the offender must attend appointments with the responsible officer or another person determined by the responsible officer, at such times and places as may be determined by the responsible officer.

Unpaid work requirement. An unpaid work requirement is a requirement that the offender must perform unpaid work. The number of hours or work must be not less than 40, and not more than 240. **An unpaid work requirement may be made only if the offender is 16 or 17 at the time of conviction.**

A court may not impose an unpaid work requirement unless after hearing (if the court thinks necessary) an appropriate officer, the court is satisfied that the offender is a suitable person to perform work under such a requirement, and the court is satisfied that provision for the offender to work under such a requirement can be made existing local arrangements.

The work must be performed at such times as the responsible officer may specify in instructions. The work must be performed during the period of 12 months beginning with the day on which the order takes effect. A youth rehabilitation order imposing an unpaid work requirement remains in force until the offender has worked under it for the number of hours specified in it, unless the order is revoked.

Programme requirement. A programme requirement is a requirement that the offender must participate in a systematic programme of activities specified in the order at a place or places so specified on such number of days as may be so specified. A programme requirement may require the offender to reside at any place specified in the order for any period so specified if it is necessary for the offender to reside there for that period in order to participate in the programme.

A court may not include a programme requirement in a youth rehabilitation order unless the programme has been recommended to the court by a member of a youth offending team, an officer of a local probation board, or an officer of a provider of probation services, as being suitable for the offender, and the court is satisfied that the programme is available at the place or places proposed to be specified.

A court may not include a programme requirement in a youth rehabilitation order if compliance with that requirement would involve the **co-operation of a person other than the offender** and the offender's responsible officer, **unless that other person consents to its inclusion**.

Attendance centre requirement. An attendance centre requirement is a requirement that the offender must attend at an attendance centre specified in the order for such number of hours as may be so specified.

If the offender is **aged 16 or over** at the time of conviction, the aggregate number of hours for which the offender may be required to attend at an attendance centre must be **not less than 12, and not more than 36**.

If the offender is **aged 14 or over but under 16** at the time of conviction, the aggregate number of hours for which the offender may be required to attend at an attendance centre must **be not less than 12, and not more than 24**.

If the offender is aged **under 14** at the time of conviction, the aggregate number of hours for which the offender may be required to attend at an attendance centre **must not be more than 12**.

A court may not include an attendance centre requirement in a youth rehabilitation order unless it has been notified by the Secretary of State that an attendance centre is available for persons of the offender's description, and provision can be made at the centre for the offender. The court must be satisfied that the attendance centre proposed is reasonably accessible to the offender, having regard to the means of access available to the offender and any other circumstances.

Prohibited activity requirement. A prohibited activity requirement is a requirement that the offender must refrain from participating in activities specified in the order, on a day or days specified in the during a period specified in the order.

A court may not include a prohibited activity requirement in a youth rehabilitation order unless it has consulted a member of a youth offending team, an officer of a local probation board, or an officer of a provider of probation services.

The requirements that may be included in a youth rehabilitation order include a requirement that the offender does not possess, use or carry a firearm.

Curfew requirement. A curfew requirement is a requirement that the offender must remain, for periods specified in the order, at a place so specified. A curfew requirement may specify different places or different periods for different days, but may not specify periods which amount to less than 2 hours or more than 12 hours in any day.

A curfew requirement may not specify periods which fall outside the period of six months beginning with the day on which the requirement first takes effect.

Before making a youth rehabilitation order imposing a curfew requirement, the court must obtain and consider information about the place proposed to be specified in the order (including information as to the attitude of persons likely to be affected by the enforced presence there of the offender).

Where a curfew requirement is made, **the order must also include an electronic monitoring requirement**, unless the court considers it inappropriate for the order to include an electronic monitoring requirement, or it will not be practicable to secure that the monitoring takes place, without the consent of some person other than the offender, and that person does not consent to the inclusion of the electronic monitoring requirement.

Exclusion requirement. An exclusion requirement is a provision prohibiting the offender from entering a place or area specified in the order for a period so specified, which **must not exceed three months**.

An exclusion requirement may provide for the prohibition to operate only during the periods specified in the order, and may specify different places for different periods or days.

Where an exclusion requirement is made, **the order must also include an electronic monitoring requirement**, unless the court considers it inappropriate for the order to include an electronic monitoring requirement, or it will not be practicable to secure that the monitoring takes place, without the consent of some person other than the offender, and that person does not consent to the inclusion of the electronic monitoring requirement.

Residence requirement. A residence requirement is a requirement that, during the period specified in the order, the offender must reside with an individual specified in the order, or at a place specified in the order.

A residence requirement that the offender reside with an individual may not be made unless that individual has consented to the requirement.

A requirement that the offender reside at a specified place may not be made unless the offender was aged 16 or over at the time of conviction. A requirement that the offender reside at a specified place may provide that the offender may reside, with the prior approval of the responsible officer, at a place other than that specified in the order.

Before making a requirement that the offender reside at a specified place, the court must consider the home surroundings of the offender. The court may not specify a hostel or other institution as the place where an offender must reside except on the recommendation of a member of a youth offending team, an officer of a local probation board, an officer of a provider of probation services, or a social worker of a local authority.

Local authority residence requirement. A local authority residence requirement is a requirement that, during the period specified in the order, the offender must reside in accommodation provided by or on behalf of a local authority specified in the order for the purposes of the requirement. The period for which the offender must reside in local authority accommodation **must not be longer than 6 months, and must not include any period after the offender has reached the age of 18**.

An order containing a local authority residence requirement may also stipulate that the offender is not to reside with a person specified in the order.

A court may not make a local authority residence requirement unless it is satisfied that the behaviour which constituted the offence was due to a significant extent to the circumstances in which the offender was living, and that the imposition of that requirement will assist in the offender's rehabilitation.

A court may not include a local authority residence requirement in a youth rehabilitation order unless it has consulted a parent or guardian of the offender (unless it is impracticable to consult such a person), and the local authority which is to receive the offender.

A local authority residence requirement may not be made unless the offender was **legally represented** at the relevant time in court, or a right to representation funded by the Legal Services Commission for the purposes of the proceedings was withdrawn because of the offender's conduct, or the offender refused or failed to apply for representation after being informed of the right to apply and having had the opportunity to do so.

A local authority residence requirement must specify, as the local authority which is to receive the offender, the local authority in whose area the offender resides or is to reside.

Mental health treatment requirement. A mental health treatment requirement is a requirement that the offender must submit, during a period or periods specified in the order, to treatment by or under the direction of a registered medical practitioner or a chartered psychologist (or both, for different periods) with a view to the improvement of the offender's mental condition.

The treatment required must be treatment as a resident patient in an independent hospital or care home, or a hospital within the meaning of the Mental Health Act 1983, but not in hospital premises where high security psychiatric services are provided, treatment as a non-resident patient at such institution or place as may be specified in the order, or treatment by or under the direction of such registered medical practitioner or chartered psychologist (or both) as may be so specified. The nature of the treatment is not specified in the order.

A court may not make a mental health treatment requirement unless the court is satisfied, on the evidence of an approved registered medical practitioner that the mental condition of the offender is such as requires and may be susceptible to treatment, but is not such as to warrant the making of a hospital order or guardianship order within the meaning of that Act. The court must be satisfied that arrangements have been or can be made for the treatment intended to be specified in the order (including, where the offender is to be required to submit to treatment as a resident patient, arrangements for the reception of the offender), and **the offender has expressed willingness to comply with the requirement**.

Drug treatment requirement. A drug treatment requirement is a requirement that the offender must submit, during a period or periods specified in the order, to treatment, by or under the direction of a treatment provider with a view to the reduction or elimination of the offender's dependency on, or propensity to misuse, drugs.

A court may not include a drug treatment requirement in a youth rehabilitation order unless it is *satisfied that the offender is dependent on, or has a propensity to misuse, drugs, and that the offender's dependency or propensity is such as requires and may be susceptible to treatment.*

The treatment required may be treatment as a resident in such institution or place as may be specified in the order, or treatment as a non-resident at such institution or place, and at such intervals, as may be so specified. The nature of the treatment is not specified in the order.

A court must not make a drug treatment requirement unless the court has been notified by the Secretary of State that arrangements for implementing drug treatment requirements are in force in the local justice area in which the offender resides or is to reside, and the court is satisfied that arrangements have been or can be made for the treatment intended to be specified in the order. The requirement must be recommended to the court as suitable for the offender by a member of a youth offending team, an officer of a local probation board or an officer of a provider of probation services, and **the offender must express willingness to comply with the requirement**.

Drug testing requirement. A drug testing requirement is a requirement that the offender must, during the treatment period of a drug treatment requirement, provide samples in accordance with instructions given by the responsible officer or the treatment provider for the purpose of ascertaining whether there is any drug in the offender's body.

A court may not include a drug testing requirement in a youth rehabilitation order unless the court has been notified by the Secretary of State that arrangements for implementing drug testing requirements are in force in the local justice area in which the offender resides or is to reside, the order also imposes a drug treatment requirement, and **the offender has expressed willingness to comply with the requirement**.

A drug testing requirement must specify for each month the minimum number of occasions on which samples are to be provided, and may specify times at which and circumstances in which the responsible officer or treatment provider may require samples to be provided, and descriptions of the samples which may be so required.

A drug testing requirement must provide for the results of tests carried out otherwise than by the responsible officer on samples provided by the offender in pursuance of the requirement to be communicated to the responsible officer.

Intoxicating substance treatment requirement. An intoxicating substance treatment requirement is a requirement that the offender must submit, during a period or periods specified in the order, to treatment, by or under the direction of a specified qualified person with a view to the reduction or elimination of the offender's dependency on or propensity to misuse intoxicating substances.

A court may not include an intoxicating substance treatment requirement in a youth rehabilitation order unless it is satisfied that the offender is dependent on, or has a propensity to misuse, intoxicating substances, and that the offender's dependency or propensity is such as requires and may be susceptible to treatment.

The treatment required must be treatment as a resident in an institution or place specified in the order, or treatment as a non-resident in a specified institution or place, at specified intervals. The nature of the treatment is not specified.

A court may not make an intoxicating substance treatment requirement unless the court is satisfied that arrangements have been or can be made for the treatment intended to be specified in the order, the requirement has been recommended to the court as suitable for the offender by a member of a youth offending team, an officer of a local probation board or an officer of a provider of probation services, and **the offender has expressed willingness to comply with the requirement**.

Education requirement.   An education requirement is a requirement that the offender must comply, during a period or periods specified in the order, with approved education arrangements made for the time being by the offender's parent or guardian, and approved by the local education authority specified in the order.

A court may not include an education requirement in a youth rehabilitation order unless it has consulted the local education authority proposed to be specified in the order with regard to the proposal to include the requirement, and it is satisfied that, in the view of that local education authority, arrangements exist for the offender to receive efficient full-time education suitable to the offender's age, ability, aptitude and special educational needs (if any), and that, having regard to the circumstances of the case, the inclusion of the education requirement is necessary for securing the good conduct of the offender or for preventing the commission of further offences.

Any period specified in a youth rehabilitation order as a period during which an offender must comply with approved education arrangements must not include any period after the offender has ceased to be of compulsory school age.

Electronic monitoring requirement.   An electronic monitoring requirement is a requirement for securing the electronic monitoring of the offender's compliance with other requirements imposed by the order during a period specified in the order or determined by the responsible officer in accordance with the order.

Where it is proposed to make an electronic monitoring requirement, but there is a person (other than the offender) without whose co-operation it will not be practicable to secure that the monitoring takes place, the requirement may not be included in the order without that person's consent.

A youth rehabilitation order which imposes an electronic monitoring requirement must include provision for making a person of a description specified in an order made by the Secretary of State responsible for the monitoring.

A court may not make an electronic monitoring requirement unless the court has been notified by the Secretary of State that arrangements for electronic monitoring of offenders are available in the local justice area proposed to be specified in the order, and in the area in which the relevant place is situated, and is satisfied that the necessary provision can be made under the arrangements currently available.

An electronic monitoring requirement must be made where the court makes either a curfew requirement or an exclusion requirement, unless the court considers it inappropriate for the order to include an electronic monitoring requirement, or it will not be practicable to secure that the monitoring takes place, without the consent of some person other than the offender, and that person does not consent to the inclusion of the electronic monitoring requirement.

Intensive supervision and surveillance. A court may make a youth rehabilitation order with intensive supervision and surveillance if the court is dealing with an offender for an offence which is punishable with imprisonment, and the court is of the opinion that the offence, or the combination of the offence and one or more offences associated with it, was so serious that a custodial sentence would be appropriate (or, if the offender was aged under 12 at the time of conviction, would be appropriate if the offender had been aged 12) in the absence of a power to make a youth rehabilitation order with intensive supervision and surveillance or a youth rehabilitation order with fostering. If the offender was aged under 15 at the time of conviction, the court must also be of the opinion that the offender is a persistent offender.

If the court makes a youth rehabilitation order with intensive supervision and surveillance, the order may include an extended activity requirement of not more than 180 days, and must make a supervision requirement and a curfew requirement with an electronic monitoring requirement, where such a requirement is required. A youth rehabilitation order with intensive supervision and surveillance may include other types of requirement, except a fostering requirement.

Fostering requirement. A court may make a youth rehabilitation order with a fostering requirement if the court is dealing with an offender for an offence which is punishable with imprisonment, and the court is of the opinion that the offence, or the combination of the offence and one or more offences associated with it, was so serious that a custodial sentence would be appropriate (or, if the offender was aged under 12 at the time of conviction, would be appropriate if the offender had been aged 12) in the absence of a power to make a youth rehabilitation order with intensive supervision and surveillance or a youth rehabilitation order with fostering. If the offender was aged under 15 at the time of conviction, the court must also be of the opinion that the offender is a persistent offender.

A fostering requirement may be made only if the court is satisfied that the behaviour which constituted the offence was due to a significant extent to the circumstances in which the offender was living, and that the imposition of a fostering requirement would assist in the offender's rehabilitation. A court may not impose a fostering requirement unless it has consulted the offender's parents or guardians (unless it is impracticable to do so), and it has consulted the local authority which is to place the offender with a local authority foster parent.

A youth rehabilitation order which imposes a fostering requirement must also impose a supervision requirement.

A fostering requirement is a requirement that, for a period specified in the order, the offender must reside with a local authority foster parent.

The period specified must end no later than 12 months beginning with the date on which the requirement first has effect and not include any period after the offender has reached the age of 18.

If at any time during the period of the requirement, the responsible officer notifies the offender that no suitable local authority foster parent is available, and that the responsible officer has applied or proposes to apply for the revocation or amendment of the order, the fostering requirement is, until the determination of the application, to be taken to require the offender to reside in accommodation provided by or on behalf of a local authority.

A court may not include a fostering requirement in a youth rehabilitation order unless the court has been notified by the Secretary of State that arrangements for implementing such a requirement are available in the area of the local authority which is to place the offender with a local authority foster parent.

A fostering requirement may not be made unless the offender was **legally represented** at the relevant time in court, or a right to representation funded by the Legal Services Commission for the purposes of the proceedings was withdrawn because of the offender's conduct, or the offender refused or failed to apply for representation after being informed of the right to apply and having had the opportunity to do so.

A fostering requirement may not be included in a youth rehabilitation order with intensive supervision and surveillance.

Breach of requirement of order

Youth court

If it is proved to the satisfaction of a youth court or magistrates court that an offender subject to a youth rehabilitation order has failed without reasonable excuse to comply with the youth rehabilitation order, the court may deal with the offender by ordering the offender to pay a fine not exceeding £250, if the offender is aged under 14, or £1,000, in any other case; by amending the terms of the order so as to impose any requirement which could have been included in the order when it was made in addition to, or in substitution for any requirement or requirements already imposed by the order; or by dealing with the offender, for the offence in respect of which the order was made, in any way in which the court could have dealt with the offender for that offence.

If the order imposes a mental health treatment requirement, a drug treatment requirement, or an intoxicating substance treatment requirement, the offender is not to be treated as having failed to comply with the order on the ground only that the offender had refused to undergo any surgical, electrical or other treatment, if in the opinion of the court, the refusal was reasonable having regard to all the circumstances.

If the court deals with the offender for the offence, the court must take into account the extent to which the offender has complied with the order. The order must be revoked.

If the order does not contain an unpaid work requirement, the court may add an unpaid work requirement with a requirement to perform between 20 and 240 hours' work. The court may not add to an existing youth rehabilitation order an extended activity requirement, or a fostering requirement, if the order does not already impose such a requirement.

If the order imposes a fostering requirement, the court may impose a new fostering requirement ending not later than 18 months from the date on which the original order was made.

If the court is dealing with the offender for the original offence, and the offender has wilfully and persistently failed to comply with a youth rehabilitation order, the court may impose a youth rehabilitation order with intensive supervision and surveillance.

If the order is a youth rehabilitation order with intensive supervision and surveillance, and the offence for which it was imposed was punishable with imprisonment, the court may impose a custodial sentence notwithstanding the general restrictions on imposing discretionary custodial sentences.

If the order is a youth rehabilitation order with intensive supervision and surveillance which was imposed following the breach of an earlier order, and the original offence was not punishable with imprisonment, the court may deal with the offender by making a detention and training order for a term not exceeding 4 months.

Crown Court

If the order made by the Crown Court contains a direction that further proceedings should be in the youth court or magistrates' court, the youth court or magistrates' court may commit the offender in custody or on bail, to be brought or appear before the Crown Court.

Where an offender appears or is brought before the Crown Court and it is proved to the satisfaction of that court that the offender has failed without reasonable excuse to comply with the youth rehabilitation order, the court may order the offender to pay a fine not exceeding £250, if the offender is aged under 14, or £1,000, in any other case; amend the terms of the youth rehabilitation order so as to impose any requirement which could have been included in the order when it was made, in addition to, or in substitution for, any requirement or requirements already imposed by the order; or deal with the offender, for the offence in respect of which the order was made, in any way in which the Crown Court could have dealt with the offender for that offence.

If the order imposes a mental health treatment requirement, a drug treatment requirement, or an intoxicating substance treatment requirement, the offender is not to be treated as having failed to comply with the order on the ground only that the offender had refused to undergo any surgical, electrical or other treatment, in the opinion of the court, the refusal was reasonable having regard to all the circumstances.

If the court deals with the offender for the offence, it must take into account the extent to which the offender has complied with the order. The order must be revoked.

If the order does not contain an unpaid work requirement, the court may add an unpaid work requirement requiring the offender to perform between 20 and 240 hours work. The court may not impose an extended activity requirement, or a fostering requirement, if the order does not already impose such a requirement.

If the original order imposes a fostering requirement, the court may substitute a new fostering requirement ending not later than 18 months from the date on which the original order was made.

If the offender has wilfully and persistently failed to comply with an order, and the court is dealing with the offender for the original offence, the court may impose a youth rehabilitation order with intensive supervision and surveillance.

If the order is a youth rehabilitation order with intensive supervision and surveillance, and the offence for which it was imposed was punishable with imprisonment, the court may impose a custodial sentence notwithstanding the general restrictions on imposing discretionary custodial sentences.

If the order is a youth rehabilitation order with intensive supervision and surveillance which was imposed following the breach of an earlier order, and the original offence was not punishable with imprisonment, the court may deal with the offender by making a detention and training order for a term not exceeding four months.

Revocation of order

If an application is made by the offender or responsible officer to the appropriate court, and it appears to the court to be in the interests of justice to do so, having regard to circumstances which have arisen since the order was made, the court may either revoke the order, or revoke the order, and deal with the offender, for the offence in respect of which the order was made, in any way in which the court could have dealt with the offender for that offence. The circumstances in which a youth rehabilitation order may be revoked include the offender's making good progress or responding satisfactorily to supervision or treatment. If the court revokes the order and deals with the offender for the original offence, the court must take into account the extent to which the offender has complied with the requirements of the order.

Subsequent conviction

Where an order **is in force** and the offender is convicted of an offence by a youth court or other magistrates' court, and the order was made by a youth court or other magistrates' court, or was made by the Crown Court with a direction that further proceedings should be in the youth court or magistrates court, and the court is dealing with the offender for the further offence, the court may revoke the order and may deal with the offender, for the offence in respect of which the order was made, in any way in which it could have dealt with the offender for that offence.

The court must not revoke the order and deal with the offender for the original offence, unless it considers that it would be in the interests of justice to do so, having regard to circumstances which have arisen since the youth rehabilitation order was made. The sentencing court must take into account the extent to which the offender has complied with the order.

If the youth rehabilitation order was made by the Crown Court, the youth court or magistrates' court may commit the offender in custody, or on bail to the Crown Court.

If an offender appears before the Crown Court while an **order is in force**, having been committed by the magistrates' court to the Crown Court for sentence, or is convicted by the Crown Court of an offence **while an order is in force**, the Crown Court may revoke the order and may deal with the offender, for the offence in respect of which the order was made, *in any way in which the court which made the order could have dealt with the offender for that offence.*

The Crown Court must not deal with the offender for the original offence unless it considers that it would be in the interests of justice to do so, having regard to circumstances which have arisen since the youth rehabilitation order was made. The Crown Court must take into account the extent to which the offender has complied with the order.

If the offender has been committed to the Crown Court to be dealt with in respect of a youth rehabilitation order following a conviction by a youth court or magistrates' court, the Crown Court may deal with the offender for the later offence in any way which the youth court or magistrates' court' could have dealt with the offender for that offence.

Part 2:

Maximum Sentences (Indictable Offences)

This part sets out the maximum sentences available to the Crown Court for the offences which are most commonly tried on indictment or dealt with in the Crown Court.

To use this part, identify the statute and section concerned by reference to the statement of offence in the indictment. Offences are listed by statute and section, with a brief reference to the nature of the offence. Where the same section creates different offences, the maximum sentence for each offence is set out separately.

Aviation Security Act 1982

Section 1 (hijacking)   **Life**
Section 2 (destroying aircraft)   **Life**
Section 3 (endangering safety of aircraft)   **Life**
Section 4 (possessing dangerous article)   **5 years**
Section 6 (inducing offence)   **Life**

Note:

Sections 1, 2, 3 and 4:

Specified offence (Criminal Justice Act 2003, Sch.15)

Scheduled offence (Sexual Offences Act 2003, Sch.5)

Sections 1, 2, 3 and 6:

Powers of Criminal Courts (Sentencing) Act 2000, s.91 applies.

Bail Act 1976

Section 6 (failing to surrender)   **12 months**

Note: Where an offender is dealt with by the Crown Court for a bail offence, otherwise than on a committal by a magistrates' court under Bail Act 1976, s.6(6), he is to be dealt with as if the bail offence were a contempt of court. An offender under the age of 18 may not be committed to custody for a bail offence.

Child Abduction Act 1984

Section 1 (taking out of United Kingdom without consent)   **7 years**
Section 2 (taking child out of lawful control)   **7 years**

Penalty provision: section 4.

Note:

Sections 1 and 2: Scheduled offence for purposes of Sexual Offences Act 2003, Sch.5.

Section 1: Offence against a child (Criminal Justice and Court Services Act 2000, Sch.4.

Offences against this Act are not specified offences for the purposes of the Criminal Justice Act 2003, Sch.15.

Children and Young Persons Act 1933

Section 1 (ill-treatment or neglect etc.)   **10 years**
Section 26 (procuring child to go abroad by false representation)   **2 years**

Note:

Section 1:

Specified offence (Criminal Justice Act 2003, Sch.15).

Offence against a child (Criminal Justice and Court Services Act 2000, Sch.4).

Scheduled offence (Sexual Offences Act 2003, Sch.5).

Companies Act 1985

Section 458 (fraudulent trading)   **10 years**
(if offence committed on or after January 15, 2007; otherwise 7 years).

For other offences, see Sch.24.

Companies Act 2006

Section 993 (fraudulent trading)   **10 years**

Computer Misuse Act 1990

Section 1 (securing unauthorised access)   **2 years***
Section 2 (unauthorised access with intent)   **5 years**
Section 3 (unauthorised modification)   **10 years****

*(if offence committed on or after October 1, 2008)
**(if offence committed on or after October 1, 2008; otherwise 5 years)

Contempt of Court Act 1981

Section 14 (contempt of superior court) **2 years**

Note: A committal for contempt is not a sentence of imprisonment or detention in a young offender institution for the purposes of Criminal Justice Act 1991, s.51(2). An offender under the age of 18 may not be committed to custody for contempt.

Copyright Designs and Patents Act 1988

Offences under s.107(1)(a), (b), (d)(iv) or (e) **10 years**
Offences under s.107(2A) **2 years**

Crime and Disorder Act 1998

Section 29(1)(a) (racially or religiously aggravated unlawful wounding) **7 years**
Section 29(1)(b) (racially or religiously aggravated assault occasioning actual bodily harm) **7 years**
Section 29(1)(c) (racially or religiously aggravated common assault) **2 years**
Section 30 (racially or religiously aggravated criminal damage) **14 years**
Section 31(1)(a) (racially or religiously aggravated causing fear of violence) **2 years**
Section 31(1)(a) (racially or religiously aggravated intentional harassment) **2 years**
Section 32(1)(a) (racially or religiously aggravated harassment) **2 years**
Section 32(1)(b) (racially or religiously aggravated causing fear of violence) **7 years**

On conviction under s.32(1)(a) or (b), the court may make a restraining order under Protection from Harassment Act 1997, s.5.

Note:

Offence under s.29:

Specified offence (Criminal Justice Act 2003, Sch.15).

Scheduled offence (Sexual Offences Act 2003, Sch.5).

Offences contrary to s.29 are not offences against a child for the purposes of the Criminal Justice and Court Services Act 2000, Sch.4.

Offence under s.31(1)(a) or (b):

Specified offence (Criminal Justice Act 2003, Sch.15).

Criminal Attempts Act 1981

Section 1 (attempted murder) **Life**
Section 1 (attempting indictable offence) **As for offence in question**

Note: Special provisions apply to attempted incest. See under Sexual Offences Act 1956.

Note: An attempt to commit an offence which is a specified offence (Criminal Justice Act 2003, Sch.15), an offence against a child under the Criminal Justice and Court Services Act 2000, Sch.4, or a scheduled offence (Sexual Offences Act 2003, Schs 2 or 5) is also a specified offence, an offence against a child or a scheduled offence. An attempt to commit an offence which is a "serious offence" for the purposes of the P.C.C.(S.)A. 2000, s.109, is not itself a "serious offence" unless it is listed as such in s.109.

Criminal Damage Act 1971

Section 1(1) (criminal damage) **10 years**

Note: if the value of the damage does not exceed £5,000 and the matter comes before the Crown Court under Criminal Justice Act 1988, ss.40 or 41, or P.C.C.(S.)A. 2000, s.6, the maximum sentence is three months.

Section 1(2) (criminal damage with intent to endanger life) **Life**
Section 1(3) (arson) **Life**
Section 2 (threatening to damage property) **10 years**

Section 3 (possession with intent)   **10 years**

Penalty provision: section 4.

Note: Arson and criminal damage endangering life (s.1(2)).

Specified offence (Criminal Justice Act 2003, Sch.15).

Scheduled offence (Sexual Offences Act 2003, Sch.5).

P.C.C.(S.)A. 2000, s.91 applies.

Criminal Justice Act 1925

Section 36(1) (making false statement to procure passport)   **2 years**

Criminal Justice Act 1961

Section 22 (harbouring escaped prisoner)   **10 years**

Criminal Justice Act 1988

Section 134 (torture)   **Life**

Note:

Section 134:

Specified offence (Criminal Justice Act 2003, Sch.15).

Scheduled offence (Sexual Offences Act 2003, Schs 2, 5).

P.C.C.(S.)A. 2000, s.91 applies.

Section 139 (possessing sharp bladed or pointed instrument)   **4 years**
(*if offence was committed before February 12, 2007; two years*)
Section 139A (possessing sharp bladed instrument, etc., near school)   **4 years**

(if offence was committed before February 12, 2007; two
   years)
Section 139A (possessing offensive weapon on school
   premises)   **4 years**
Section 160 (possessing indecent photograph of child)   **5 years**
(If the offence was committed on or after January 11, 2001; otherwise six
months).

Note:

Section 160:

Specified offence (Criminal Justice Act 2003, Sch.15).

Scheduled offence (Sexual Offences Act 2003, Sch.3), if the indecent
photographs, etc. showed persons under 16 and (if the offence was
committed after May 1, 2004) the offender was over 18 or sentenced to a
term of imprisonment of at least 12 months (see s.131).

Offence against a child (if victim under 18) Criminal Justice and Court
Services Act 2000, Sch.4.

Criminal Justice Act 1993

Section 61 (insider dealing)   **7 years**

Criminal Justice (International Co-operation) Act 1990

Section 12 (manufacturing or supplying scheduled substance)   **14 years**
Section 19 (having possession of a Class A controlled
   drug on a ship)   **Life**
Section 19 (having possession of a Class B controlled
   drug on a ship)   **14 years**
Section 19 (having possession of a Class C controlled
   drug on a ship)   **14 years**

Note: Offences under ss.12 and 19 are drug trafficking offences for the
purposes of the Drug Trafficking Act 1994 and the Proceeds of Crime Act
2002, Sch.2.

Criminal Justice and Public Order Act 1994

Section 51 (intimidating witness)   **5 years**

Criminal Law Act 1967

Section 4 (assisting offender)

Sentence for principal offence fixed by law	**10 years**
Maximum sentence for principal offence 14 years	**7 years**
Maximum sentence for principal offence 10 years	**5 years**
Otherwise (normally five years)	**3 years**

Criminal Law Act 1977

Section 1 (conspiracy to commit offence punishable by life imprisonment)	**Life**
Section 1 (conspiracy to commit offence for which no maximum is provided)	**Life**
Section 1 (conspiracy to commit offence with specified maximum term)	**Maximum term for offence in question**
Section 51 (bomb hoax)	**7 years**

Customs and Excise Management Act 1979

Section 50 (importing undutied or prohibited goods)	**7 years**
Section 68 (evading prohibition of exportation)	**7 years**
Section 170 (evading duty, or prohibition)	**7 years**

Note: Where an offence under ss.50, 68 or 170 relates to Class A drugs, the maximum is life imprisonment; where the offence relates to Class B or Class C drugs, the maximum is 14 years.

Where an offence under ss.50, 68 or 170 relates to goods prohibited by the Forgery and Counterfeiting Act 1981, ss.20 or 21, the maximum sentence is 10 years.

Where an offence under ss.50, 68 or 170 relates to certain prohibited weapons within the meaning of the Firearms Act 1968, s.5(1) (excluding weapons falling within ss.5(1)(b) or 5(1A)(b) to (g)), the maximum is 10 years.

Section 170B (taking preparatory steps)   **7 years**

Offences involving the importation or exportation of controlled drugs are drug trafficking offences for the purposes of the Drug Trafficking Act 1994 and the Proceeds of Crime Act 2002, Sch.2.

Offences involving the importation or exportation of controlled drugs: P.C.C.(S.)A. 2000, s.91 applies.

Offences involving importation of indecent materials:

Specified offence (Criminal Justice Act 2003, Sch.15)

Scheduled offence (Sexual Offences Act 2003, Sch.3, if the indecent photographs etc. showed persons under 16 and (if the offence was committed after May 1, 2004) the offender was over 18 or sentenced to a term of imprisonment of at least twelve months (see s.131).

Domestic Violence, Crime and Victims Act 2004

Section 5 (causing or allowing death of child)   **14 years**

Explosive Substances Act 1883

Section 2 (causing explosion likely to endanger life)   **Life**
Section 3 (attempting to cause explosion, or possessing
   explosive substance with intent)   **Life**
Section 4 (making or possessing explosive substance)   **14 years**

  Note:

  Sections 2 and 3:

  Specified offence (Criminal Justice Act 2003, Sch.15).

  Scheduled offence (Sexual Offences Act 2003, Schs 2, 5).

  Sections 2, 3 and 4:

  P.C.C.(S.)A. 2000, s.91 applies.

Firearms Act 1968

Section 1 (possessing firearm without certificate)   **5 years**

Section 1 (possessing shortened shotgun) **7 years**

Section 2 (possessing shotgun without certificate) **5 years**

Section 3 (selling firearm, etc.) **5 years**

Section 4 (shortening shotgun) **7 years**

Section 5 (possessing, etc., prohibited weapon) **10 years**

Section 16 (possessing firearm with intent to endanger life) **Life**

Section 16A (possessing firearm with intent to cause fear of violence) **10 years**

Section 17 (using firearm to prevent arrest, or while committing scheduled offence) **Life**

Section 18 (carrying firearm with intent to commit offence) **Life**

Section 19 (carrying firearm other than an airweapon in public place) **7 years**

Note: If the firearm is an imitation firearm, the maximum sentence for an offence committed **before October 1, 2007** is six months; after that date, 12 months.

Section 20 (trespassing with firearm) **5 years**

Section 21 (possessing firearm as former prisoner, etc.) **5 years**

Penalty provision: Schedule 6, as amended by Criminal Justice and Public Order Act 1994, Sch.8.

Note:

Sections 16, 16A, 17(1) and (2), 18:

Specified offence (Criminal Justice Act 2003, Sch.15).

Scheduled offence (Sexual Offences Act 2003, Schs 2, 5).

Serious offence (P.C.C.(S.)A. 2000, s.109).

P.C.C.(S.)A. 2000, s.91 applies.

Section 5 (with exceptions).

Required minimum sentence applies (Firearms Act 1968, s.51A).

Sections 16, 16A, 17, 18, 19, 20(1).

Required minimum sentence applies if firearm is a prohibited weapon.

Forgery and Counterfeiting Act 1981

Section 1 (making false instrument with intent) **10 years**

Section 2 (making copy of false instrument with intent)   **10 years**
Section 3 (using false instrument with intent)   **10 years**
Section 4 (using copy of false instrument)   **10 years**
Section 5(1) (custody or control of false instrument with intent)   **10 years**
Section 5(2) (custody or control of false instrument, no intent)   **2 years**
Section 5(3) (making machine, etc., with intent)   **10 years**
Section 5(4) (making machine, etc., no intent)   **2 years**

Penalty provision:

Section 6.

Fraud Act 2006

Section 1 (fraud)   **10 years**
Section 6 (possession of article for use in fraud)   **5 years**
Section 7 (making or supplying article for use in fraud)   **10 years**

Identity Cards Act 2006

Section 25(1) (possession of false identity document with intent)   **10 years**
Section 25(3) (possession of apparatus for making false identity document with intent)   **10 years**
Section 25(5) (possession of false identity document etc without intent)   **2 years**
Section 27 (unauthorized disclosure)   **2 years**
Section 28 (providing false information)   **2 years**

Immigration Act 1971

Section 24A (obtaining admission by deception)   **2 years**
Section 25 (facilitating illegal entry)   **14 years**
Section 25A (assisting asylum seeker)   **14 years**
Section 25B (assisting entry in breach of deportation order)   **14 years**

Incitement to Disaffection Act 1934

Section 1 (seducing member of forces from duty)   **2 years**

Section 2 (possessing document, etc.) **2 years**

Penalty provision: section 3.

Indecency with Children Act 1960

Section 1 (gross indecency with child) **10 years**
(If the offence was committed on or after October 1, 1997; otherwise two years).

Note: This Act was repealed by the Sexual Offences Act 2003 with effect from May 1, 2004, but it is thought that its practical effect has been preserved by the Interpretation Act 1978, s.16, See note to Sexual Offences Act 1956.

Specified offence (Criminal Justice Act 2003, Sch.15).

Offence against a child (Criminal Justice and Court Services Act 2000, Sch.4).

Scheduled offence (Sexual Offences Act 2003, Sch.2).

P.C.C.(S.)A. 2000, s.91 does not apply.

Indecent Displays (Control) Act 1981

Section 1 (displaying indecent matter) **2 years**

Penalty provision: section 4.

Infanticide Act 1938

Section 1 (infanticide) **Life**

Note:

Specified offence (Criminal Justice Act 2003, Sch.15).

Offence against a child (if victim under 18) Criminal Justice and Court Services Act 2000, Sch.4.

Scheduled offence (Sexual Offences Act 2003, Schs 2, 5).

P.C.C.(S.)A. 2000, s.91 applies.

Infant Life (Preservation) Act 1929

Section 1 (child destruction) **Life**

Note:

Specified offence (Criminal Justice Act 2003, Sch.15).

Scheduled offence (Sexual Offences Act 2003, Sch.5).

P.C.C.(S.)A. 2000, s.91 applies.

Knives Act 1997

Section 1 (marketing combat knife) **2 years**
Section 2 (publishing material) **2 years**

Mental Health Act 1983

Section 126 (possession of false document) **2 years**
Section 127 (ill-treating patient) **5 years**
(if the offence was committed on or after October 1, 2007; otherwise two years)
Section 128 (assisting absconded patient) **2 years**

Merchant Shipping Act 1995

Section 58 (endangering ship) **2 years**

Misuse of Drugs Act 1971

Section 4(2) (producing Class A drug) **Life**
Section 4(2) (producing Class B drug) **14 years**

Section 4(2) (producing Class C drug)	**14 years**
Section 4(3) (supplying Class A drug)	**Life**
Section 4(3) (supplying Class B drug)	**14 years**
Section 4(3) (supplying Class C drug)	**14 years**
Section 5(2) (possessing Class A drug)	**7 years**
Section 5(2) (possessing Class B drug)	**5 years**
Section 5(2) (possessing Class C drug)	**2 years**
Section 5(3) (possessing Class A drug with intent to supply)	**Life**
Section 5(3) (possessing Class B drug with intent to supply)	**14 years**
Section 5(3) (possessing Class C drug with intent to supply)	**14 years**
Section 6(2) (cultivating cannabis plant)	**14 years**
Section 8 (occupier of premises permitting supply, etc. of Class A drugs)	**14 years**
Section 8 (occupier of premises permitting supply, etc. of Class B drugs)	**14 years**
Section 8 (occupier of premises permitting supply, etc. of Class C drugs)	**14 years**
Section 9 (opium)	**14 years**
Section 11(2) (contravention of directions)	**2 years**
Section 12(6) (contravention of prohibition on prescribing in relation to Class A drug)	**14 years**
Section 12(6) (contravention of prohibition on prescribing in relation to Class B drug)	**14 years**
Section 12(6) (contravention of prohibition on prescribing in relation to Class C drug)	**14 years**
Section 13(3) (contravention of prohibition on supplying in relation to Class A drug)	**14 years**
Section 13(3) (contravention of prohibition on supplying in relation to Class B drug)	**14 years**
Section 13(3) (contravention of prohibition on supplying in relation to Class C drug)	**14 years**
Section 17(4) (giving false information)	**2 years**
Section 18 (contravention of regulations, etc.)	**2 years**
Section 20 (assisting offence outside United Kingdom)	**14 years**
Section 23 (obstructing search)	**2 years**

Penalty provision: Schedule 4.

Note: Offences under ss.4(2) or (3), 5(3), 20, 49, 50 and 51 are drug trafficking offences for the purposes of the Drug Trafficking Act 1994. Offences under ss.(2) or (3), 5(3), and 8 are drug trafficking offences for the purposes of the Proceeds of Crime Act 2002, Sch.2.

Section 4(3):

Offence against a child (if drugs supplied to person under 18) Criminal
Justice and Court Services Act 2000, Sch.4.

Obscene Publications Act 1959

Section 2 (publishing obscene article, or having article
  for publication)   **3 years**

Offences against the Person Act 1861

Section 4 (soliciting to murder)	**Life**
Section 16 (threatening to kill)	**10 years**
Section 18 (wounding with intent to cause grievous bodily harm)	**Life**
Section 20 (unlawful wounding)	**5 years**
Section 21 (choking, etc., with intent)	**Life**
Section 22 (administering drug with intent)	**Life**
Section 23 (administering noxious thing to endanger life)	**10 years**
Section 24 (administering noxious thing to injure, aggrieve or annoy)	**5 years**
Section 27 (abandoning child)	**5 years**
Section 28 (causing grievous bodily harm by explosion)	**Life**
Section 29 (using explosives with intent, throwing corrosive substance with intent)	**Life**
Section 30 (placing explosive substance with intent)	**14 years**
Section 31 (setting spring gun, etc.)	**5 years**
Section 32 (endangering safety of railway passengers)	**Life**
Section 33 (throwing object with intent to endanger rail passenger)	**Life**
Section 34 (endangering rail passenger by neglect)	**2 years**
Section 35 (causing grievous bodily harm by wanton driving)	**2 years**
Section 36 (obstructing minister of religion)	**2 years**
Section 38 (assault with intent to resist arrest)	**2 years**
Section 47 (assault occasioning actual bodily harm)	**5 years**
Section 58 (procuring miscarriage)	**Life**
Section 59 (supplying instrument, etc.)	**5 years**
Section 60 (concealment of birth)	**2 years**

Note: Offences under the following sections are specified offences for the
purposes of the Criminal Justice Act 2003, Sch.15: ss.4, 16, 18, 20, 21, 22,
23, 27, 28, 29, 30, 31, 32, 35, 37, 38, 47.

Offences under the following sections are offences against a child (if victim is under 18) for the purposes of the Criminal Justice and Court Services Act 2000, Sch.4: ss.16, 18, 20, 47.

Offences under the following sections are scheduled offences for the purposes of the Sexual Offences Act 2003, Sch.5: ss.4, 16, 18, 20, 21, 22, 23, 27, 28, 29, 30, 31, 32, 35, 37, 38, 47.

Official Secrets Act 1911

Section 1 (act prejudicial to safety of state)   **14 years**
Penalty provision: Official Secrets Act 1920, s.8(1)

Official Secrets Act 1920

Section 1(1) (gaining admission to prohibited place)   **2 years**
Section 1(2) (retaining document, etc.)   **2 years**
Section 3 (interfering with police officer or sentry)   **2 years**

Penalty provision: section 8(2).

Official Secrets Act 1989

Section 1 (disclosing information)   **2 years**
Section 3 (Crown servant making disclosure)   **2 years**
Section 4 (unauthorised disclosure)   **2 years**
Section 5 (unauthorised disclosure by recipient)   **2 years**
Section 6 (unauthorised disclosure)   **2 years**

Penalty provision: section 10.

Perjury Act 1911

Section 1 (witness making untrue statement)   **7 years**
Section 1A (false statement for foreign proceedings)   **2 years**

Prevention of Corruption Act 1906

Section 1 (corruptly accepting consideration, etc.)   **7 years**

Prevention of Crime Act 1953

Section 1 (possessing offensive weapon)   **4 years**

Prison Act 1952

Section 39 (assisting escape)   **10 years**

Prison Security Act 1992

Section 1 (prison mutiny)   **10 years**

Protection from Eviction Act 1977

Section 1 (depriving residential occupier of occupation)   **2 years**

Protection from Harassment Act 1997

Section 3 (breach of injunction)   **5 years**
Section 4 (causing fear of violence)   **5 years**

The court may make a restraining order (s.5).

Protection of Children Act 1978

Section 1 (taking, distributing, possessing, publishing
    indecent photograph of child)   **10 years**

(If the offence was committed on or after January 11, 2001; otherwise
three years).

Penalty provision: section 6.

Note:

Section 1:

Specified offence (Criminal Justice Act 2003, Sch.15).

Offence against a child (if victim under 18) Criminal Justice and Court Services Act 2000, Sch.4.

Scheduled offence (Sexual Offences Act 2003, Sch.3, if the indecent photographs etc. showed persons under 16 and (if the offence was committed after May 1, 2004), the offender was over 18 or sentenced to a term of imprisonment of at least twelve months (see s.131).

Public Bodies (Corrupt Practices) Act 1889

Section 1 (public servant soliciting or accepting gift)   **7 years**
  The court may order payment of the value of the gift, etc., to be paid to the employing body, and may disqualify offender from public office.

Penalty provision: section 2.

Public Order Act 1936

Section 2 (unlawful organisation)   **2 years**

  Penalty provision: section 7.

Public Order Act 1986

Section 1 (riot)	**10 years**
Section 2 (violent disorder)	**5 years**
Section 3 (affray)	**3 years**
Section 18 (using words to stir up racial hatred)	**7 years**
Section 19 (distributing material to stir up racial hatred)	**7 years**
Section 20 (performing play to stir up racial hatred)	**7 years**
Section 21 (distributing recording to stir up racial hatred)	**7 years**
Section 22 (broadcasting programme)	**7 years**
Section 23 (possessing material to stir up racial hatred)	**7 years**

Penalty provision: section 27(3).

Section 38 (contaminating goods)   **10 years**

Note: offences against the following provisions are specified offences for the purposes of the Criminal Justice Act 2003, Sch.15: ss.1 (riot), 2 (violent disorder), 3 (affray).

Representation of the People Act 1983

Section 60 (personation)   **2 years**

Road Traffic Act 1988

Section 1 (causing death by dangerous driving)   **14 years**
Section 2 (dangerous driving)   **2 years**

Section 2B (causing death by careless or inconsiderate
  driving)   **5 years**
Section 3A (causing death by careless driving, having
  consumed alcohol)   **14 years**
Section 3ZB (causing death by driving while unlicenced,
  disqualified or uninsured)   **2 years**
Section 4(1) (driving while unfit)   **6 months**
Section 5(1) (driving with excess alcohol)   **6 months**

Penalty provision: Road Traffic Offenders Act 1988, Sch. 2.

Note:

Sections 1, 3A:

Specified offence (Criminal Justice Act 2003, Sch.15).

Scheduled offence (Sexual Offences Act 2003, Sch.5).

Serious Crime Prevention Act 2007

Section 44 (encouraging or assisting commission of
offence) . . . if the anticipated offence is murder, life
imprisonment, otherwise the maximum sentence for the
anticipated or reference offence.

Section 45 (encouraging or assisting commission of
offence, believing it will be committed) . . . if the anticipated offence is murder, life imprisonment, otherwise the
maximum sentence for the anticipated or reference
offence.
Section 46 (encouraging or assisting commission of one
or more offences) . . . if the anticipated or reference
offence is murder, life imprisonment, otherwise the maximum sentence for the anticipated or reference offence.

If the offence whose commission is encouraged or assisted is a specified
offence for the purposes of the Criminal Justice Act 2003, Sch.15, an
offence under ss 44, 45 or 46 is also a specified offence for that purpose.

Sexual Offences Act 1956

Most sections of the Sexual Offences Act 1956 are repealed with effect
from May 1, 2004, by the Sexual Offences Act 2003. References in other
statutes (such as the P.C.C.(S.)A. 2000, s.161) are also for the most part
repealed by the Sexual Offences Act 2003. The liability of an offender to be
sentenced for a sexual offence committed before May 1, 2004, depends on
the Interpretation Act 1978, s.16, which provides:

> "Without prejudice to section 15, where an Act repeals an enactment,
> the repeal does not, unless the contrary intention appears,—
>   (c) affect any right, privilege, obligation or liability acquired,
>   accrued or incurred under that enactment;
>   (d) affect any penalty, forfeiture or punishment incurred in respect
>   of any offence committed against that enactment;
>   (e) affect any investigation, legal proceeding or remedy in respect
>   of any such right, privilege, obligation, liability, penalty, forfei-
>   ture or punishment; and any such investigation, legal proceed-
>   ing or remedy may be instituted, continued or enforced, and
>   any such penalty, forfeiture or punishment may be imposed, as
>   if the repealing Act had not been passed."

It appears that this section preserves the effect of the Sexual Offences
Act 1956, and preserves the effect of statutory provisions referring to
provisions of that Act, in respect of offences committed on or before May 1,
2004.

Section 1 (rape)	**Life**
Section 2 (procurement of woman by threats)	**2 years**
Section 3 (procurement by false pretences)	**2 years**
Section 4 (administering drugs)	**2 years**

Section 5 (intercourse with girl under 13)	**Life**
Section 6 (unlawful sexual intercourse with girl under 16)	**2 years**
Section 7 (intercourse with defective)	**2 years**
Section 9 (procurement of defective)	**2 years**
Section 10 (incest by man with girl under 13)	**Life**
(attempt, seven years)	
Section 10 (incest by man)	**7 years**
(attempt, two years)	
Section 11 (incest by woman)	**7 years**
(attempt, two years)	
Section 12 (buggery with person under 16)	**Life**
Section 12 (buggery with animal)	**Life**
Section 12 (buggery of person under 18 by person over 21)	**5 years**
Section 12 (other forms of buggery)	**2 years**
Section 13 (indecency by man over 21 with man under 18)	**5 years**
Section 13 (indecency by males)	**2 years**
Section 14 (indecent assault on woman)	**10 years**

(If the offence was committed on or after September 16, 1985: otherwise two years, unless the victim was under 13 and her age was stated in the indictment, in which case the maximum is five years).

Section 15 (indecent assault on male)	**10 years**
Section 16 (assault with intent to bugger)	**10 years**
Section 17 (abduction)	**14 years**
Section 19 (abduction of girl under 18)	**2 years**
Section 20 (abduction of girl under 16)	**2 years**
Section 21 (abduction of defective)	**2 years**
Section 22 (causing prostitution)	**2 years**
Section 23 (procuring girl under 21)	**2 years**
Section 24 (detention in brothel)	**2 years**
Section 25 (permitting premises to be used by girl under 13)	**Life**
Section 26 (permitting premises to be used)	**2 years**
Section 27 (permitting defective to use premises)	**2 years**
Section 28 (causing prostitution of girl under 16)	**2 years**
Section 29 (causing prostitution of defective)	**2 years**
Section 30 (living on earnings of prostitution)	**7 years**
Section 31 (controlling prostitute)	**7 years**
Section 32 (man soliciting)	**2 years**
Section 33A (keeping brothel used for prostitution)	**7 years**

Offences under the following sections are specified offences for the purposes of the Criminal Justice Act 2003, Sch.15: ss.1, 2, 3, 4, 5, 6, 7, 9, 10, 11, 14, 15, 16, 17, 19, 20, 21, 22, 23, 24, 25, 26, 27, 28, 29, 32, 33. (offences contrary to s.13 are not specified offences).

Offences under the following provisions are offences against a child for the purposes of the Criminal Justice and Court Services Act 2000, Sch.4, if the victim is under 18: ss.1, 2, 3, 4, 5, 6, 7, 9, 10, 11, 12, 13, 14, 15, 16, 17, 19, 20, 21, 22, 23, 25, 26, 27, 28, 29, 30, 31.

Offences under the following provisions are sexual offences for the purposes of the Sexual Offences Act 2003, Sch.3, if the required conditions are satisfied: ss.1, 5, 6 (if offender 20 or over), 12 (if other party under 18), 12 (if offender over 20 and other party under 18), 14 (if victim under 18, or offender sentenced to 30 months or more or to a hospital order), 15 (if victim under 18, or offender sentenced to 30 months or more or to a hospital order), 16 (if victim under 18), 28 (if girl under 16).

All offences under the Sexual Offences Act 1956, except for offences under sections 30, 31, 33, 34, 35 and 36 were "sexual offences" for the purposes of the P.C.C.(S.)A. 2000, s.161.

P.C.C.(S.)A. 2000, s.91 applies to all offences punishable with imprisonment for 14 years or more, and to offences under ss.14 and 15.

Sexual Offences Act 2003

Section 1 (rape)	**Life**
Section 2 (assault by penetration)	**Life**
Section 3 (sexual assault)	**10 years**
Section 4 (causing sexual activity with penetration)	**Life**
Section 4 (causing sexual activity without penetration)	**10 years**
Section 5 (penetration of child under 13)	**Life**
Section 6 (assault of person under 13 by penetration)	**Life**
Section 7 (sexual assault on person under 13)	**14 years**
Section 8 (causing person under 13 to engage in sexual activity involving penetration)	**Life**
Section 8 (causing person under 13 to engage in sexual activity without penetration)	**14 years**
Section 9 (sexual activity with person under 16)	**14 years**
Section 10 (causing person under 16 to engage in sexual activity)	**14 years**
Section 11 (sexual activity in presence of person under 16)	**10 years**
Section 12 (causing person under 16 to watch sexual act)	**10 years**
Section 13 (child sex offence committed by person under 18)	**5 years**
Section 14 (arranging child sex offence)	**14 years**
Section 15 (meeting person under 16 with intent following grooming)	**10 years**

Section 16 (abuse of trust by sexual activity)   **5 years**

Section 17 (abuse of trust by causing sexual activity)   **5 years**

Section 18 (abuse of trust by sexual activity in presence of child)   **5 years**

Section 19 (abuse of trust by causing child to watch sexual act)   **5 years**

Section 25 (sexual activity by person over 18 with family member under 18)   **14 years**

Section 25 (sexual activity by person under 18 with family member under 18)   **5 years**

Section 26 (person over 18 inciting family member under 18 to engage in sexual activity)   **14 years**

Section 26 (person under 18 inciting family member under 18 to engage in sexual activity)   **5 years**

Section 30 (sexual activity involving penetration with person with mental disorder)   **Life**

Section 30 (sexual activity not involving penetration with person with mental disorder)   **14 years**

Section 31 (causing or inciting sexual activity involving penetration by person with mental disorder)   **Life**

Section 31 (causing or inciting sexual activity not involving penetration by person with mental disorder)   **14 years**

Section 32 (engaging in sexual activity in presence of person with mental disorder)   **10 years**

Section 33 (causing person with mental disorder to watch sexual act)   **10 years**

Section 34 (offering inducement to person with mental disorder to engage in sexual act involving penetration)   **Life**

Section 34 (offering inducement to person with mental disorder to engage in sexual act not involving penetration)   **14 years**

Section 35 (inducing person with mental disorder to engage in sexual act involving penetration)   **Life**

Section 35 (inducing person with mental disorder to engage in sexual act not involving penetration)   **14 years**

Section 36 (causing person with mental disorder to watch sexual act by inducement etc.)   **10 years**

Section 37 (causing person with mental disorder to watch third party sexual act by inducement etc.)   **10 years**

Section 38 (sexual acts involving penetration by care worker with person with mental disorder)   **14 years**

Section 38 (sexual acts not involving penetration by care worker with person with mental disorder)   **10 years**

Section 39 (care worker inciting person with mental disorder engage in sexual act involving penetration)   **14 years**

Section 39 (care worker inciting person with mental disorder engage in sexual act not involving penetration)   **10 years**

Section 40 (care worker engaging in sexual act in presence of person with mental disorder)	**7 years**
Section 41 (care worker causing person with mental disorder to watch sexual act)	**7 years**
Section 47 (paying for sexual service involving penetration by person under 13)	**Life**
Section 47 (paying for sexual service by person under 16)	**14 years**
Section 47 (paying for sexual service by person under 18)	**7 years**
Section 48 (causing person under 18 to become involved in prostitution or pornography)	**14 years**
Section 49 (controlling prostitution by person under 18)	**14 years**
Section 50 (facilitating prostitution by person under 18)	**14 years**
Section 52 (causing or inciting prostitution)	**7 years**
Section 53 (controlling prostitution for gain)	**7 years**
Section 57 (arranging arrival for purposes of prostitution)	**14 years**
Section 58 (facilitating travel for purposes of prostitution)	**14 years**
Section 59 (facilitating departure for purposes of prostitution)	**14 years**
Section 61 (administering substance with intent to enable sexual activity)	**10 years**
Section 62 (committing offence with intent to commit sexual offence)	**10 years**
Section 63 (trespass with intent to commit sexual offence)	**10 years**
Section 64 (sexual penetration of adult relative)	**2 years**
Section 65 (consenting to sexual penetration by adult relative)	**2 years**
Section 66 (intentional exposure)	**2 years**
Section 67 (observing private act)	**2 years**
Section 69 (sexual act with animal)	**2 years**
Section 70 (sexual penetration of corpse)	**2 years**

Note: Offences under the following provisions are specified offences for the purposes of the Criminal Justice Act 2003, Sch.15: ss.1, 2, 3, 4, 5, 6, 7, 8, 9, 10, 11, 12, 13, 14, 15, 16, 17, 18, 19, 25, 26, 30, 31, 32, 33, 34, 35, 36, 37, 38, 39, 40, 41, 47, 48, 49, 50, 52, 53, 57, 58, 59, 61, 62, 63, 64, 65, 66, 67, 69, 70.

Offences against the following provisions are offences against a child (if the victim is under 18) for the purposes of the Criminal Justice and Court Services Act 2000, Sch.4: ss.1, 2, 3, 4, 5, 6, 7, 8, 9, 10, 11, 12, 13, 14, 15, 16, 17, 18, 19, 20, 21, 22, 23, 24, 25, 26, 30, 31, 32, 33, 34, 35, 36, 37, 38, 39, 41, 47, 48, 49, 50, 52, 53, 57, 58, 59, 60, 61, 62, 63, 66, 67.

Offences against the following provisions are scheduled sexual offences for the purposes of the Sexual Offences Act 2003, Sch.3, if the required conditions are satisfied: ss.1, 2, 3*, 4, 5, 6, 7*, 8, 9, 10, 11, 12, 13*, 14*, 15, 16, 17, 18, 19*, 25*, 26*, 30, 31, 32, 33, 34, 35, 36, 37, 38*, 39*, 40*, 41*, 47*, 48*, 49*, 50*, 51, 52, 53, 57, 58, 59, 61, 62*, 63*, 64*, 65*, 66*, 67*, 69*, 70*.

Conditions apply to provisions marked with asterisk. See Current Sentencing Practice H11–1G.

Offences against the following provisions are sexual offences for the purposes of the P.C.C.(S.)A. 2000, s.161: any provision of Pt 1 of the Act except ss.52, 53, or 71.

Sexual Offences (Amendment) Act 2000

This Act is repealed by the Sexual Offences Act 2003; but see the note to the Sexual Offences Act 1956.

Section 3 (abuse of position of trust) **5 years**

Note: Offence against a child (if victim under 18) Criminal Justice and Court Services Act 2000, Sch.4.

Scheduled offence (Sexual Offences Act 2003, Sch.3) if offender 20 or over.

Suicide Act 1961

Section 2 (aiding suicide) **14 years**

Theatres Act 1968

Section 2 (giving obscene performance) **3 years**

Theft Act 1968

Section 7 (theft) **7 years**
Section 8 (robbery) **Life**
Section 9 (burglary of dwelling) **14 years**

Section 9 (burglary of building other than dwelling)	**10 years**
Section 10 (aggravated burglary)	**Life**
Section 11 (removing object from public place)	**5 years**
Section 12A (aggravated vehicle taking resulting in death)	**14 years**
Section 12A (aggravated vehicle taking not resulting in death)	**2 years**

Note: if the offence is aggravated vehicle taking by reason of causing damage, and the value of the damage does not exceed £5,000, the offence will normally be dealt with as a summary offence and the maximum sentence is six months.

Section 13 (abstracting electricity)	**5 years**

Section 15 (obtaining by deception)	**10 years**
Section 15A (obtaining money transfer by deception)	**10 years**
Section 16 (obtaining pecuniary advantage)	**5 years**
Section 17 (false accounting)	**7 years**
Section 20 (destroying valuable security etc.)	**7 years**
Section 22 (handling)	**14 years**

Note: offences against the following provisions are specified offences for the purposes of the Criminal Justice Act 2003, Sch.15): 8, 9 (burglary with intent to cause grievous bodily harm, cause criminal damage, or rape: not burglary with intent to steal) ss.9, 12A (aggravated vehicle taking involving death).

An offence of burglary with intent to rape a child is an offence against a child (if the intended victim is under 18) for the purposes of the Criminal Justice and Court Services Act 2000, Sch.4.

Offences under the following provisions are scheduled offences for the purposes of the Sexual Offences Act 2003, Sch.5: s.1 (theft) ss.8, 9, (burglary with intent to cause grievous bodily harm, cause criminal damage or steal), ss.10, 12A (aggravated vehicle taking involving death).

Note that burglary with intent to rape contrary to s.9 is a specified offence for the purposes of the Criminal Justice Act 2003 but not a scheduled offence for the purposes of the Sexual Offences Act 2003. The definition of burglary is amended by the Sexual Offences Act 2003 to omit references to an intent to rape; offences which would formerly have been charged as burglary with intent to rape will now be charged as trespass with intent, contrary to s.63.

Theft Act 1978

Section 1 (obtaining services)   **5 years**
Section 2 (evading liability, etc.)   **5 years**
Section 3 (making off without payment)   **2 years**

Penalty provision: section 4.

Value Added Tax Act 1994

Section 72 (fraudulently evading VAT, etc.)   **7 years**

Violent Crime Reduction Act 2006

Section 28 (using another to hide weapon etc.)

If weapon is weapon to which Criminal Justice Act 1988,
 s.141 or 141A applies   **4 years**
If weapon is prohibited weapon (with exceptions) and
 offender is over 16   **10 years**
Other cases   **5 years**

Part 3
Charts and Tables

Restraints and Restrictions (for details, see the relevant topic in the text)

Antisocial Behaviour Order (Crime and Disorder Act 1998, s.1C)

Any offence, harassment of persons not of same household. Any restriction imposed by court.

Banning Order

Football related offence. Not to attend football matches, to report to police when supported team playing abroad.

Curfew Order (or Curfew Requirement of Community Order)

Any offence. To remain at specified place during specified times.

Disqualification from Directing Company, etc.

Offence in connection with management of company.

Disqualification from Driving (P.C.C.(S.)A, s.147)

Any offence. Disqualified from driving motor vehicle.

Disqualification Order

Offence against child. Not to work with children.

Drink Banning Order

Any offence committed while under the influence of alcohol.

Exclusion Order (or Exclusion Requirement of Community Order)
Any offence.

Exclusion Order (Licensed premises)

Offence of violence on licensed premises. Exclusion from specified licensed premises.

Restraining Order (Prevention of Harassment Act)

Offence against ss.2 or 4 of the Act. Any restriction imposed by court.

Sexual Offences Prevention Order

Any offence listed in Sexual Offences Act 2003, Schs 3 or 5. Any restriction necessary to protect public from serious sexual harm.

Travel Restriction Order

Any drug trafficking offence for which sentence of four years' imprisonment or more is imposed—mandatory unless inappropriate; minimum two years.

Dangerous Offenders—Adults

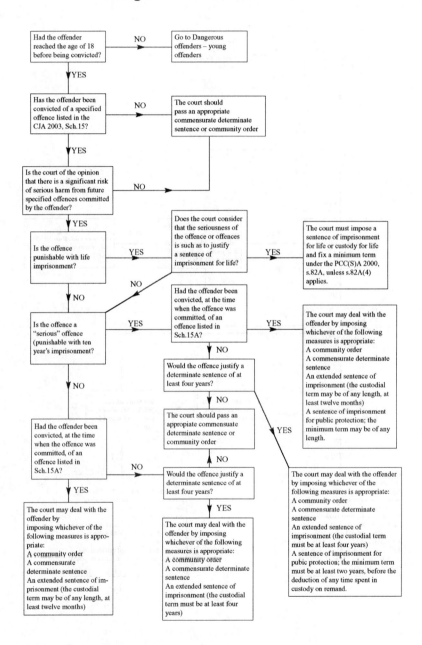

Note: in this table, "imprisonment for life" includes "custody for life", and "imprisonment" includes "detention in a young offender institution", if the offender is 18 and under 21 on the day of the conviction.

Dangerous Offenders—Young Offenders

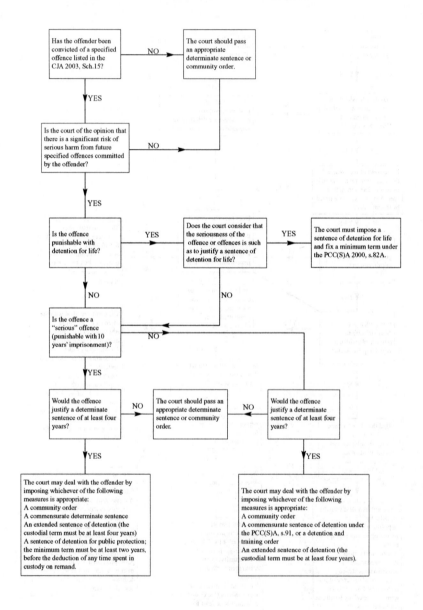

Disqualification Orders
(Criminal Justice and Court Services Act 2000)

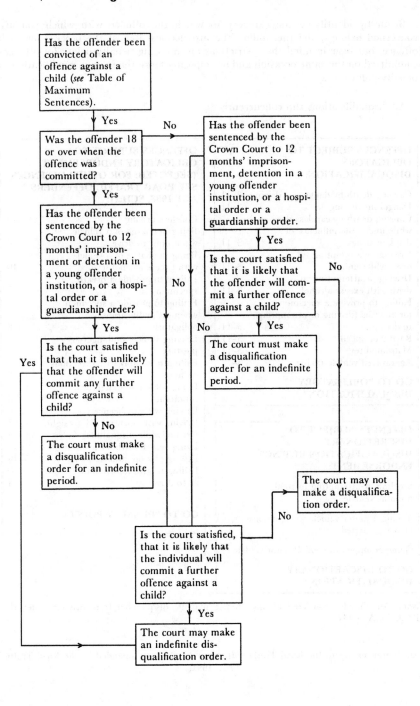

Disqualification from Driving

Begin by identifying the category to which the offence with which you are concerned belongs, and then follow the instructions. Repeat the process for each offence, but bear in mind the restrictions on imposing penalty points for offences committed on the same occasion and on imposing more than one disqualification in penalty point cases.

All disqualifications run concurrently.

OFFENCES SUBJECT TO OBLIGATORY DISQUALIFICATION:

Causing death by dangerous driving	3–11
Dangerous driving	3–11
Causing death by careless driving while under the influence of drink or drugs	3–11
Driving or attempting to drive while unfit	3–11
Driving or attempting to drive with excess alcohol	3–11
Failing to provide a specimen for analysis (driving or attempting to drive)	3–11
Racing or speed trials	3–11
Manslaughter	3–11
Aggravated vehicle taking	3–11

GO TO "OBLIGATORY DISQUALIFICATION"

OFFENCES SUBJECT TO DISCRETIONARY DISQUALIFICATION BUT NOT ENDORSEMENT:

Stealing or attempting to steal a motor vehicle

Taking a motor vehicle without consent, or being carried

Going equipped to steal a motor vehicle

GO TO DISCRETIONARY DISQUALIFICATION

OFFENCES SUBJECT TO OBLIGATORY ENDORSEMENT (SELECTED; FOR OTHER OFFENCES SEE ROAD TRAFFIC OFFENDERS ACT 1988, SCH.2):

Careless driving	3–9
Being in charge of a vehicle when unfit to drive	10
Being in charge of a vehicle with excess alcohol level	10
Failing to provide a breath specimen	4
Failing to provide a specimen when disqualification not obligatory	10
Leaving vehicle in dangerous position	3
Failing to comply with directions or signs	3
Using vehicle in dangerous condition	3
Driving without licence	3–6
Driving with uncorrected eyesight	3
Driving while disqualified	6
Using vehicle without insurance	6–8
Failing to stop after accident	5–10
Failing to give information as to driver	3

GO TO "PENALTY POINTS"

Note: An offender convicted of any offence may be disqualified from driving under the P.C.C.(S.)A., s.147.

All references are to the Road Traffic Offenders Act 1988 as amended by the Road Traffic Act. 1991.

Obligatory Disqualification

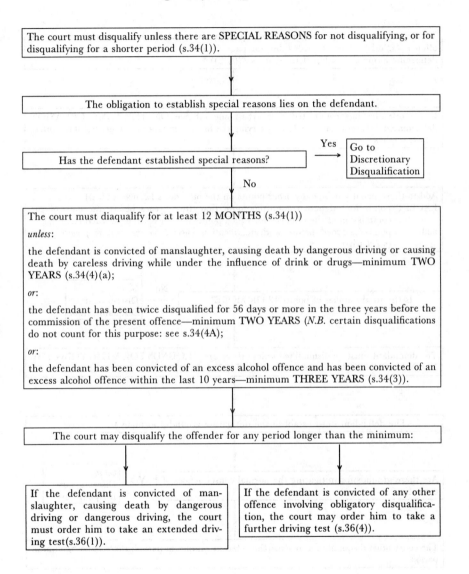

The court must disqualify unless there are SPECIAL REASONS for not disqualifying, or for disqualifying for a shorter period (s.34(1)).

The obligation to establish special reasons lies on the defendant.

Has the defendant established special reasons?
→ **Yes** Go to Discretionary Disqualification
No

The court must diaqualify for at least 12 MONTHS (s.34(1))

unless:

the defendant is convicted of manslaughter, causing death by dangerous driving or causing death by careless driving while under the influence of drink or drugs—minimum TWO YEARS (s.34(4)(a);

or:

the defendant has been twice disqualified for 56 days or more in the three years before the commission of the present offence—minimum TWO YEARS (*N.B.* certain disqualifications do not count for this purpose: see s.34(4A);

or:

the defendant has been convicted of an excess alcohol offence and has been convicted of an excess alcohol offence within the last 10 years—minimum THREE YEARS (s.34(3)).

The court may disqualify the offender for any period longer than the minimum:

If the defendant is convicted of manslaughter, causing death by dangerous driving or dangerous driving, the court must order him to take an extended driving test(s.36(1)).

If the defendant is convicted of any other offence involving obligatory disqualification, the court may order him to take a further driving test (s.36(4)).

Penalty Points

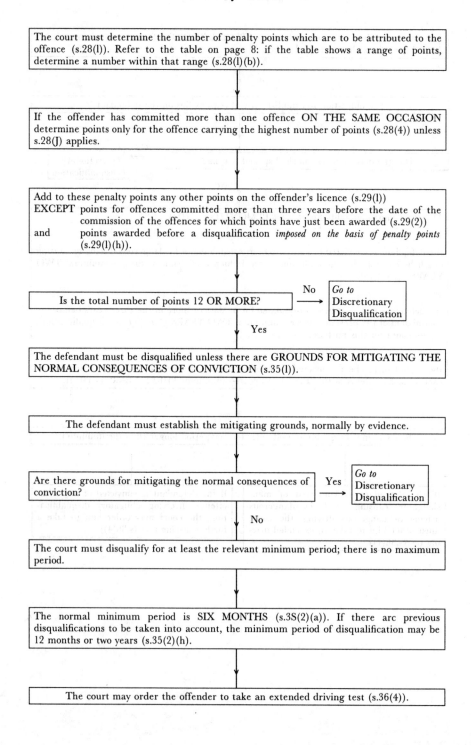

The court must determine the number of penalty points which are to be attributed to the offence (s.28(l)). Refer to the table on page 8: if the table shows a range of points, determine a number within that range (s.28(l)(b)).

If the offender has committed more than one offence ON THE SAME OCCASION determine points only for the offence carrying the highest number of points (s.28(4)) unless s.28(J) applies.

Add to these penalty points any other points on the offender's licence (s.29(l))
EXCEPT points for offences committed more than three years before the date of the commission of the offences for which points have just been awarded (s.29(2))
and points awarded before a disqualification *imposed on the basis of penalty points* (s.29(l)(h)).

Is the total number of points 12 OR MORE? — No → Go to Discretionary Disqualification

Yes

The defendant must be disqualified unless there are GROUNDS FOR MITIGATING THE NORMAL CONSEQUENCES OF CONVICTION (s.35(l)).

The defendant must establish the mitigating grounds, normally by evidence.

Are there grounds for mitigating the normal consequences of conviction? — Yes → Go to Discretionary Disqualification

No

The court must disqualify for at least the relevant minimum period; there is no maximum period.

The normal minimum period is SIX MONTHS (s.3S(2)(a)). If there arc previous disqualifications to be taken into account, the minimum period of disqualification may be 12 months or two years (s.35(2)(h).

The court may order the offender to take an extended driving test (s.36(4)).

Discretionary Disqualification

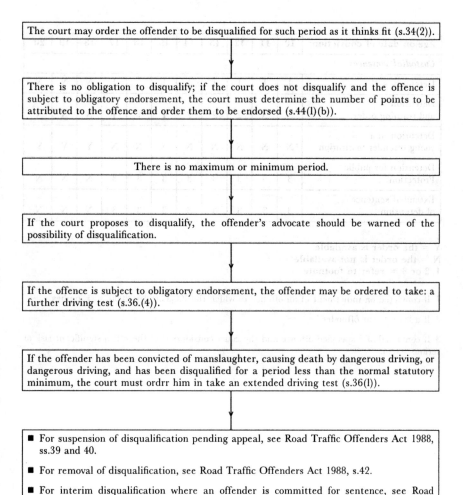

The court may order the offender to be disqualified for such period as it thinks fit (s.34(2)).

There is no obligation to disqualify; if the court does not disqualify and the offence is subject to obligatory endorsement, the court must determine the number of points to be attributed to the offence and order them to be endorsed (s.44(l)(b)).

There is no maximum or minimum period.

If the court proposes to disqualify, the offender's advocate should be warned of the possibility of disqualification.

If the offence is subject to obligatory endorsement, the offender may be ordered to take: a further driving test (s.36.(4)).

If the offender has been convicted of manslaughter, causing death by dangerous driving, or dangerous driving, and has been disqualified for a period less than the normal statutory minimum, the court must ordrr him in take an extended driving test (s.36(l)).

- For suspension of disqualification pending appeal, see Road Traffic Offenders Act 1988, ss.39 and 40.

- For removal of disqualification, see Road Traffic Offenders Act 1988, s.42.

- For interim disqualification where an offender is committed for sentence, see Road Traffic Offenders Act 1988, s.26.

- For disqualification where sentence is deferred, see Road Traffic Offenders Act 1988, s.26(2).

Road Traffic Offenders Act 988, ss.34A, 34B and 34C make provision for a court to order an offender convicted of alcohol-related offences to attend a course of a kind approved by the Secretary of State, This power is available only to magistrates' courts which have been designated for the purpose under Road Traffic Act 1991 s.3(3).

Sentences for Young Offenders

Age on date of conviction:	10	11	12	13	14	15	16	17	18	19	20
Custodial sentences:											
Detention s.91	1	1	1	1	1	1	1	1	N	N	N
Detention and training order	N	N	2	2	2	Y	Y	Y	N	N	N
Detention in a young offender institution	N	N	N	N	N	N	N	N	Y	Y	Y
Detention for public Protection	3	3	3	3	3	3	3	3	N	N	N
Extended sentence of detention (YOI)	3	3	3	3	3	3	3	3	N	N	N

Y = the order is available
N = the order is not available
1, 2 or 3 = refer to footnote

1 If convicted on indictment of an offence to which the P.C.C.(S.)A. 2000, s.91 applies.

2 If a "persistent offender".

3 If convicted of a specified offence and the court considers that there is a significant risk of serious harm.

Subject: Sentencing Referencer 2009 Sentences for Young Offenders p.292

Importance: High

I have become aware that the chart covering sentences for young offenders is some
does not directly refer to two possible sentence options. It does not include any refe
Young Offenders' Institution for Public Protection or an Extended Sentence of Deter
Offenders' Institution in the available custodial sentence options for offenders aged
in mind when using this chart.

Dr Paul Burns

Community Sentences

Age on date of conviction:	10	11	12	13	14	15	16	17	18	19	20
Action plan order	Y	Y	Y	Y	Y	Y	6	6	N	N	N
Attendance centre Order	Y	Y	Y	Y	Y	Y	6	6	1	1	1
Community order (Criminal Justice Act 2003)	N	N	N	N	N	N	7	7	2	2	2
Community punishment Order	N	N	N	N	N	N	6	6	1	1	1
Community rehabilitation Order	N	N	N	N	N	N	6	6	1	1	1
Community punishment and Rehabilitation order	N	N	N	N	N	N	6	6	1	1	1
Curfew order	3	3	3	3	3	3	6	6	1	1	1
Drug treatment and testing order	N	N	N	N	N	N	6	6	1	1	1
Exclusion order	3,5	3,5	3,5	3,5	3,5	3,5	5	5	5	5	5
Referral order	4	4	4	4	4	4	4	4	N	N	N
Reparation order	5	5	5	5	5	5	5	5	N	N	N
Supervision order	Y	Y	Y	Y	Y	Y	6	6	N	N	N

Y = the order is available
N = the order is not available
1, 2, 3, 4, 5, 6 , 7 = refer to footnote

1 If the offence was committed before April 4, 2005.

2 If the offence was committed on or after April 4, 2005.

3 Maximum period of order is three months.

4 Mandatory if compulsory referral conditions apply.

5 If the court has been notified that arrangements are available.

6 If the offence was committed before April 4, 2009.

7 If the offence was committted after April 4, 2009.

Note: discharges are available in all cases.

592   PCCA 000

formerly 5.53 of C+4PA